Realism in green politics

Social movements and ecological reform in Germany

Helmut Wiesenthal
edited by John Ferris

Manchester University Press
Manchester and New York

Distributed exclusively in the USA and Canada by St. Martin's Press

Published by Manchester University Press
Oxford Road, Manchester M13 9PL, UK
and Room 400, 175 Fifth Avenue, New York, NY 10010, USA

Distributed exclusively in the USA and Canada
by St. Martin's Press, Inc., 175 Fifth Avenue, New York,
NY 10010, USA

British Library Cataloguing-in-Publication Data
A catalogue record for this book is available from the British
Library

Library of Congress Cataloging-in-Publication Data

Wiesenthal, Helmut.
    Realism in green politics : social movements and ecological reform
in Germany / Helmut Wiesenthal ; edited by John Ferris'.
        p. cm. — (Issues in environmental politics)
    Includes bibliographical references.
    ISBN 0–7190–3701–8
        1. Grünen (Political party)   2. Green movement—Germany (West)
    3. Germany (West)—Politics and government—1982–   I. Ferris, John.
    II. Title. III. Series.
    JN3971.A98G72383   1993
    322.4'4'0943—dc20   93–78

ISBN 0 7190 3701 8 *hardback*

Photoset in Linotron Sabon
by Northern Phototypesetting Co Ltd, Bolton

Printed in Great Britain
by Biddles Ltd, Guildford and King's Lynn

Contents

Acknowledgements

Most of these essays first appeared as articles in 'alternative' journals and newspapers in Germany. In some of the more theoretical chapters it has seemed appropriate to provide full notes and references, in others that were more journalistic this did not seem appropriate.

Chapter 1 first published in *Kommune*, 2:4 (1984), pp. 31–46. Reprinted in G. Falkenberg and H. Kersting (eds.) *Eingriffe im Diesseits*, Essen: Klartext Verlag (1985).
Chapter 2 first published in two parts in *Kommune*, 5:9 (1987), pp. 39–45, and 5:11 (1987), pp. 43–7.
Chapter 3 'The Greens and the decline of the social movements', *Gewerkschaftliche Monatshefte*, 39:5, (1988), pp. 289–99.
Chapter 4 first published in *Links*, 16:169 (Apr. 1984), pp. 8–9.
Chapter 5 first published in *Wechselwirkung*, 6:22 (Aug. 1984), pp. 9–13.
Chapter 6 first published in *Kommune*, 6:9, (1988), pp.43–8.
Chapter 7 first published in E. Hildebrandte (ed.) *Ökologischer Konsum. Schriftenreihe des Instituts für ökologische Wirtschaftsforschung*, No.25/89, (Berlin:IÖW, 1990) pp. 21–32.
Chapter 8 appeared in *Frankfurter Rundschau* (14/15 Nov. 1989).
Chapter 9 was specially written for this volume.
The versions of the articles published in the book were revised, and where appropriate extended, for English-language readers.

As editor I am indebted to the following people for their work and support. To Margaret Curran for her skilful and sensitive translation. To Helmut Weisenthal for explaining at length the intricacies of green politics in Germany and his hospitality in Bielefeld and Bremen. For discussions about die Grünen and social movements with Claus Offe, Norbert Kostede and Johannes Berger, at the Universities of Bielefeld and Bremen. To Dick Geary for his advice on German language and political culture. To Richard Purslow, my editor at Manchester University Press for his encouragement and commitment. Financial support for the translation was made available by the University of Nottingham. I have attempted to the best of my editorial ability to ensure that the translated text is accessible and 'readable' in English. Inevitably something is lost in even the best translations and some of my interventions may have resulted in misinterpretations and inaccuracies. For any such errors I am responsible. My hope is that this book will contribute to the debates within the ecological movement about a strategy for change and therefore bring forward, however modestly, the transition to an ecologically responsible and socially just society.

John Ferris
August 1992

John Ferris

Introduction: Political realism and green strategy

I Strategy and ideology in green politics

These essays by Helmut Wiesenthal reflect a realist perspective towards green politics and first appeared as contributions to the strategy debates among German Greens in the 1980s. They now appear in English at a time when there is considerable uncertainty about the role and purpose of green political parties. The new social movements associated with the emergence of green parties seem to have declined in significance, though the ecological and social problems that gave rise to them in the 1970s and 1980s are no less pressing than they were.

The Greens and new social movements called for a new type of politics and a new agenda. Ecocentric thinkers have provided a detailed critique of prevailing patterns of production and consumption and called for changes in lifestyle. They have also elaborated visions of a new 'post-industrial' order. Although many journalists and commentators tend to see ecological politics as another kind of 'single-issue' politics it is evident that the green agenda is more ambitious. These essays by Helmut Wiesenthal are premised on the assumption that the green agenda is more than a form of 'single-issue' politics. At the same time the perspective he adopts is strategic rather than normative. The emphasis is on how, given present starting-points, it might be possible to achieve democratic renewal and an ecologically responsible society.

This book is structured in a way that, hopefully, will assist readers to make connections between normative and strategic agendas in contemporary green politics. It seems to me indisputable that green politics needs a vision of what an ecologically sustainable society might look like. At the same time it is equally clear that Greens need to address strategic questions if they wish to achieve such a society, and it is evident that more attention has been given to the former than the latter. These essays focus on this deficit in green political thought. This introductory chapter seeks to provide a broad over-view of green normative theory as well as an introduction to the context of Wiesenthal's approach to green strategy. The essays in Part I are theoretical and analytic in character and explore the structural preconditions for a feasible green strategy in the context of Germany in the 1980s. The essays in Part II draw on the analytic framework and address particular topics that were widely seen as relevant to the green agenda in Germany during the 1980s (e.g. alternative technology, economic questions, ecological consump-tion, and social policy issues like flexible working-time and basic income proposals). The concluding chapter looks at green politics in Germany from the perspective of German reunification after 1989.

The experience of the German Greens is important because they were able to achieve a degree of electoral success that has eluded Greens elsewhere. They therefore had more power and influence than other green parties in Europe. Participation in local and regional government exposed the German Greens (even as a minority party) to dilemmas that Greens elsewhere were able to avoid. These dilemmas were essentially strategic decisions. Should political parties with different aims and policies be tolerated? Should Greens be willing to participate in coalitions with parties who do not share their ecological objectives? More concretely, should Greens be prepared to 'scale down' ecological demands in order to secure advances in other areas of policy? These and similar questions were faced in Germany during the 1980s and the experience is in my view relevant to Greens seeking power elsewhere. The merit of Wiesenthal's approach to these strategic questions is that he demon-strates the inherent complexity of a feasible political strategy in modern industrialised societies. His critique of radical funda-mentalism is based on his awareness of complexity and the simplistic and self-defeating nature of the strategies advocated by the radicals in die Grünen. This is a critique of means rather than norms. 'Willed social change', with all the risks this implies of unintended conse-quences, means that Greens have necessarily to be specific and pragmatic in their reform proposals if they wish to be taken seriously by voters. Nevertheless he argues that there are more opportunities for ecological reforms than many radicals are prepared to accept, attached as they are to an ethic of ultimate ends.

These essays were originally written by Wiesenthal as an active member of die Grünen, not as a social scientist presenting research in scholarly journals. They represent a point of view in the fiercely argued strategy debate and were intended to serve a political purpose. Nevertheless it is important to stress that the expertise that informs these arguments is that of a political sociologist acting as 'party intellectual' – they are more than personal opinion. Wiesenthal is a social scientist offering his expertise to die Grünen. For this reason Wiesenthal refrains from directly addressing the normative debates that are important in the field of green politics. His concern is not green ideology, except if and when it leads to what he would regard as self-defeating strategies. Indeed Wiesenthal views the main strategic problems facing Greens as arising from contradictory demands for emotionally satisfying ideas and instrumentally appropriate knowledge rather than alternative ideas as such.

The debates that took place in West Germany within die Grünen led some American and English authors coming from very different intellectual and political traditions to view the German Greens as overly contentious and still committed to some version of 'old left' politics that Greens elsewhere had transcended.[1] It is widely acknowledged by German social scientists that West Germany represented something of a special case in European political development that is related to the post-war political constitution and the specific circumstances that led to the formation and composition of die Grünen in the late 1970s.[2] While this 'peculiarity of the Germans' position has some validity I would argue that the strategic problems that faced die Grünen and ecological movements in Germany in the 1980s have more general relevance to ecological politics. They are inherent in a political position that advances a broad programme of social change, as Greens certainly do.

Apart from the issues mentioned above I also think it is worth drawing attention to the very different social scientific traditions that prevail in Germany and the English-speaking world. This seems very evident when we consider the normative debates in green political theory in the English language literature and the critical social scientific approaches that prevail in Germany. The overview of political ecology given below starts from different methodological assumptions than those addressed by Wiesenthal in the rest of the book. It is offered here as an extension of Wiesenthal's essays which arose from the particular context of West Germany during the 1980s.

Although green 'new paradigm' authors often write as if there is a unified and coherent green ideology from which a decentralist neo-anarchist strategy self-evidently emerges, it seems to me essential to demonstrate in this context that this is not the case. There are very real and important differences in the normative visions being offered. What people believe does have a bearing on political action in terms of the strategy pursued and concrete political demands. Wiesenthal is committed to generally agreed green principles but in these essays he is much more interested in how means and ends can be combined in an effective green political strategy. The question that seems worth posing here is whether the ideas now being advocated by 'deep ecology' could in practice be supported by the kind of realist strategy advanced by Wiesenthal, given that deep ecology seems to rest on somewhat arbitrary metaphysical foundations. Deep ecology has a large element of 'non-negotiability' built in and Wiesenthal's position implies not closing options and actively seeking consensus wherever possible. Moreover deep ecologists have explicitly rejected 'anthropocentric reformism'.[3]

Part II of this chapter will provide an overview of current normative debates within green politics, and Part III an introduction to the realist critique of radical fundamentalism as well as the context for which the essays collected here were written.

II Normative debates in political ecology

The term political ecology is used here to describe what other authors simply call environmentalism. It is used in this chapter to distinguish our concerns from those that come under the labels of 'environmental science' and 'environmental studies'. Political ecology can be said to embrace social scientific and philosophical approaches to environmental problems. A broad label is useful because no single disciplinary perspective is able to adequately address the range of issues raised by environmental problems. There have been a number of attempts to classify the variety of political positions within political ecology. In Britain an early typology was produced by O'Riordan.[4] This is still cited, although now rather dated. O'Riordan makes a basic distinction between ecocentric and technocentric approaches to environmental issues.

Ecocentric approaches would now be labelled 'green', while the technocentric approaches described by O'Riordan are the familiar kinds of managerial and technological response to environmental problems produced by mainstream politics for which environmental issues are simply another category of problem that has to addressed. There are further subdivisions with O'Riordan's categories. On the ecocentric side there is a distinction between those who adhere to bio-ethics (deep environmentalism) and those who adopt anarchist principles for organising social and community life as a response to ecological problems (self-reliant communalism). The technocentrics are labelled 'cornucopians' and 'accommodators' by O'Riordan. The 'accommodators' are environmental reformers who acknowledge that there are problems to be addressed by managerial and technical means. The 'cornucopians' are economic conservatives who argue the case for sticking with 'normal' free market processes and relying on technological innovation to overcome resource deficits or other environmental problems.

It is already evident in O'Riordan's typology that environmental issues transcend the terms of the established left–right spectrum of ideas. What we are presented with are clusters of ideas that at some points converge and at others diverge from conventional left–right typologies. Ecological concerns raise issues that simply cannot be classified in left–right terms. The technocentric spectrum in O'Riordan's typology is now seen by some authors as outside the frame of green politics. Recent literature has focused on the debates within ecocentrism.[5]

Debates within ecocentrism

Building upon earlier attempts to classify green political thought, Robyn Eckersley provides a definition of environmentalism that excludes the technocentric position identified by O'Riordan. Environmental thought generally is viewed as having emerged as a reaction to mainstream liberal and socialist ideology. It also rejects 'industrialism'. For Eckersley the main criterion for evaluating green political thought is whether it is anthropocentric or ecocentric. She identifies four themes within ecocentrism which have emerged over the past three decades: participation, survival, emancipation, and ecology. During the 1980s these strands came together to constitute in broad terms what is now known as 'green politics'.

Drawing upon typologies produced by other ecocentric authors,[6] she seeks to identify and defend a pure ecocentric position uncontaminated by 'anthropocentrism'. She considers that the major currents of modern green politics have given insufficient attention to articulating the theme of ecology in any kind of detail or to exploring the social and political implications of different kinds of environmental postures. The themes of participation and emancipation belong unequivocally in Eckersley's account to leftist and liberal traditions dating back to the eighteenth-century Enlightenment but given new life by the 'new left' during the 1960s. Survivalism and ecology as complexes of ideas have associations with nineteenth-century science, in particular with evolutionary theory and scientific ecology.

Central to Eckersley's purpose is the aim of sharpening the distinction between anthropocentrism and ecocentrism. She outlines an historically derived typology with five major clusters of ideas and political responses. These are: (i) Resource Conservationism, (ii) Human Welfare Ecology, (iii) Preservationism, (iv) Animal Liberation, and (v) Ecocentrism. In Eckersley's ordering, which follows historical chronology, this appears as a progressive movement from darkness to light. As environmental history it is interesting and informative but what is worthy of note in the context of this chapter is the way in which the clusters are associated in one way or another with 'anthropocentrism'. Eckersley pays a great deal of attention to the 'new left' themes of participation and emancipation, mainly as critique to purge them of human self-interest arguments which she thinks (along with the deep ecologists) fail to adequately protect species which are of no interest or use to humankind.

Eckersley notes the role of 'survivalism' in green thought and its association with authoritarian neo-Malthusianism and social Darwinism but draws, in my opinion, the overly comfortable conclusion that it has served mainly to encourage the search for more 'deep seated cultural transformations' that would foster more cooperative and democratic responses to the environmental crisis. She does not provide a sustained critique of biocentric conservatism which has, and continues to play an important role in bioethical arguments. This is not the place to develop this point but a closer scrutiny might have led her to a more sceptical defence of contemporary ecocentrism thought, especially as she comments that the German Greens were primarily human interest orientated.

It is however relevant here to state that normative ecocentric arguments were not central to the West German strategy debates to which Wiesenthal's arguments were an important contribution, although they did surface in the positions of some of the fundamentalist protagonists (e.g. Rudolf Bahro who resigned from die Grünen over the issue of animal rights.) There is a sense in which the normative theorists of green politics in the English-speaking world and the die Grünen political activists and theorists are talking past each other. They are addressing quite different agendas. Wiesenthal cannot be classified as 'technocentric', nor on the other hand should he be classified as 'communalist' in terms of O'Riordan's typology. He explicitly rejects the bioethics of deep ecology and therefore the emphasis given by Eckersley to the distinction between anthropocentrism and ecocentrism. He is primarily concerned with *how* to bring about change. He takes the basic principles as given even if they are philosophically problematic. The main problems facing Greens in his analysis have more to do with established instititutional structures and political power.

Andrew Dobson has called for more attention to be given to green strategy.[7] A good starting-point for this strategic emphasis is the German strategy debates of the 1980s which outlined many of the key issues for green politics. In the English-speaking world it sometimes seems as if green normative debate is regarded as strategic debate. Wiesenthal's approach cuts across these normative debates and brings us back to the dominant structures of power and the complexity inherent in any programme of 'willed social change'. The main thrust of Wiesenthal's arguments is aimed at justifying political action in the contemporary situation where there are no ready-made solutions to environmental problems or the possibility of unchallengable beliefs on which to base action. Self-doubt and scepticism are built in with his approach. The normative debates among English-speaking Greens seem to me to be about 'politically correct' beliefs, rather than what should count as effective political action. For this reason they seem likely to generate more 'self-defeating fundamentalism' of the kind that was the target of Wiesenthal's critique in the die Grünen debates.

III The realist critique of green fundamentalism

For most of the period when the essays collected here were written (between 1984 and 1991) Helmut Wiesenthal was a research associate of Claus Offe at Bielefeld University and the Centre for Social Policy at Bremen University. The collaborative research in political sociology at Bielefeld and Bremen was informed by a distinctive methodology that Wiesenthal used in his role of policy advisor to die Grünen and in intra-party debates. Two particular sociological perspectives inform Wiesenthal's approach in the essays collected here, one positively and the other negatively.

The positive influence is rational choice theory, and in particular the approach associated with Jon Elster.[8] The negative influence was the dominance of systems theory in mainstream German sociology. Wiesenthal made an important contribution to the reception of Elster's rational choice approach in Germany by introducing and editing a selection of his essays.[9] Unlike Elster he was not particularly interested in reconstructing or defending 'analytic Marxism' as rigorous social science. The reason for adopting this approach was because of dissatisfaction with certain aspects of systems theory, especially the way in which it excluded concepts of political action, contingency and agency. From the perspective of green politics Wiesenthal held the view that rational choice could help Greens achieve social and ecological reforms and avoid electorally costly mistakes.

Wiesenthal's most influential essay on green politics, 'Green rationality', published here for the first time in English, was directly influenced by rational choice concepts. It was widely debated in green realist circles following its publication in *Kommune* in 1984. It also provides the analytic approach for the other essays written during the 1980s. An important element in the arguments developed is the perspective of methodological individualism which is used against the leftist arguments of the eco-socialists and fundamentalists. In the early 1980s Wiesenthal felt that leftist social theory in Germany had been effectively incapacitated by systems perspectives which left little room for concepts of political action and agency. It had in effect become a social science of constraints, telling us what could not be done but offering little in the way of positive action. The overly structuralist theories of Althusser and others proclaimed stronger constraints than could be justified theoretically or empirically. Concepts which hinted at 'choice', 'feasible options', 'uncertainty and contingency', 'dilemma' were excluded from theory because they were 'idealist'. The turn to rational choice by Wiesenthal was guided by the need to strengthen concepts that could justify 'choice' and 'decision'. Wiesenthal does not argue that rational choice can provide ethical values. What it offers is the possibility of rational strategy and an intellectual toolbox for limiting risks and avoiding unnecessary costs.

Two particular kinds of systems theory have been fashionable in German sociology during the 1980s. The first was the theory of communicative action elaborated by Habermas which was influential on the left.[10] The second was the more conservative structural functionalist approach associated with Niklas Luhmann which emphasises the complexities and self-steering properties of social systems.[11] There is little scope for planned social change in Luhmann's theory. Critical theory as elaborated by Habermas places a virtual taboo on strategic thinking because of its supposed instrumentality, even while seeking to defend utopian aspirations. Wiesenthal acknowledges the value of the utopian claims of leftist theory and its opposition to forms of domination and inequality but considers the participatory ethic of discourse offered by Habermas as having limited political use to those seeking change.[12] Life is short and politics and policy-making require urgent decisions to be made: the talking has to stop and action must be agreed at some time. Normal politics requires participants constantly to make and justify policy decisions. How do we justify necessary sacrifices of equality in one case while insisting on equal outcomes elsewhere? Political parties and social movements, like the German Greens who are involved in power have to assume such responsibility. They cannot afford the luxury of endless discourse. Rational choice provides, Wiesenthal thinks, the concepts to facilitate such choices and inform strategic decisions. The substance of Wiesenthal's critique of radical fundamentalism is that it was failing to identify appropriate institutions to abolish injustice and advance ecological reforms. Necessary and feasible changes were being sacrificed on the altar of emotional desires for 'total system change' – everything or nothing.

Luhmann's structural functionalism is influential in less direct ways. It provides a persuasive account of the complexity of structural relations and system properties that offers little scope to those seeking radical change, or even modest reforms. In Luhmann's portrayal of social systems there is no 'centre' and they are 'self-steering', there are no levers available to those who wish to shape the future. This theory can be used by those who wish to defend as much as possible of the status quo from reforming initiatives. It effectively excludes concepts of agency and is effectively immobilising because it is difficult to see how it could address preferences for moral choice and social change.

Wiesenthal accepts that modern social systems are indeed very complex and inherently 'disorganised' and that this does appear to impose certain constraints on generalised utopian aspirations, especially with the collapse of Marxism and the historical theory of progress. However the contingency and uncertainty that emerges from this 'disorganisation' thesis means that there will be opportunities for concrete reforms advanced by Greens. It is also feasible to envisage scope for institutional learning. We are confronted by ecological and social problems that we do not yet know how to address practically. Rational choice it is argued can perhaps help us to avoid some of the pitfalls of irreversibility.[13] Normative ideology provides motives to learn, perhaps, but does not supply answers to concrete problems. The implication of this for Greens, according to Wiesenthal, is that they should argue for a willingness to engage in social experiments in order to find sustainable institutional solutions and reject abstract utopias based on obsolete notions of 'total system change'. Even within complex 'centre-less' systems there are opportunities for practical reforms and institutional learning.

The strategy debate in die Grünen

Die Grünen as a political party arose directly from the activities of the diverse social movements that came together in the late 1970s, notably the ecological, the anti-nuclear/peace, and other radical alternative networks. So long as they were united in hostility to the established political parties and the governing coalition the relationship ran smoothly enough. Strategic and tactical questions could be set aside, consciousness-raising and 'building a majority' was seen as more important. This situation changed following the successful intervention by die Grünen in the 1983 elections. Unity based on hostility to established parties became problematic now that Greens were sitting together on the opposition benches with the SPD (Sozialdemokratische Partei Deutschlands). Should they join forces with the SPD against the right-wing coalition? How was social change to be achieved? What should be the role of die Grünen in Parliament? What links should there be between parliamentary and extra-parliamentary activity? Should elected representatives engage in confrontational political demonstrations and publicly defend activists who used violence against the police? These and similar questions now became pressing and forced the strategy debate on to the agenda. This strategy debate was the immediate context of the essays collected here and they cannot be properly understood without some reference to this context and the main divisions within die Grünen.[14]

There were a variety of groupings in die Grünen. The four major currents were; (i) eco-libertarians, (ii) realists, (iii) fundamentalists and (iv) eco-socialists. The eco-libertarians (who were never numerically significant) were economic liberals who believed that there was a market road to an ecological society and they rejected the left-wing prescriptions of eco-socialism. The fundamentalists did not have a single clear political identity but included most of those who prioritised ecological issues like nature conservation and animal rights and attracted those committed to versions of 'opting out' of mainstream society. The eco-socialists insisted on the interrelationship of social and ecological questions and the need to oppose the capitalist state. Most were still Marxist in their political orientation. The centre ground was occupied by the political realists who argued for forms of co-operation with other parties where possible, for example the SPD in some regions and local government areas and in Parliament on certain issues. The eco-socialists and fundamentalists were in effect advocating revolutionary change, while the eco-liberals and realists were calling for structural reforms. Radical ecological feminists, like Jutta Ditfurth, were also very influential within the fundamentalist wing of the party.

It is true to say that the German Greens have been caricatured by the media, and by naive foreign green commentators who visited Germany briefly and then went away to write books that presented die Grünen as locked into incomprehensible and irrelevant disputes over dogma.[15] However the divisions that emerged among German Greens were not at all simple and as events elsewhere have subsequently shown, hardly unique. Similar divisions have since emerged in the British and American green movements. Where Germany was perhaps unique was that no official Communist Party was allowed to exist under the post-war constitution and that Marxists were effectively driven into the radical alternative groups that became part of die Grünen. Eco-socialism seems therefore to have been stronger in Germany than elsewhere.

From the launch of die Grünen in 1979 there has been a sustained

attempt by members collectively to define a new economic model
that transcends both capitalism and state communism (and because
of its historical association with social democratic industrial growth
policies the 'mixed economy' model of post-war Europe). This
search for a way to a new economic model was at the heart of the
strategy debate. All sides in the debates in Germany took this search
seriously (elsewhere, particularly in Britain and North America,
ecocentric thinkers have preferred to simply prioritise ecological
questions and set aside related social and economic issues). In no
other country has such a lively and wide-ranging intellectual debate
occurred over the design of an alternative social order. Despite the
slogan 'neither left or right but forward' it has not been possible to
define a new economic model or find a 'third way' with any plausibility. The importance of the strategy debates in Germany is that the
outline of the terrain that green politics will have to explore in more
depth in the coming years was marked out. The central issue in the
strategy debates was between the realists who argued for reformist
restructuring of the 'industrial society' and co-operation where possible with other parties and the radical fundamentalists (including
the eco-socialists) who were committed to the idea of creating a new
kind of ecological society from the 'bottom up' by 'building a
majority'. Whether reformist or revolutionary, all currents of the
German Greens adhered to a radical vision of the future.[16]

Self-defeating radicalism?
Wiesenthal's objection to 'radicalism' within the green and alternative movements is not with the values proclaimed or ends that are
pursued but to the fact that they are impossible to realise with the
strategies being advocated. In the key theoretical essay 'Green
rationality' (chapter I) he deals comprehensively with the reason why
the 'radical' strategies are self-defeating. It is not necessary to sum-
marise the whole of this long chapter here but his arguments against
'green fundamentalism' are worth reviewing in some detail because
they form the basis of everything that follows, and if true have much
wider application than Germany in the 1980s. Firstly he argues that
old strategy (inherited from the workers' movement) of seeking to
build a majority is in current conditions impossible to achieve.
Simply informing people about the impending catastrophic
apocalypse, as both the ecological and peace movements did, does
not necessarily produce the desired result. Either people find the

prediction implausible against the test of personal experience or because they believe it might well accept such an end fatalistically – 'there is nothing I can do'. The commitment one gains therefore is likely to be no greater than that which has been neutralised. There is a tendency to recruit people who are looking for something else here and now other than preventing the apocalypse or creating the new society, e.g. contact with people like themselves, enjoyment of political activity, power in all its forms, etc. Mobilisation results in recruiting either a large number of poorly motivated followers or inadequate numbers of supporters of a rather utopian disposition. On the one side a lack of will to act; on the other a poor grasp of political reality.

If radicalism is confined to protest and education – telling people the 'facts' – and this results in increased support a paradoxical situation is arrived at. Such an opposition would have the power to act but in acting one would give lie to the arguments often used in mobilising, namely that the 'exterminist system is bankrupt', 'parliamentary democracy is a sham', etc. At such a point the radical opposition would either have to join the game, by tolerating or going into coalition with other parties, or taking the blame if the parties representing the 'bigger evil' ended up with power as a consequence of green abstinence. Power would result in compromising on the basic demands. Petra Kelly was not alone in worrying that the Greens would become a 'power-seeking party' like any other.

This social movement attitude to social change based on extra-parliamentary opposition found expression in the green alternative list thesis in Hamburg in 1983, namely that the radical opposition cannot realise its aims inside Parliament. As the voters discover this they will become politically active outside Parliament. Underlying this thesis is the assumption that mobilisation on the streets is the 'real' force for change. Wiesenthal provides a number of cogent reasons for rejecting this thesis but he thinks the main error is that a minority party fighting for parliamentary seats is not likely to convince voters of the uselessness of Parliament while blaming the currently ruling group in Parliament for prevailing conditions. The basic choice facing the die Grünen with the GAL (Green Alternative List) thesis was either become a party of reform or attempt to follow a revolutionary route to change, despite the logical inconsistencies.

The other radical course was that proposed by Bahro, which was not so much political as cultural. The Bahro position, which is widely

shared in the international green movement, is for an autarkical
solution. Greens should opt out of industrial society by adopting a
new lifestyle and living in small self-sufficient communities. Eventually the communes would demonstrate a qualitatively better way
of life that others would wish to adopt. This strategy depends on
individuals desiring, and of being able, to change themselves and
renouncing the security and benefits of the present order. Moreover
it would depend on the relevant dispositions for changing identities
already being widespread in the population. Wiesenthal is not totally
unsympathetic to this position, especially as it does much to promote
processes of change targeted at institutional structures and makes
clear to individuals what the personal costs and benefits would be.
Ultimately however he finds it implausible because radical beliefs
have a fatal tendency to segregation and sectarianism (rather than
integration and expansion). The fact is that modern societies are
irreversibly differentiated and this poses a real obstacle to radicalism
founded on shared collective beliefs. He rejects as impossible the idea
of a 'radical majority'. The rejection of 'green fundamentalism' is
partly based on logical analysis, identifying the internal contradictions. It is also based on empirical sociological observations
and knowledge of modern capitalist–industrial society.

Social complexity and multiple conflicts
Although Wiesenthal is sparing and sceptical in his use of glib
sociological shorthand phrases like 'post-modern' and 'post-
industrial', his political and sociological frame of reference is firmly
grounded in the awareness that the industrial society that gave rise to
the traditional workers' movement and the old left–right conflict is
disappearing and giving rise to new and more complex social divisions with multiple lines of conflict. In German sociology this new
and uncertain situation has been characterised by Ulrich Beck as the
'Risk Society',[17] that is to say a society where individual biographies
are no longer governed by tradition or once-and-for-all decisions.
Individuals are exposed to the need to constantly re-invent their
biographies and make decisions affecting life chances in the absence
of clear social parameters. The traditional 'normality' pattern is in a
constant state of crisis and restructuring. Habermas likewise speaks
of the 'new uncertainty' in addressing similar phenomena. There is a
renewed emphasis in contemporary sociology on 'individualisation'
and the societal risks associated with this. Contrary to widespread

social and political debate around notions of post-modernity Wiesenthal's position on this is not normative. In effect he is saying 'this is how it is' and any green strategies must therefore address this social reality and its inherent uncertainties and risks. He refers in various places to living through a 'conjuncture of transition'. The old order has not completely disappeared and the new order is far from being firmly established. The realist arguments with the eco-socialists revolve around acceptance of this interpretation more than normative values as such. The objection to eco-socialist proposals is that they are based on too much irrelevant 'Marxist baggage' from the past.

The Greens and the social movements to which they relate as a party are caught up in what seem to be historically unprecedented conflicts. They were, and are, still involved in the left–right conflict over the distribution of opportunities and political power. At the same time they are caught up in a second conflict, and oppose those (both left and right) who want distribution to be seen in purely quantitative terms rather than as something to be seen in qualitative material terms (that is say a conflict about environmental/natural conditions and 'quality of life'). Greens do not assume that 'more is better'. Given this 'transverse axis' of conflict, it is no longer appropriate to fall back on the old social democratic or Marxist strategic concepts to bring about social change because they do not adequately address the ecological agenda or the multiple lines of conflict that are now recognised to have emerged.

The emergence of the social movements in the late 1970s brought to the surface issues and conflicts that were outside the scope of the old left–right conflict. In particular they were not issues of class and structures of privilege. As often as not the issues and problems taken up by the movements were the unintended consequences of action. Many arose from the trend to using large-scale technology and the incalculable risks associated with such projects e.g. cumulatively environmentally damaging effects of the increasing use of chemicals, energy waste, transport systems, urban development, housing policy, etc. There were also social as well as physical effects, e.g. of marginalisation of social groups and categories like ethnic minorities, the mentally ill, women, etc. These new conflicts could not be fitted into a schema of clear-cut causation, nor was it possible to identify a single social adversary to whom blame could be attached. The issues are extremely varied and this is reflected in the range of social movement motivations. It is not possible to reduce them to a simple formula. There is no necessary continuity or link between the conflicts, for example, opposition to chemical pollution in a specific locality or the protests of marginalised groups of people living in inadequate housing projects.

Those who protest against chemical pollution or nuclear power do not necessarily attach themselves to the struggle for ecologically safe agriculture or alternative energy proposals. From a social viewpoint, being affected by one problem does not automatically engender a willingness to take collective action with respect to a range of issues. Those who oppose an open-cast coal mine near their property and welcome help from an organisation like Friends of the Earth do not necessarily become committed eco-activists across a range of environmental issues. Wiesenthal concludes by observing that, given the multiplicity of the conflicts and the particularity of each one, the identification of protagonists who can be unified across all issues is a virtual impossibility. Although the disposition to oppose threats is widespread this generally means only in relation to specific areas of the process of change.For this reason it makes little sense to proceed from the idea that the precondition for social change is a generalised radicalism that transcends all the separate issues and is directed at the 'system' as a whole. Wiesenthal argues that established politics has the effect of producing highly specific negative impacts on people while pursuing general objectives. Ordinary politics produces a steady stream of negatively affected minorities that are unasked for by anyone and are only possible because the unwitting majority who are not affected acquiesce in them. In brief the basic conditions with which we start are a product of the system itself. Complexity and the pressure of problems to be solved do not militate against the idea that the ecological movements can succeed but they should lead us not to expect that all participants in conflict will score highly on some scale of 'radical awareness' or that this is at all necessary for social change. Wiesenthal's account of how social change occurs reflects very clearly the methodological individualism of his approach to strategy.

In terms of those who act, social change is brought about by and through multiple conflicts which is variable and restricted to the particular. The actors are different in each case. What preserves unity and continuity are a few general principles and eventually the institutional changes that are brought about. Change is the result of individual conflicts rather than a precondition for radical action. He is sceptical of advocacy urging cultivation of pure philosophies and the need to 'act' (these personal passions in his sceptical view are on a par with amateur sports, academic ambition, managerial obsession, DIY activity, etc. It seems to him pointless and counterproductive to bank on stoking up passionate convictions).

General principles
Wiesenthal's 'realism', although pragmatic with respect to means and tactics, is grounded on two general principles which he believes can guide decision-making and fulfil the subjective 'need' for a general orientation of values. These provide for him the moral core of green politics ('that is to say the essential, uncircumventable substance of all new claims'). These principles are 'preservation' and 'emancipation'. The preservation principle is common to all 'green' demands, that is to say it is what makes 'green politics' green as opposed to 'red' or 'blue'. Ecological demands, however, relate in specific instances to differing 'objects' and this, according to Wiesenthal, gives rise to a paradox. Such demands may relate to ethically unacceptable threats (e.g. the loss of a particular species or habitat) or, on the other hand, the focus may be on finite resources and their role as 'raw materials'. From the first perspective society appears as the cause of the threat, in the second society is itself threatened. For this reason Wiesenthal holds that rational policies can only be formulated on middle ground, not at the extremes.

Wiesenthal's position on this, it seems to me, sets him very clearly apart from those who advocate extreme positions on the spectrum of environmental values. On the one hand the deep ecology demand for the total preservation of life is self-contradictory because there are no conceivable circumstances in which humanity could evade living at the 'expense of nature'. At the technocratic (or to use the language of the deep ecologists 'anthropocentric' or 'human interest') extreme natural resources only appear to be the focus of concern. From an ecocentric perspective, however, what is at issue is a structure of needs shaped by 'industrial' requirements and the aim of green politics is to change the productive base of society so that as much as possible of it (society) can be preserved unchanged. Applying the preservation principle is fraught with problems because each case must be specified and must be done by balancing ethical norms and those of a more material/economic character. Individual identities are built on both; we need economic and aesthetic satisfaction. For

this reason Wiesenthal argues that green politics is not unconstrained when it comes to reinterpreting existing norms about what
should be preserved. Ethical norms that fail to coincide with peoples'
view of themselves would miss the mark and do little to encourage
political activity.

The emancipation principle addresses human needs and refers
mainly to the freedom of action demanded by individuals. It does
not, according to Wiesenthal, apply to blanket social categories or
class *per se*. Autonomy of action is constrained by normative and
structural factors and impedes progressive reforms. This is why
structural reforms that do not change patterns of discrimination or
changes in norms without changes in structural disadvantage often
fail to achieve what was aimed at. Wiesenthal considers that the
women's movement has been the most rigorous supporter of the
emancipation principle to date because it has demanded structural
and normative change. In so far as emancipation refers explicitly to
human needs it could be said to have been relegated by ecocentric
activists and thinkers who prioritise ecological preservation (e.g. the
deep ecologists).

By identifying a minimal number of basic principles of green
politics, Wiesenthal hopes to make it possible for other green ideas to
be seen as instrumental and secondary rather than fundamental.
Issues like grass-roots democracy, parliamentary activity, electoral
participation, etc., are simply means and should be related to issues
of power and distribution. Among the indispensable secondary goals
of the Greens are the restraint of power and the equalisation of
distributional policies. Wiesenthal calls for the articulation of a new
principle of progress that differs from that associated with socialism,
but nevertheless picks up on issues 'left over' from the old conflicts
like distributional justice and restraint of power, and incorporates
lessons from the new conflicts that create greater opportunities for
developing more autonomous life styles.

Concrete utopias
The critique of fundamentalism and the elaboration of the premisses
of a viable realist strategy in Part I is followed in Part II of the book by
essays concerned with the preconditions of reform and specific
reform proposals that have been widely discussed in green and
alternative circles. Wiesenthal bases his strategy for change on the
argument that change has necessarily to proceed from existing

preferences and values in society, that is to say from specific rejections of policies and specific advocacy of alternative proposals. These positive proposals he calls 'concrete utopias'. Politically this means multiple and particularised conflicts that can lead to new and more radical preferences. His criterion of success is summarised in the following way: 'creation of more, or qualitatively better, possibilities of action (options). This means additional choices both in shaping life at the individual and collective levels and in moulding living conditions in accordance with ecological and emancipatory values. Put more simply; the central problem in every case is to find a way to live according to new values.'

The practical reforms addressed by Wiesenthal include issues like alternative technology, working-time policies, basic income proposals and the possibility of green social policies, and ecological consumption. All these issues have of course been discussed widely in green circles beyond Germany. The discussion in these essays, is in my view, more focused than usual because it is directly related to the theoretical position elaborated in Part I and the particular context of Germany in the 1980s. Central to Wiesenthal's strategy for ecological reform is the idea that there must be societal structural reforms to make it possible for people to live in ecologically responsible ways. Both current values and structural mechanisms 'lock' people into unsustainable 'lifestyles'. The room for manoeuvre at individual or collective levels is presently very narrow. The 'emancipation' (more 'lifestyle' options) principle is therefore crucial for realising the 'preservation' (ecological) principle, and this is why most of the essays are concerned with economic and social policy. One problem with normative proposals from deep ecologists is that while they address value change they ignore the structural preconditions of 'living' the values advocated. How would it be feasible for the populations of highly urbanised regions like Europe to live lives of 'self-reliant independence' without radical changes in housing, transportation, employment, health and many other areas of public policy? If the deep ecologists want us to 'return to the country' this would seem self-defeating in terms of saving wilderness. Interdependence is a reality that cannot be wished away by normative thought.

Alternative technology
Wiesenthal approaches the issue of alternative technology (AT)

critically and notes the seeming 'hopelessness' of many of the small-scale and fragmentary initiatives in this field in terms of the gap between aspirations and achievement. From one perspective it is nothing more than 'a catalogue of the concrete deficits of the industrial society' – 'a counter-vision to the rather gloomy pictures of progress associated with industrial capitalism and state socialism'. The importance however of AT as it has emerged is that it challenges the notion of the 'technological fix'. Not every problem has a technical solution. It also asserts values other than 'economic efficiency', and can also help establish ethical, participatory, communicative and aesthetic criteria. Part of the larger green programme of change is precisely to challenge the reigning orthodoxies of neoclassical economics and calculations of cost-effectiveness. AT, according to Wiesenthal, plays a highly important role in enabling people to imagine technical alternatives to current production. The consistency of these observations is directly related to Wiesenthal's theoretical position regarding people's degree of freedom to organise their lives and the opening up of options for action that would otherwise not be available. The principles of emancipation and preservation come together in AT.

Ecological consumption
In the essay on ecological consumption Wiesenthal uses his knowledge of Luhmann's systems theory and rational choice theory to illustrate his more general thesis that it is feasible to envisage collective action that is not based on a uniformity of motives (i.e. in the face of the attachment of fundamentalists and those in die Grünen who adhere to nineteenth-century socialist models of change within the green and alternative movements). Central to Wiesenthal's arguments is the idea that it is neither feasible or necessary for Greens to establish a normatively founded majority. Political fundamentalists of all kinds start from this outdated premiss. He acknowledges that consumer politics are always problematic and disenchanting. All the evidence to date on this subject demonstrates that consumers are not readily amenable to organisation in forms that can exercise effective power and influence on companies selling un-ecological products. Moreover, although the State could introduce stronger regulatory measures, its power should not be overestimated. Unco-ordinated individual action in such a sphere may even be counterproductive in some circumstances. Wiesenthal concludes on the basis of classical

choice theory that the idea of 'ecological consumption' is indeed a generalised concern with an insufficient mobilising force.

Two ways forward from this dilemma are proposed to strengthen the idea of ecological consumption. Firstly, that employees within companies might be enlisted to the cause of preventing 'ecological irresponsibility'. This would mean organising 'consumer protection' from the sphere of production and extending it into that of consumption. Although difficult, it would present fewer problems than that of creating an all-embracing consumer organisation. This might be supported by industrial law and the protection of workers' rights, areas where there are already many precedents. Secondly, it is possible to envisage collective action from the base of heterogeneous consumer coalitions. Specialised consumer organisations might organise themselves under an 'umbrella organisation' that represented a variety of ecological interests, e.g. nature conservation, health, transport, ecological agriculture, etc. Such an organisation would be based on a plurality of motives. Social movement research has already revealed that the dynamic behind their emergence came from a diversity of motives for participation and readiness to act, not, as is often claimed, from unitary motives and values. Whether or not Wiesenthal's proposals are taken up, or likely to be successful in the sphere of ecological consumption, they illustrate very concretely his approach to problems of collective action in highly complex differentiated societies and the irrelevance of obsolete social theory that ignores heterogeneity and the plurality of values that constitute the starting-point of all current proposals for social change.

Towards green social policies

A central issue in green political thought since the early 1970s has been the dependence of the major industrial societies on economic growth. This has implications for individual and collective choice. A common green response has been to argue the case for 'limits to growth' and to advocate zero-growth. On the individual level such arguments are accompanied by calls for 'voluntary simplicity' and 'self-reliance'. Wiesenthal argues that few people are likely to feel content in the no-man's land between catastrophic scenarios and self-help slogans. In reality of course the vast majority of people who live in the most industrialised societies simply do not have opportunities to opt for 'simple life' solutions. Most households are dependent upon the labour market (directly or indirectly) for income (or past participation in the labour market). The prime mechanism for distributing income is the labour market. Unless and until those who are dependent upon the capital dominated labour market are able to win at least a degree of autonomy the arguments against 'growth' seem likely to fall on deaf ears. Green social policies therefore are seen by Wiesenthal as a precondition for people who want to effect changes in the structures on which they presently depend.

Opportunities of securing an 'alternative' livelihood beyond the extortionate conditions offered by the capitalist labour market are important. This is not simply a question of equity, important as this is, but of creating the space for registering protest more effectively and engagement with the social experiments that will be necessary to build an ecologically sustainable society. Wiesenthal does not envisage a total opting out: 'What we need are options for ordinary normal people, ways of surviving materially in communication with others and without loss of self-worth when the firm closes down. When the stress of the job is too much, when you want to swap jobs with your partner.' What is being called for here is a drastic redistribution of working-time, a break in the relation between income and work via guaranteed basic income schemes, as well as the creation of neighbourhood initiatives, co-operatives, etc. Fundamentally there should be alternative modes of existence to those currently offered by conventional labour markets. These proposals and related issues are discussed in Chapters 4 and 8. Wiesenthal draws two important conclusions from his reflections about these issues. Firstly, it is not enough to criticise and condemn the status quo. It is also necessary to embark on positive pragmatic measures. Secondly, one of the basic tenets of eco/emancipatory politics must be no progress at the cost of social insecurity. The initial responses to limits to growth were either to advocate a strategy that implied virtually universal insecurity or to defend growth (despite the evidence of environmental damage) as essential for human welfare. The case for a guaranteed basic income scheme and more flexible working-hours policy is discussed in 'Unheeded problems and enticing utopias'. While neither of these type of proposals (there are a number of variants of both currently on offer) can be regarded as social policy panaceas they do begin to address the green/alternative emancipatory objective of increasing the options open to individuals. For Wiesenthal green politics should always be concerned with policies that create new options, especially in conditions where there is a high degree of social and economic heterogeneity. The main aims of guaranteed basic income schemes and flexible working-time proposals are, firstly to meet the objections of those who say that ecologically dictated limits to production and consumption would result in hardship for the poor and most vulnerable members of society and, secondly, to accommodate the plurality of values and interests that now exist.

A new beginning for the Greens?

The final chapter written after German reunification reviews the conditions that gave rise to die Grünen, outlines some of the 'peculiarities of the Germans' and forcibly restates the case for a strategically orientated view of green politics. Firstly, such a perspective would seek to offer pragmatic solutions to problems as well as a moral critique. Secondly, in rejecting 'emotionally satisfying' fundamentalism Wiesenthal argues that green politics needs to develop a tolerance of ambiguity and the existence of multiple rationalities. The strategy debate to some extent reflected the special circumstances in Germany, but the divisions that have now opened up in green movements in other countries like Britain and America demonstrate that green politics are not only 'new politics' with few precedents to fall back on but are also inherently complex. It is no longer enough to proclaim the impending catastrophe and offer simplistic moral self-help solutions, if it ever was – something more is needed.

The ecological problems that have risen up the agenda everywhere over the past decade are quite properly seen as important and urgent but it seems unlikely that they can be resolved with narrowly environmentalist policies founded on a rejection of 'industrialism'. Although there will always a temptation to simplify issues to make them cognitively manageable and amenable to political intervention, the German experience demonstrates it is not enough for Greens to confine themselves to ecology, ecological values and the critique of industrialism. As Wiesenthal points out, the German Greens from the very beginning concerned themselves with the full range of global and social themes, as well as pursuing an ambitious programme of a movement of democratic and moral renewal. Single-issue green politics aimed solely at ecological and related conservation problems would be self-defeating. The objection to deep ecology from a realist perspective, therefore, is not whether their philosophical arguments for a rejection of anthropocentrism are valid but that their agenda is too narrow and fails to adequately address the 'human' emancipation principle that is essential to green politics that aspire to more than single-issue status. From a political or sociological rather than philosophical perspective the point made by Wiesenthal is particularly telling: 'The fact that the moral fundamentalism of radical ecology, or of 'deep ecology', is geared to the generation only of the need for action but not of alternatives for action, is what makes it politically weak. Viewed thus, fundamentalism is parasitic, because it remains dependent on the readiness of those with 'other' motives to engage in pragmatic action.' Thus have we witnessed, in Britain, the hijacking of ecological values and themes by the Conservative government under Margaret Thatcher as well as business interests who certainly had motives 'other' than the realisation of the ecological and emancipatory objectives which Greens and alternative movement supporters have sought to realise. Paradoxically it seems that radical fundamentalism plays into the hands of the 'technocentrics' and those who seek to preserve the status quo. The value of Wiesenthal's contribution to the German debates, in my view, is that it demonstrates that it is not only the German Greens who need a 'new beginning'. It also develops a coherent reformist position that is consistent with mainstream ecocentric thinking and is opposed to the kinds of technocentric thinking outlined by O'Riordan.

Notes

1 C. Spretnak and F. Capra, *Green Politics* (London: Paladin, 1985).

2 W. Hulsberg, *The German Greens – A Social & Political Profile*, (London: Verso, 1988).

3 B. Devall and G. Sessions, *Deep Ecology: Living as if Nature Mattered* (Salt Lake City: Peregrine Smith Books, 1985).

4 T. O'Riordan, *Environmentalism*, 2nd edn (London: Pion, 1981).

5 R. Eckersley, *Environmentalism and Political Thought – Toward an Ecocentric Approach* (London: UCL Press, 1992).

6 Eckersley mentions in this context J. Rodman, 'The Liberation of Nature?', *Inquiry*, 20 (1977), pp.83–145. Also W. Fox, *Toward a Transpersonal Ecology: Developing New Foundations for Environmentalism* (Boston: Shambhala, 1990).

7 A. Dobson, *Green Political Thought* (London: Unwin Hyman, 1990).

8 J. Elster, *Sour Grapes* (Cambridge: Cambridge University Press, 1983).

9 H. Wiesenthal, 'Introduction', in J. Elsher, *Subversion der Rationalität* (Frankfurt: Campus, 1987).

10   J. Habermas, *The Theory of Communicative Action Vol 2: Life World and System, A critique of Functionalist Reason* (Boston: Beacon, 1987) (translated by Thomas McCarthy).

11   N. Luhmann, *Ecological Communication* (Cambridge: Polity, 1989).

12   See, for example, the interview with Wiesenthal by John Ely and Volker Heins in *Capital Nature Socialism*, No. 3 (1989) (Santa Cruz, USA).

13   For a detailed philosophical reflection on technology and the reversibility thesis see H. Jonas, *The Imperative of Responsibility: In Search of an Ethics for the Technological Age* (Chicago: Chicago University Press, 1984).

14   Hulsberg, *The German Greens*.

15   Spretnak and Capra, *Green Politics*.

16   Hulsberg, *The German Greens*.

17   U. Beck, *Risk Society* (Cambridge: Polity, 1992).

PART I

1

Green rationality

Reflections on a strategy for our age

I What is the strategy debate about?

At the beginning of 1983 on the first Bundestag election after the collapse of the SPD/FDP (Sozialdemokratische Partei Deutschlands/ Freie Demokratische Partei) government, the Greens captured their place in the parliamentary system. A few weeks later they started a debate, which has gone on to this day, not only about their parliamentary role but also about strategies to influence society. There is no guarantee at all that the subjects which give rise to the most heated debate are in fact the ones that are truly at issue. For a number of reasons, and in some cases this happens unconsciously, the burning issues are only rarely discussed in their 'raw' form. More often it is secondary questions – which may be simpler, more topical, and more pressing, and which seem less damaging – that dominate, because with them the lid is left tightly on the bubbling broth of controversy. Anyone who fails to heed this as the arguments beat their way round the bush, or who entertains the innocent notion that the 'SPD toleration/coalition' debate, for example, is really about what it says, and not about something else (e.g. the 'hotter' question of 'revolution or reform'), soon gets their fingers burnt.

Hence the strategy debate amongst the Greens is dominated by a whole range of (undoubtedly important) issues, each prompted by some topical consideration: conditions for political toleration, the State's monopoly on power, radicalism in political programmes, the feasibility of coalitions and alliances, participation in government, and so on. But the surprisingly high degree of conflict associated with these issues can be explained only by reference to the fundamental issues which their discussion simultaneously also raises. These are the question of how we go about attaining a radical transformation of society, or, in more concrete terms, of what counts as correct and incorrect or ineffective action on the part of the Greens (or of the social movements) as they make their way towards an ecological, non-authoritarian, demilitarised society. Also the question of what character a 'better' society would have in institutional terms. Would it take the form of a soviet-based socialist democracy, a global patchwork of communities of 3,000 inhabitants, a market economy with eco-socialist constraints, or a continuation of the present system with technologically improved means?

Although there are obvious links between these basic questions, they are not identical. The 'How?' of practical politics is a question that necessarily confronts all those faced with decision-making alternatives (e.g. political toleration at what price?). On the other hand, the 'Whither?' question assumes a controversial character only when political commitment is underpinned by a specific philosophical outlook (in such a case, one simply 'knows' that no kind of socialism/ only socialism can cure our ills). It immediately becomes obvious why the 'big' questions of 'How?' and 'Whither' cannot merely be debated, voted on, and filed away. Current answers to the 'Whither?' question smack noticeably of the arbitrary or of credal finality, the 'How?' question, meanwhile, is rightly regarded as being too important to be 'settled' by majority vote or doctrinal pronouncement.The reason for this question being such a 'hot' one, however, probably lies elsewhere. Anyone who believes they have the 'right' answer necessarily feels doubly unsure about their belief. Firstly, because of the great uncertainties that lurk in their own arguments and which can therefore be exploited by anyone of a different opinion in order to support the opposite viewpoint. Secondly, because of historical experience, which can supply any number of examples of failure but practically no usable dogmas for radicals seeking change. Even though in facing the outside world the parties concerned adhere to the 'impact–information–understanding–political activity–social change' strategic model, now known to be inadequate, they are unable to ward off self-doubt. This, amongst other things, explains the tendency to dogmatise questions of strategy and proposed solutions.

How can one break out of this quandary and arrive at strategically 'workable' views of social reality, without abandoning one's political objective? No doubt primarily through a broad and open discussion that avoids degeneration into ideological warfare. Insistence on intelligible argument and logical consistency, however, far from being abandoned, should actually be made more stringent. The reflections that follow are intended as a contribution to this discussion, and not at all as a basis for new dogmas. They take as their starting-point the still widespread view that the changes sought can be achieved, and can only be achieved, by gradually 'securing a majority'(II). An 'alternative' frame of reference for strategic analysis is proposed – one that seems better suited to social conditions and conflictual situations than do either the 'majority' model or recourse to the Leninist party concept (III). On the basis of a working hypothesis positing a multiple conflict structure, a number of conclusions are then drawn in respect of the political strategy of the Greens (IV).

II   Securing a majority as a means to radical change?

All the various currents of opinion within the Greens are agreed on this one point: that the prime objective is not to improve the existing system but to bring about 'a fundamental change in this society' (Trampert).[1] This may take the form of a 'partial dismantling of the industrial system' (Kretschmann),[2] or of a 'radical U-turn by society away from the industrial system' (Bahro),[3] but at all events, what is being proposed is some kind of 'new and as yet largely unknown social model that transcends not only capitalism but industrialism itself'.[4]

In so far as their aim of bringing about radical change is not mere lip-service but arises out of a well-founded awareness of crisis, the Greens belong to the tradition of workers' parties that have pursued a similar aim. Such parties, however, could still hope to attain their goal by a two-track route. Firstly they relied on the effects of history, which it was assumed was producing an 'upward evolution' of society (and possibly also still of 'nature'). Secondly they could count on human insight and readiness to organise (people as it were needed only to act at the right moment, to facilitate the birth of the new). Nowadays, of course, only the second track remains as a route to a consciously moulded future.

Although the myth of progress has now pretty well universally lost its mystique, the conclusions that necessarily follow from the disappearance of the idea that salvation is ultimately inevitable have not by any means all been drawn. It is true that, because of the manifest inappropriateness of putschist strategies and the general rejection of these, it is recognised that the force needed for change can only develop out of people's free determination to act together (collective action). However, fragments of the old myth still creep into the notions as to how collective action comes about, for example in the shape of supposedly 'objective' laws governing the assimilation of experience and the readiness to act, or in the presumption that there is a clear link between the gravity of problems and the radicalness of social reactions (radical in respect of the readiness to act and the goal of the action). Furthermore, people often behave as though 'society' could be 'conquered' step by step by the social movements, like a battlefield or, more appositely, a desert. The transformation of the whole is conceived of as a product of gradual, cumulative, quantitative progress.

One of the central aspects of this conception reappears in the mobilisation strategies of many movements that challenge the established order. This is the idea of the individual as a measure of the success of the organisation. Seen from this perspective, people stand either on one side or the other, they are either 'for' or 'against'. The 'strength of the movement' can be gauged from their absolute or relative numbers. The notion that in order to open up the possibility of radical change one has gradually to work one's way to a majority through a process of cumulative, quantitative growth, thereby becoming the 'strongest force', is one that is also deeply rooted in the minds of green politicians.[5]

Of course, no green 'quantum strategist' is so narrow-minded as to insist on an absolute numerical majority (e.g. 50.1 per cent of the population). The point is to underline the need for a 'relatively large number' of (active and passive) supporters. When the feasibility of securing a majority is at issue, however, this quantitative distinction is not of decisive significance. What matters is rather the qualitative determination of the majority in the sense of support for a programme that has (first) to be recognised as necessary in order (secondly) for people to be prepared to endorse it despite the drawbacks to themselves.

But a majority whose composition is qualified in this way is impossible to achieve. Why? When, in mobilising for radical politics, one applies the traditional 'impact–information–political struggle' formula and has, in order to get people to commit themselves, to begin by informing them about impacts they have not yet experienced, and the relevant options for redress and resistance, a more or less insurmountable dilemma crops up. Informing people about impending catastrophes does not automatically produce the desired result, let alone exclusively that result. It also produces other, unwanted effects. Either the radical analysis is not accepted, on account of its radicalness, e.g. because people measure the plausibility of the prediction against their own personal experience, in other words against the past, despite the fact that this is particularly inappropriate in the case of historically unprecedented dangers. Or else there is that dash of religiosity or trust in science which means that the predicted catastrophes are 'believed in' to such a degree that they are held to be unavoidable. The eco/peace movement is affected by both these fallacies. There is a fascination with doomsday visions and a tendency to ossify social processes in negatively charged structural concepts ('the system', 'capitalism', or 'industrialism' are viewed as forces which, though still personalised, are beyond influence). In extreme cases, the result is that the calculated commitment that one neutralises is as great as the ideologised following one wins over. Mobilisation becomes a balancing-act teetering between too much and too little plausibility.

What was true of the radical self-education of the student movement is confirmed in the mobilisation problems of the new social currents. The radicalisation of analyses and aims leads to 'strategic self-intimidation'.[6] The success of attempts at mobilisation thus runs up against a particular constraint on motivation long before the selected goal (a 'relatively large number' of supporters) is attained. Only those individuals who are looking for something else here and now, something other than the prevention of the catastrophe or the creation of a new society, will be prepared to commit themselves. That something else is contact with kindred spirits, the enjoyment derived from organisational activities and politics, conflict and discussion, power in all its permutations, etc.

Although one can see a gateway here for all kinds of irrational, utopian, and egoistic motives, one should not forget that it is, to a large extent, real social problems which overtax purely 'rational' approaches, since there is no promise of success for the commitment that is called for here and now. Without emotion and utopian vision, i.e. without the 'power of belief' (belief, amongst other things, in one's own strengths) the movement would not exist at all.[7]

However, the green/alternative movement also tries to make up for the lack of rationality in quasi-rational ways, namely by attempting partially to anticipate, in its organisational practice and in the development of an individual political culture, some of the features of the situation it aims to bring about. This allows it on the one hand to recruit motivated support and reduce to some extent the need for utopias; on the other hand, however, the claim to be a 'new type of party'[8] becomes a risky kind of hallmark. It has often to be asserted against better judgement and it therefore repeatedly engenders disappointment.

The essential point to retain here is that mobilisation involves a dilemma whereby one can recruit either poorly motivated supporters in relatively large numbers, or inadequate numbers of followers of predominantly utopian, emotional, or purely organisational bent (and who have a tendency to be blind to reality). On the one hand there is a lack of will to act, on the other a poor grasp of reality. Hence there is very little possibility of mustering any active majorities. Against the background of this dilemma, it becomes clear why many proposals and 'instant remedies' come to nothing. We need, in particular, to examine the internal logic of the 'strategies of radicalisation' that currently predominate.

Radicalism as a programme?

Deliberately narrowing down one's political focus exclusively to the fundamental and radical, and directing it at explicitly identified opponents, implies reliance on the educational power of publicised facts and/or on the notion that future social developments will make one's own radical position comprehensible. If activity is confined to accusation and education, resulting in increased support, the situation becomes paradoxical. Because one has greater scope for action, one has the possibility of altering the social process, but by so doing one would give the lie to one's own arguments. Given this Cassandra-like paradox, an oppositional force remains credible only so long as it is assumed to have the will to intervene and act. If, however, it fails to avail itself of the opportunities for action, if the potential threat of a growing opposition remains unexploited, those who criticise unsatisfactory situations will themselves be blamed for the perpetuation of those situations. This is because, whether one is a parliamentary party or a grass-roots group, once one is 'strong' enough to have acquired a right of veto, even abstaining from action is seen as a positive decision (in favour of the status quo). The option of a coherent opposition exploiting its involvement in order to present its own position and to demonstrate the limits of Parliament's legitimacy and power to shape political life is thus a specious one. But what criterion may be used to measure the success of this kind of fundamental opposition? Definitely not an increasing share of the vote! This would put the proponents of fundamental change in the awkward position of either having to join in – by tolerating, or forming coalitions with, other parties – or being 'to blame' if a grand coalition representing the greater evil ended up governing despite the existence of an objective alternative. Thus when Petra Kelly says, 'Yes, sometimes I worry that the Greens will suddenly get 13 per cent of the vote and become a power-seeking party. It would be better if we stayed at around 6 or 7 per cent but didn't compromise on our basic demands',[9] this runs counter to the goal of acquiring political influence but is perfectly logical in terms of how radicals see themselves.

For a radical parliamentary opposition, therefore, only failure can count as success, because this failure at least pays for itself in ideological terms,[10] the 'impenetrability of the system' provides proof of the dangerous nature of that system and underlines the need to bring about fundamental changes.

Radicalism through failure?
Since the securing of votes is thus not a measure of success, the radical opposition places its hopes in a kind of 'learning through disappointment'. When – so runs the thesis of the GAL (green/alternative list) politicians in Hamburg – the voters discover that the radical opposition cannot realise its aims inside Parliament, they, the voters, will themselves become politically active as a social movement outside Parliament.

Participation in parliamentary activity is here viewed as promoting the mobilisation of real, extra-parliamentary forces. However, at least three preconditions must be fulfilled for this to work. First, the voters – all proto-revolutionaries who have soberly weighed up the facts beforehand – must be convinced that an increase in the proportion of votes won (indeed winning the majority of the seats in Parliament) does not signify any real gain in power. Secondly, the voters must also genuinely have the same political goals as the political organisation that is pursuing this strategy. There has never been a time, even in the history of the labour movement, when either of these conditions was fulfilled – let alone both simultaneously – and it is highly doubtful whether the subject-matter of the ecological debate is sufficiently explosive to act as a mobilising and unifying force.[11] Thirdly, the activists in the organisation, if no one else, have to be schizoid in their thinking: they have to decide on programmes, fight elections, and convince all those potential voters they can reach that they should go out and vote, merely in order to be able afterwards to confirm that precisely this kind of effort is pointless. This approach, whose immediate effect is a 'self-frustrating' one, is not a strategy but a 'recipe for failure'.[12] It is also familiar from the history of the labour movement and whose only 'certain' effect is to transform party workers into asocial cynics.

What amounts to the decisive error, however, is that signalled in the first precondition: a party that finds itself in the minority will not be able to convince its voters of the pointlessness of Parliament, because it has no choice but to identify prevailing conditions with the ruling party, in other words is constantly implying the opposite. The voters would be immune to this parliamentary illusion only if they could 'see through' the situation from the outset, in other words if they were not dependent on the information they received via the parliamentary microphones and green/alternative leaflets. But such a situation presupposes the existence of that which the radical opposition is still only aiming to bring about, namely revolutionary awareness.

A satisfactory outcome is no more assured if one banks on the objective course of the market economy and capitalism and believes that one can 'render the dire even direr by talking about it'.[13] In the first place, the allegedly 'educational' effects of the economic crisis, under way since 1975, are also used by the established parties in cooking up their own particular broth; and in the second place, we have even fewer clues now than in earlier times about how to 'bind together' the very heterogeneous and, indeed, partially contradictory interests involved 'in such a way that the interests are not curtailed'[14] and that 'broader sections of the population'[15] are reached through radicalisation. Winfried Kretschmann has pointed out that no consensus can be presupposed on the question of what the referential scale or goal of 'radicalisation' should be.[16]

There are indications that, in the absence of objective norms, decisions on these matters are taken in accordance with the need of those who are politically active to project a certain identity. The very attempt to use the new campaign slogan 'opposition to the state' to forge strategic unity between the parliamentary organisation and the social movements[17] paves the way for the demise of the orthodox concept of radicalisation. Whilst efforts to seek out untapped support are undertaken chiefly in working-class circles, it would seem that the anarchist-style hostility to the state must drastically reduce the movement's appeal to workers. Such an approach would constitute an attempt to latch on to a variant of 'working-class consciousness' that has a tenuous historical basis but no basis at all in the present day.

The retreat away from the dilemma posed by radical mobilisation and towards the issue of an anarchist mobilisation of the (theoretical!) workers' movement must be viewed as a circuitous and energy-draining detour leading to a parting of the ways between sectarianism and explicit operation as a party of reform. As an attempt to maintain a revolutionary course despite all the inherent contradictions, however, it displays admirable consistency. In this it contrasts sharply with the ideas of 'realist politicians of radical intent'[18] who, though they stress their 'rejection of revolution' appear to have no strategic approach of their own. The proposals put forward by the eco-libertarians in November 1983 seem to advocate seeking refuge from the dilemma set out above by turning to matters of internal organisation.

Radicalism through a change of identity?

The strategy propounded by Rudolf Bahro also relies on a radicalised approach to analysis and to the elaboration of a political programme, but this radicalisation is not so much political as cultural. The clearly defined goal of establishing communities for working and living which are autonomous/tending to autarkical has a definite advantage compared with all other projected goals in the green/alternative spectrum: it has already been worked out in sufficient detail to make clear to each individual what personal costs and sacrifices would be occasioned by a radical break with the evils of the industrial society.

For this reason, a pro-opt-out attitude of any practical significance can only come about where the new life style is regarded as having a high inherent value, independent of its effects as regards humanity. The condition for success here is ultimately the continued transformation of culture and values, in the course of which it becomes subjectively easier to take at least the first step into the opting-out process. For, in contrast to objectives that are more demanding in institutional terms, Bahro's proposal is subject to a daily popularity test, which in most cases turns out negatively. Everyone could avail him/herself of the social and material 'advantages' of the simple life if he/she 'only' wanted to.

It may be seen from the degree of religiosity necessitated by this strategy that even the required cultural change hardly offers sufficient incentive, and that people curtail the options that are still open to them voluntarily. In fact, taking the opt-out step – which represents a kind of 'renunciation of one's interests' – already calls for the sort of 'new' person whom only community-based socialisation can actually engender. This means ultimately banking on people's effecting a radical mental and social change in themselves, so that one is offering a tautological solution to civilisation's crisis: equipped with a different identity, people are different.

A strategy that relies on individuals' transforming themselves implies a considerable degree of denial of organisational democracy and openness. Why? Anyone who seriously resolves to become 'different' will, in their own interests, want to safeguard themselves against any changes to their resolution once it is made, in other words will resort to mechanisms by which they obligate themselves not to make any alterations to their choices. The most obvious means of doing this, and the one that is most common in sect-like groups, is the preventive renunciation of one's rights in case of 'backsliding'.[19] One freely consents to no longer being taken seriously if one suddenly reverts to asserting 'A' instead of 'B'. Even the mildest versions of self-commitment require a certain degree of renunciation of autonomy and democracy. Now a quasi-religious attitude does not sit particularly well with the autonomous leanings and grass-roots democracy of the social movements. Moreover, when plugging into conservative values, Bahro dispenses with any distinction between the different nuances which values such as preservation and protection, security and community, mutual help and solidarity can assume.

These values, all of which are stressed to some degree in the social movements, have a quite different practical significance depending on whether they are set alongside moral concepts of order and authority, of the traditional roles of the sexes within the family, of loyalty to the State and national pride, or whether they appear in conjunction with the quite different concepts of democracy and autonomy, self-realisation and co-operation, cultural identity and international solidarity.

Yet we should not throw out the baby with the bathwater. Deliberately assuming a position that is opposed to narrow-minded orthodox socialist thinking, Bahro emphasises the view – which has also been revived in alternative culture – that the readiness which people who wish to live in different structures display in regard to learning and effecting changes in themselves does much to promote processes of change targeted at institutional structures. The question of how one can ensure that as many people as possible develop 'radical' leanings, in the sense of aiming at green/alternative objectives, is at any rate a more sensible and more pressing one than the question of how radical politicians who feel their identity threatened can protect themselves from the dangers with which success in political practice confronts them.

All the dilemmas documented above may be summarised in a theorem on the impossibility of radical majorities. The first step is the notion that the will to effect comprehensive institutional changes necessarily also embraces the readiness of 'those who will it' to effect changes in themselves – so that they 'fit in with' changed social institutions. This dual readiness to change, which also applies to changed identities, does not come about only as a result of the persuasive power of rational argument. On the contrary, it presupposes the existence of the relevant dispositions in world view and attitudes. These would have to be (a) collectively distributed from the outset, (b) exempt from everyday disputes (which have a fragmenting effect), and (c) largely free of verifiable claims to truth. But social reality flies in the face of these premises. It engenders attitudes that are (a) predominantly subjectively differentiated, (b) tied up with everday problems, and (c) subject to revision in the light of experience. Furthermore, the majority of radical beliefs have a fatal tendency to mutual segregation (rather than integration and expansion). However uncertain one deems the role of radical thinking to have been in historical upheavals, the current obstacles to radicalism would seem, in view of the irreversible differentiation of society, to be beyond doubt.[20]

III   Politics within the framework of a new logic of conflict?

Both the Greens and the new social movements to which they relate as a political party are caught up in a conflict different from that faced by earlier movements and the party-style organisations associated with them. Since the mid-1970s, there has been talk of a second conflictual axis, one that cuts across the traditional left–right alignment rather than being congruent with it.[21]

Up to now, however, the thesis of the transverse axis has not been particularly 'popular' outside the realms of political science; indeed, it has proved a double irritation – to those who much preferred to be clearly on the left rather than 'out front' and athwart the axis, and to those who fancied they were already 'out front' and were forced to realise that there was actually not very much going on there. Yet there is something valid in the notion of a second dimension. The whole green/alternative movement quite clearly interacts with two axes of conflict, both of which are important. Firstly, it is involved in the left–right conflict over the distribution of opportunities and political power. Secondly, it opposes all those, whether on the left or on the right, who want questions of distribution to be viewed in purely quantitative terms, rather than in qualitative, material terms (in other words as questions about specific natural and social living conditions), and who daily use the instruments of power at their disposal (and which they have secured/preserved in the aforementioned struggle over distribution) in order to enforce this narrow perspective.

A second strategic dilemma
Given the existence of these two conflictual axes, one soon comes a cropper if one tries to apply traditional strategic concepts. Hence there is a tacit but deeply-rooted consensus amongst Greens that certain established revolutionary ideas should not now be given currency. There is no longer any trust in the institutionalism that was once much fostered in social-democratic circles, and there is now little or no belief in the notion, deriving from that institutionalism, that social change can be directed by technocratic means. Instead of assuming that in order for society and its human payload to take a turn for the better, one has 'only' to alter a few structures, people now realise that some degree of transformation has to take place in people, at least at the same time, if not right 'at the outset'. After all, simply taking on board all the aspirations engendered by this society just as they are would mean that the shop would continue to be run as it is run today.

But if social change can happen only in conjunction with a change of identity, how can one build on people's existing ('old') intentions and objectives? Further doubts as to the decisive significance of individual intentions and objectives arise from a quite different quarter, namely the fact that the efficacy of individual intentions is manifestly not solely a question of power. For even social groups which, in their own and in our estimation, have an exceptionally great degree of power (owners of capital; economic, political, and military management-elites) have so far not managed, despite numerous and continuing attempts, to achieve this. Namely, to use their superior power not just piecemeal and in order to extend their own positions of power, but in order to alter the foundations of society, in other words those personal and institutional values that transcend constitutions and other official norms. Examples here are markets, ideologies, family relations. Even the most brutal and most disruptive changes, for example those that took place in China during the 1960s (the Cultural Revolution) and in Kampuchea (the Pol-Pot regime) have not produced the result intended, namely a radically different society.

Precisely because of this, those in positions of power react extremely sensitively when the system which even they cannot direct (or cannot direct purposefully or effectively) becomes subject to further turbulence as a result of plans by less powerful groups to effect changes in it. Their inability to direct the system then expresses itself as a fear of being unable to repair even the smallest 'alternative' cracks without the plaster starting to crumble at other, completely different, points. Thus the status quo is doubly protected from change, by power monopolies and by the complexity of the system, and less powerful head-on opposition is doubly likely to experience defeat. Where even superior power could not produce the effect one would like it to, rickety alternative projects operating with inadequate means are definitely not going to be tolerated.

Radical political opposition groups regularly draw the wrong conclusions from such situations, namely that they have been particularly canny in their choice of target, possibly even that they have struck at the 'heart of the system'. Why else would the powerful react so strongly? But in fact repression is not a good indicator of the effectiveness of strategies that call the system into question. Previously, this kind of reaction would have been described as the system's 'strategem for defending itself', but nowadays one has at least to allow for the possibility that there is no volitional-cum-logical link between the action and the reaction, one reason being that the powerful do not (cannot) themselves always know when and where they are being subjected to effective attack. If one recognises this lack of a connection, one then at least understands how it comes about that inappropriate strategies (selected against the background of a misinterpretation of the true situation) tend to promote narrow-mindedness and dogmatism rather than successful learning experiences and adjustment.

Rational radical strategies thus face not only an 'internal' dilemma (in relation to their self-imposed goal of securing a majority in favour of radical objectives, cf. Section II) but also an 'external' one, determined by the outside context. This external dilemma consists in the fact that, because of the complexity of the system known as the 'industrial society' (a system whose weak points are not determined by 'simple' causal relations), willed social change has enormous and largely unknown problems to contend with when it comes to aims and means, and one effect of this is that the movements which are challenging the system are receiving systematically distorted, or indeed downright false, 'learning stimuli'. Given that there is no sure link between the appropriateness and efficacy of political actions on the one hand, and the vehemence of the reaction against them or of the repressive 'responses' to them (mostly originating from the State), even a slight tendency to wishful thinking and dogmatism is enough to ensure that, armed with the best intentions, one will head at full speed for the most adamantine parts of the system, where one will inevitably founder on the complexity of that system or on the insurmountably superior power of the State.[22]

Assuming that dissident social movements are at all capable of rational self-education and a rational choice of strategy (this precondition will not be universally or automatically satisfied), the prime task, ahead of the resolution of any organisational problems, is to throw some light on the links between objective problems, social action, and the reactions one is looking for from society. If there is any kind of window of opportunity for willed change, then it is here, in the typology of the 'new' conflicts, that we are likely to find it.

Multiple conflicts: diversity, uncertainty, participation
Since the rise of the new social movements, we have grown used to people pointing out the originality of the issues with which they deal.

They are not issues of class in the sense of being about social structures of privilege and how these predetermine who is positively or negatively affected (in an objective sense) or how affectedness is perceived (subjectively). Again, they relate to consequences of social action that are unintended (and more often unwitting) rather than intended (and witting). Such effects include the trend towards large-scale technology with its incalculable risks, the cumulative environmentally damaging effects of the increased use of chemicals, of energy waste, of traffic, and of housing policy; the marginalisation of certain social groups and categories, and so on. Viewed globally, these issues (or the circumstances which give rise to them) do not fit into a scheme of clear-cut causation, nor do they tally with the notion that all the conflicts are caused by one and the same social adversary, who can be blamed for 'deliberately' engineering them. Hence it is no coincidence that abstract conceptual terms ('industrialism',' the industrial society', 'capitalism', 'capital') fill – or ostensibly fill – the 'slots' in the definitions of causes and opponents.

The nature of the conflicts may be clarified by sorting them according to three commonly used criteria.[23] From an objective point of view, what we are dealing with here is an extremely varied set of issues, and this fully reflects the range of motivations within the grass-roots movement. The objective pressure of particular problems constitutes at best only one of several factors at the origin of the movement, and this in itself prevents the extraordinary diversity of the issues from being reduced to one simple formula. It is often more important, for example, that there has been a change in the social interpretation of a problem and in the notions of legitimacy relevant to it, or that individuals believe their values to be under threat. The particular motivations can be highly specific, but in many cases the transcendent idea in all the conflicts might be defined as 'the safeguarding and restoration of endangered lifestyles or ... the implementation of reformed ones' (Habermas).[24] The reasons that are cited for the actions point to dangers engendered by the social structure: 'costs and negative effects of the prevailing economic and political rationale ... a qualitative change in the methods and effects of government and of social control', and the fact that 'political and economic institutions ... have lost all capacity for self-correction and self-restraint' (Offe).[25]

From a chronological point of view, there is no mechanism inherent in the state of affairs itself (or rather in the objective character of the issues) which ensures continuity between the conflicts There is no guarantee of any 'evolution of the contradictions'. Indeed the 'new' conflicts are notable for their discontinuity. Thus, for example, the opposition to nuclear power stations contained no inherent trend towards increasing integration (e.g. in the shape of a struggle for a new, positively defined concept of energy provision). And it is just as unlikely, for example, that the self-help movement in psychiatric medicine will work itself up to the level of a global political struggle for new institutions and living conditions that safeguard health.

From a social point of view, as has already been said, the defining characteristic is the heterogeneity of those involved. Typical here were, and still are, conflicts concerning the use of space for industrial or infrastructure purposes. In these disputes, almost all the groups that are physically affected (from large farm-owners to young people without jobs or training-places) – and not just middle-class people affected only on an 'ideas' level – find themselves on the same side. However, the facile thesis that being affected automatically engenders a readiness to undertake collective action is one that stands in need of correction. It is likely that there are always a number of factors at work here, and only in combination do they account for the genesis of joint social or political activities. First, there is a common negative concept of reality (that is to say, agreement at least about what one does not want – the fact that one is personally affected undoubtedly plays what is often a decisive role as a trigger here). Secondly, there is a vague consensus about suitable means and forms of actions (e.g. coming together in a 'one-point' initiative for the purpose of direct action). Thirdly, there is a mimimum of resources of the kind found particularly amongst academically trained members of the middle classes (time, money, knowledge). Fourthly, there are already networks in existence between individuals (thus, for example, the Greens would not have got off to such a good start had it not been for the communication and organisational work done by those in pre-existing radical 'contact group' networks.

In one respect something of a link may be traced between the social provenance of the protagonists in the new social movements and the issues that concern them. The dangers described above are more easily perceived from certain 'social quarters' than, for example, from the standpoint of the clash between labour and capital. Those quarters are the ones occupied by the educated and by (primarily young) outsiders. The one group enjoy, so to speak, prominent access to the contradictions of society as cognitively graspable entities, the other group – in their capacity as structurally 'super-fluous' individuals – experience those contradictions as an intense threat to their own identity. What is decisive here, however, is that the particularities relating to social structure do not show through in the formulation of the issues. The social claims put forward by these groups are often of a general nature, formulated to accommodate all those actually or potentially affected.[26]

It is important to bear in mind that discontinuous conflicts over particularised issues and attracting a heterogeneous set of par-ticipants are not shaped exclusively 'objectively', and cannot be engineered by any political elite. Once they have got going, they can, given organisational skill, political astuteness, and a few chance factors, work up to quite a degree of political explosiveness. The conficts, however, are bound to lose some of their political effective-ness if they are put to work by third parties for their own purposes (for example, in order to reinforce party interests), and even more so if they are 'reassigned' by third parties from one issue to another.

Since it is probably true that capitalist industrial society has become too complex for the considerable degree of potential conflict it contains to develop into a fully-fledged catastrophe (of the kind one could expect in more simply structured social systems of the nineteenth century). What we observe instead is 'a whole collection of sectoral crises and instances of social disintegration occurring on a permanent basis' (Hirsch),[27] the problem outlined above may be very crudely summarised as follows: how can a dynamic of social change develop out of the heterogeneity, complexity, and lack of synchrony of the 'new' conflicts?[28]

The answer to this question will only emerge when we have disengaged ourselves from a number of obvious but now invalid assumptions and have accepted the idea of the complexity of existing conditions. We must start by taking leave of the notion of cumulative learning. It is not the case that individuals become more and more aware as they move from one action to the next (in simplified hypotheses, this means from one general election to the next), finally concluding that it is 'the system itself' or 'the conditions regulating property' or some other root-of-all-evil that should be tackled.

In contrast to this idea of cumulative radical consciousness, there would seem to be an urgent need to think through the new conflictual logic in a way that takes account of the status or role of the social protagonists. In so doing, one should be ready to accommodate the notion of a new kind of link between issues, individuals, and social change (that link is not necessarily historically new but may be new in theoretical terms). This necessary change of perspective would have to take as its starting-point the observation, borne out by experience and theoretical deliberation, that, given both the multiplicity and the individual peculiarities (particularity) of the conflicts, the emergence of identical protagonists who can be 'unified' across what would seem to be all conflicts and issues, is an impossibility. Instead, what we have – and this is the central thesis of the present section – are very widely distributed instances of readiness to act, but ones that always relate only to very small areas of the whole process of change. This is because we cannot count either on a steady increase, at the individual level, in awareness of the interests involved or in readiness to act, or on there being a 'proper' sequence (e.g. from peripheral to central) in the issues, interests, and conflicts.

In concrete terms: the varied nature of people's situations (this includes differences in social and cognitive 'proximity' to issues), and of other social ties, constraints, and values, (which, for example, influence the way interests are prioritised) makes itself felt in a number of ways. Many of those participating in the peace movement, for example, did not involve themselves in the ecological issue, many ecologically motivated people did not support feminist demands, the desire to halt the spread of the nuclear industry or of private transport is not identical with 'radical' objectives such as that of achieving exclusively solar-based energy consumption or the renunciation of all kinds of private motorised transport, a 70-year-old, after much hesitation, decides 'just' (?) to take part in a census boycott but sticks to his view that schoolchildren really ought to be taught some manners. For many different reasons individual political activity varies greatly at different stages of life and does not (as the cumulative thesis would have it) increase in accordance with the objective pressure of particular problems or the need for political action. Yet all these deviations from the ideal of political activity are not exceptions; they are typical of normal involvement in social conflict. The participants only ever participate in the totality of the conflicts in a specific and partial way (they literally 'take part').

Whether this specific, purely sectional character of individual

experience of conflict and of readiness to become involved is something new, in other words a product of the complex network of social
differentiations operating in conjunction with a certain degree of
scope for individual adjustment and orientation, can only be
accepted here as one plausible explanation amongst several. Ideas
about politically active individuals becoming ever more 'aware' and
'radical' should probably be regarded as an error of older revolutionary theory. Whatever the case, the typology of conflict associated
with the new social movements (and probably also with the workers'
movement, if it were to revive under specific circumstances) 'produces' social change primarily as a result of the activity of individuals
whose experience, motivation, and action are particularised. As a
result, it makes little sense, at the level of individual awareness, to
start out from the idea that the precondition for, and motive force of
change is a radicalism that transcends all the issues and is directed at
the whole of society. To take this fact into account, however, in no
way precludes the conflicts having radical effects on social institutions; on the contrary, given that it constitutes an improved understanding of the processes of change (processes that are quite
definitely open to influence), it should actually foster such an
outcome.

Two further arguments demonstrate the strategic superiority of
this approach. First, the particularity of people's experience of conflict and the varied ways in which they are affected (these may be
positive as well as negative, for example, with respect to access to
resources and opportunities for interaction). In other words, the
basic conditions with which we start are a product of the system.
Within these conditions, established politics has the effect of producing highly specific negative impacts on people (these impacts are
often bunched together), whilst pursuing general, across-the-board
political objectives. Hence regular politics produces a steady stream
of negatively affected minorities in its attempt to push through
decisions that are not asked for or supported by any majority and are
only legally 'possible' because they are acquiesced in individually by
an unwitting majority of non-affected people.[29]

If the specific political identities[30] thus produced now had to be
passed through the filter of out-and-out radical, possibly philosophical, dogmas before they were allowed to be considered politically
relevant or 'mature', the effect would be to reinforce quite considerably the filter-effect of existing structures. If it were only those

people who also collected radical Brownie-points in other areas of debate such as peace, women's issues, energy, and ecology, which are also products of the system's complexity and the existing power-structures, this would have an even graver effect than the much-maligned policy of 'patching-up capitalism'. It would be tantamount to unceremoniously 'stabilising the system' by deliberately neutralising the greater part of the forces that might become opposi-tional. There is therefore no choice but to respect the actual multi-plicity of individual political identities – along with the particular histories they bring in terms of experience, orientation, and preferences as the only possible basis for an alternative kind of politics; and to do so even, indeed precisely, where one is seeking to change existing preferences.

Secondly, people's habit of concentrating their involvement on one issue at a time is no less 'rational' than the traditionally preferred 'across-the-board' radicalism, and indeed, the reason for this is that the gamut of social demands generated by the promises and failures of the industrial society is far from being free of contradictions in itself. People are not to blame for this, and one does not by any means have to share the world-view of an organisation like I. G. Bergbau or of a bureaucrat at the energy department to have doubts about the logical and social compatibility of all the different demands (e.g. the demand for long-term security in living conditions, for untouched natural areas, for easily assimilable socio-technical systems, for com-munal forms of ownership based on principles of solidarity, for grass-roots decision-making procedures, for individual autonomy, for self-fulfilment at the workplace etc.).

The point at issue here is that if the 'need' for ever more radical awareness is not going to be confined to purely negative concepts ('destroy what is destroying you'), one has to live with the idea that people have in their heads a variety of visions (which probably change from time to time) of positive situations, and these visions would lose their political force if they were subjected to external pressure to conform. One should also bear in mind that the norm to which people would be required to make their demands conform would almost inevitably have to be determined arbitrarily; as a result, it would always remain open to dispute. In addition, one would not be able to exclude the possibility that the complexity of social relations has become too great for all the relevant issues and interconnections to be integrated in the minds of the politically

active. This excess pressure of problems does not militate
systematically against the notion that social movements can succeed,
but it is does militate against the idea of subjecting participant
awareness to measurement against 'standards of quality' that are
unattainable.

Complex transformations

In terms of those who carry it out, social change that is brought
about through multiple conflict is variable and restricted to the
particular. The people who conduct the conflicts are different in each
case. The things that ensure unity and continuity, in the sense of
some kind of 'development', are a few general principles and values
shared by all and eventually the institutional changes that are
brought about. In other words, the results of successful individual
conflicts rather than the preconditions for them.

'Pure' philosophies of life and a correspondingly acute sense of the
need to act in the cause of 'revolution' are not decisive here.
Cultivating an attitude that is uncompromisingly 'revolutionary' or
in fundamental opposition to the system lies in the same realm as
quite personal passions such as serious amateur sports, semi-
professional music-making, enthusiastic do-it-yourself, academic
ambition, managerial obsession (also to be found amongst
politicians), and so on. It seems pointless, indeed counterproductive,
to bank on an increase in passionate convictions.

Equally, it is misleading to suppose that there is a 'barrier because
people's outlook is tied into the system' (Bahro). The notion that
everything is so difficult only because 'capitalism has created within
individuals a psychological structure that conforms to its own
requirements' is an erroneous belief implanted by the mechanical
rehearsal of popular Marxist arguments.[31] According to this view,
there would have to be a kind of self-conquering act of the will before
anti-capitalist politics could or should get under way. But that which
here occupies the place of some kind of personalised 'power', namely
'capitalism', is nothing more than society itself. The problem 'how is
change possible?' always concerns both sides, the institutional structures (or the real situation) and the preferences of those who are
taking action/being affected.

But starting-points for changes on both sides of the 'system' that is
society are to be found only within that system; 'outside' there is
nothing, since the as yet non-existent cannot be either a cause or

basis of current action. What remains therefore is merely the existing preferences for specific rejections and concrete 'utopias', that is to say for multiple but particularised conflicts. The preferences that are born out of real situations and existing values provide the only route out of those situations, a route which will, if we choose to follow it, lead us to new and possibly 'more radical' preferences.

A change in individual desire is necessary for the process of transformation to make any progress (of course, other preconditions must be fulfilled for 'progress' to occur). Stated very crudely, one might imagine a stage-by-stage process in which specific preferences lead to changes in the conditions which gave rise to them and to which they relate. Within this ongoing process new conditions and new preferences develop, and these may, if successfully 'worked through' politically, lead to a change in conditions (e.g. in other areas of action), and so on. Strategically speaking, it would hardly be sensible to aim to achieve unity, or even linear uniformity, in the individual steps of the conflict or between one conflict and the next – unless one has a preference for the 'aesthetics' of mass organisation and revolutionary rhetoric to the effectiveness of action.

The following factors, on the other hand, may be considered positive:

(1) One important precondition of the 'subjective transformation' that has to take place at the same time as the overall transformation, namely, the fulfilment of the 'change yourselves' postulate, can only exist in conjunction with specific conflicts/issues. This is because the 'begin with yourself' approach can only ever relate to one section of a person's identity, alongside which a lot of other things must remain unchanged. As an appeal to transform oneself entirely, it is completely absurd.

(2) Because of the particularity of the conflicts, the threshold from individual desire to collective action is lower than in the case of a comprehensive programme of social transformation. Procedures for reaching agreement on objectives and means tend to be simpler and thus more promising. The prospect of having a large number of people participating makes the goal appear achievable and makes the corresponding preferences seem 'realistic'. As the adversaries would see it, this approach offers one advantage which, in certain circumstances, could be decisive. The militants are harder to identify and, because they only deviate slightly from the 'average' members of the population, it is very difficult to single them out and take

action against them.

(3)   By acknowledging that particularised conflicts have the same motive force in social change as was formerly claimed for aspirations to revolutionary organisation, one avoids the credibility pitfall mentioned above. It is positively incomprehensible that impending catastrophes should be evoked but that any attempt to intervene in their development should be rejected on the grounds that this would achieve 'nothing' and would 'only' gain time. Here too, the old faith in the future that was a feature of the labour movement immediately shines through. Within the framework of the mode of thought peculiar to it, that movement had much more ground to believe that its options for action would improve with time. As far as the ecological crisis is concerned, however, the opposite is true. A policy of wait and see will not bring solutions any nearer. Time swallows up the options for action.

Criteria of success
I am not concerned here to criticise or appraise specific components of the green/alternative package, which now covers practically all the areas dealt with by a departmentally organised politics. What does need to be done is to establish a level of discussion about political strategy at which concrete routine political demands, current extra-parliamentary conflicts, and the dynamics of complex trans-formations can be viewed (and of course represented) not as oppo-sites or alternatives, and thus as irreconcilable, but as related.

What should count as success may be summarised very generally as the creation of (more or qualitatively better) possibilities of action (options). What is meant by this is additional choices both in shaping life at the individual and collective levels and in moulding living conditions in accordance with ecological and emancipatory values. Put more simply: the central problem in every case is to find a way to 'live according to new values'.

Here again, two sides of social change come into play: the material/structural and the normative. In material terms, what is at issue here is the possibility of not having to concentrate one's atten-tion as an individual solely on the problems of securing one's exist-ence, and of having to spend as short a time as possible on this. This is the precondition for securing options and new possibilities at the subjective/normative level. Such options imply improved access to values which are 'objective' *vis-à-vis* existing social problems and problems of social development, which aim to give 'everyone' the chance to be involved in shaping society. This would lend purpose to the idea of using collective action to realise the values involved. Since there is no automatic solution here, nor any ideal methods of 'developing awareness', the only possiblity left is that individuals will learn through political activity. To increase the likelihood of individuals being confronted with insights and values which, in terms of the explanations and guidance they offer, are 'better suited' to the experiences and perceived problems than are exclusively traditional values.

Those who are active in the new social movements must, of all people, realise to what degree each of their own personal 'alternative' life-histories has been fostered by basic material security, by some degree of disengagement from restricted thought and behaviour and, most importantly, by relatively easy access to the stores of social knowledge. In other words, typical middle-class living conditions, socialisation, and education.

The struggle for life and autonomy of action
Although an increase in options can, very generally, be described as probably the most important criterion of success in multiple conflicts, it is practically impossible to identify in advance those issues which will constitute the breaking-points in future conflicts. All one can do is to offer a few cautious provisional observations on the current situation.

Apart from conflicts that are concerned with defending existing options for shaping one's life, including all the issues involving use of land, environmental protection, and industrialisation, there seems to be another, extremely important area of debate emerging at another level, namely the question of distribution of income or access to sources of income. The reason why this issue is becoming so crucial is that the central distributive mechanism – the 'labour market' – leaves a large and ever growing number of people 'out of account', and these people's claims to opportunities of securing an autonomous existence therefore remain unsatisfied. This is a problem for which a whole range of options for action going beyond the 'growth solution' have been proposed. These include redistributing existing work by introducing shorter working-hours, excluding certain categories of workers (women, older people, foreigners), introducing a minimum income that would be paid whether one is in

work or not and promoting the opportunities of securing a livelihood which exist within the informal or alternative economy.

The income problem makes itself felt particularly acutely when a
work-force is threatened with redundancy and calls for the continuation of a production process which in itself is a matter of
indifference to it. But what attracts so much attention in such cases is
only a particularly pronounced example of the interdependence that
prevails generally. The phenomenon of peoples depending on situations which they often do not just not care about but actually find
unpleasant, and yet still feel obliged to defend because this is the only
way they can provide for themselves, is a widespread one. It is a type
of dependence which those affected can generally only replace with
another dependence of the same kind but which they are unable to
remove individually. Dependence on the labour market or (in even
more general terms) on income is one important and effective
mechanism (but not the only one!) by which society safeguards itself
against various 'designs for change'. The traditionally recommended
antidote – getting rid of 'paid work', the undisputed root of all evil,
by 'abolishing capital-based relations' – is logical but ineffective,
since in order to bring this about, the very dependencies in question
would have to have been removed already, or at least considerably
slackened.

In the course of the history of the labour movement, attempts to
reduce people's dependence on a capital-dominated labour market
have attracted the label 'reformist'. It may today seem a paradox of
the history of ideas that the concrete attempts to win workers some
independence from capital – as an autonomous base for action –
were denounced from the standpoint of the 'revolutionary', no less,
as an expression of wrong thinking. This applies to all attempts to
launch a co-operative movement as well as to early socialist models
of community as developed within the framework of an 'island
strategy'.[32] A sober analysis on the basis of modern strategic theory
shows, however, that just these kinds of routes are very probably the
only ones open to people if they want to effect a change in the
structures on which they themselves depend.

In concrete terms: all opportunities of securing an 'alternative'
livelihood, outside the extortionate conditions offered by the labour
market in the interests of the economically and politically powerful,
are important. It would be too much of a digression here to enter into
a comparison of the concrete alternatives (transferred income, the

drastic redistribution of labour, self-help initiatives and neighbourhood projects, co-operatives, etc.). But even a quick glance at
possible criteria of suitability reveals what might be at least one of
the issues here. What is required is not a vision of how to achieve a
total 'opting-out', a vision that is comprehensible only to those
involved in the now distant alternative culture. What we need are
options for ordinary normal people, ways of 'surviving' materially in
communication with others and without loss of self-worth when the
firm closes down; when the stress of the job is too much, when you
want to swap jobs with your partner; when the options for collective
counteraction have been exhausted to no avail or have not even got
into gear but where an individual retreat would have little or no
political effect.

This undoubtedly multifarious 'second net' need not be so big as to
carry 'everyone' at once. To achieve the desired effect, namely the
ability to register protest more effectively from within the system
when one is either less dependent on its operations or is able to
choose between alternative modes of existence, requires far less than
this, even though this 'less' would constitute a minor social revolution in comparison with the present situation. Finally, there are
grounds for believing that options for substituting or complementing
one's livelihood will be all the more 'secure' the more concretely they
are organised. Space, working materials, communication networks,
self-managed funds, can in some cases offer more security after
dismissal than individual rights to payments.[33]

The effect of 'reformist' advances towards greater independence
from the labour market extends to both social levels. It produces
something resembling an 'Archimedean point', a deliberately
increased distance between centralised operations of the economic
system and individual living conditions. Only from this somewhat
'safe' distance are people able to apply effective levers to their
circumstances. Two obvious conclusions for political action follow
from this: in the struggle to secure choices as to how life is shaped,
criticism and indictment of the status quo are not enough. It is also
essential to have the courage to embark on positive, thoroughly
pragmatic measures which, in isolation, will always seem and probably will be inadequate. In addition, one should adhere to one of the
basic tenets of ecological/emancipatory politics: no progress at the
cost of social insecurity!

Beyond the economic principle: a second scale of values
Administratively, there is almost nothing one can do to 'recruit' more people to those systems of values in which ecological/emancipatory goals occupy a prime position. Such a change can happen only as part of a 'voluntary' reorientation. What one can and should do, however, is to strengthen the notion of the 'normality' of such values, to bolster the legitimacy of corresponding social claims and, most importantly, to defend claims to autonomy and self-fulfilment – as voiced originally by the women's movement – against attempts to make them conform to economic factors or naturalistic principles.[34]

The conflict of values and the importance of new and perhaps unconventional attitudes should not be underestimated, especially as they challenge conservative values. Such attitudes, like new 'material' options, have a strategic significance: in real conflicts they make it possible for individuals both to view the disadvantages and costs which their participation brings in terms that are other than purely economic, that is to say, as an investment leading to the fulfilment of 'qualitative needs' and to opt for 'indirect strategies' in order to achieve their objectives.[35] The thinking here is basically quite simple: sacrifices of a material/economic kind (e.g. the time and money spent on political activity) must appear as benefits on a second 'scale' if one wishes to count on something more than purely irrational action.

As an aid to understanding here, one should recall the strategic deficit suffered by a purely materialistic doctrine, which regards reference to subjective values as an 'idealist' deviation from the goal of securing resources. But in the light of an exclusively economic rationale, the material costs of collective action must inevitably appear as a 'step backwards'. Because success is so uncertain anyway, these costs seem too 'high'.[36] In this sense, ecological/emancipatory values, qualitative claims to autonomy in shaping one's life, are perhaps the most precious capital held by the ecological and other new social movements. It would be imprudent to squander this capital – for example in opportunistic attempts to 'extend the alliance' – by subordinating such claims to (undoubtedly justified) economic aspirations, especially at a time when even the trade unions will be increasingly dependent on motives of this sort in order to secure a minimum of influence over working conditions. The fact that the demand for a 'new way of working' has retained its

persuasiveness – indeed, has become even more persuasive – despite
unemployment and uncertainty in regard to livelihood indicates that
there is some hope as far as the progress of the conflict at the
value-level is concerned.

IV   The functions of the party in anonymous social change

The idea of social change as a product of asynchronous, particularised conflicts involving varying sets of non-radical protagonists is hard to square with the current concepts of what the
relation should be between movements and party. One thing is clear
however. Social conflicts are not 'staged' using administrative
means, they seem rather, looking at them with hindsight, to 'happen'. Apart from being able to provide organisational help in the
initial phases, and possibly having the chance to get any positive
results of the conflict 'ratified' by Parliament, the main task of a party
such as the Greens will be to adopt a positive attitude to conflicts that
are under way, in order to encourage extra-parliamentary movements and accelerate the dynamic of social change.

At the same time, however, the proposed projection of multiple
individual conflicts into one overall dimension – namely, securing
greater scope for the realisation of ecological/emancipatory values –
involves a great many preconditions. A political organisation acting
alongside and between the various conflicts is undoubtedly needed in
order to ensure continuity, gather and preserve experiences, and
safeguard the claims made during the conflicts against partisan
attempts at distortion or perversion. Only from the oversimplified
perspective of 'grass-roots groups parliamentarising themselves' was
it possible for it to seem as if the Greens were an appendage, an
organisational offshoot of initiatory politics. Their own particular
character, which is substantially different from that of a movement,
has now emerged more clearly, and there are indications that the
party is encountering special problems in the competition to recruit
members and win votes.

It would seem that, even when the pitfall associated with
radicalism (cf. Section II) has successfully been circumvented, the
phase of defining party tasks and identifying the special status of the
party *vis-à-vis* the social movements and conflicts will still not be
over. The problems listed below – which have been chosen arbitrarily rather than systematically – are intended to show what kinds

of tasks and dangers a party organisation can expect to meet as it tries to provide productive back-up to complex transformations.

Principles
Maintaining a productive attitude to autonomously conducted conflicts means reinforcing those factors which promote the change that is being sought and criticising anything that threatens to block, divert, or set it back. However obvious and simple this definition is, its practical realisation will remain a matter of dispute because, in the face of the various claims that have currency within the movements and the party, not always the same thing is defined as success. For this reason, it seems worth at least attempting to set out some 'highest' principles or guides to decision-making. A further motive for doing so is the subjective 'need' for very general guidelines.

The nub of the political objectives pursued in green politics, that is to say the essential, uncircumventable substance of all 'new' (i.e. 'across the board') claims in regard to political content and form, may – on the basis of programmes, statements, internal disputes, and the end-result of the process of self-recruitment that takes place as people join or leave the party – be summarised in two postulates: preservation and emancipation.

The preservation postulate[37] is common to all 'ecologically' formulated demands but relates in each case to quite different 'objects'. At the one extreme of ethically/aesthetically experienced threat, it applies to all natural resources endangered by industrialisation and civilisation (in particular, of course, the different forms of life). At the other extreme, the focus is the problem of resources faced by the industrial society and civilisation (the prime issue here is that of finite resources and their importance as raw materials). This preservation aspect is paradoxical on two counts. In the first place, there is a curious reversal in the way the problem is viewed at either extremity (in one case society appears as a cause of the threat, in the other it seems itself to be threatened). In the second place, it is clear that rational political objectives can be formulated only in the median area, not at the extremities.

Given that human beings are themselves part of nature, the ethical/aesthetic extreme postulating the total preservation of life[38] is self-contradictory. There are no conceivable circumstances under which we could avoid living 'at the expense of nature'. At the industrialistic extreme, on the other hand, natural resources only appear to be the focus of attention. In reality, what is at issue is a structure of needs shaped by industrial requirements, and the idea is to alter the production base of that structure so that as much of it as possible can be preserved unchanged. To the extent that needs depend directly on the production base, at this extremity too we come up against a contradiction. Needs are to be reformed in order that they can survive as unchanged as possible.[39] Application of the preservation postulate is therefore fraught with problems. What is meant by 'preserve' is not predetermined; its contents must be specified – and this must be done by weighing and balancing ethical norms and aesthetic/communicative claims[40] and also claims of a more material/economic nature.

In contrast to some facile notion of a hierarchy of needs, the two sorts of claims can hardly be played off against each other, so individual identities are built simultaneously on both. Economic satisfaction can hardly compensate for aesthetic loss, and vice versa. The conclusion is evident. Green/alternative politics is not really free (in the sense that it is unconstrained) to reinterpret existing definitions of problems in line with ideas of what should be preserved and of what should, in certain circumstances, be taken on board as a result of that preservation. Nor is it free to shift these definitions in another direction as it pleases. Attempts of this kind would miss the mark in that they would fail to coincide with people's view of themselves, and they would rapidly dampen willingness to engage in political activity.

The emancipation postulate scarcely needs explanation. It should be said, however, that it does not apply to blanket social categories, or indeed to class *per se*. It seems rather to relate primarily to the freedom of action demanded by individuals. Both normative and structural constraints on autonomy of action emerge as problems here, which is why proposed 'one-dimensional' solutions (improvements in structure but no change in discriminatory norms, or alterations in norms with persisting structural disadvantage) are regularly criticised and tend to be 'underestimated' (as a precondition for further progress). To date, the women's liberation movement seems to have been the most important supporter of a rigorous postulate of emancipation.

To identify preservation and emancipation as 'highest' principles is to acknowledge the different character of the other major ideas dealt with in alternative politics: these ideas are instrumental rather than goal-related. This is undoubtedly the case for the principle of 'grass-roots democracy' and for the socialist inheritance of the Greens. Procedures based on grass-roots democracy, and the vision of socialist institutions, originate in a (historical) context of ideas that only approximately 'hit home' as far as the claims that arise in present-day conflicts are concerned. This is why, in regard to ecological and emancipatory priorities in particular, recourse to 'tradition' always causes difficulties. These difficulties can hardly be got rid of by subordinating the new values to old, purely instrumental principles.

For success at the normative level of claims and values, two aspects in particular seem important. First, because of the understandable need for harmony there is undoubtedly a constant temptation for conservatives to discredit the sole medium in which social change takes place, namely social conflicts, as constituting lawlessness, instability, disorder, or an unwanted by-product of action. Instead of accepting objectives such as 'governability' and calm,[41] we should be aiming at precisely the opposite, promoting greater tolerance of conflict and demonstrating that to accept the (non-violent) working-out of conflicts as normal is an important condition of change. Particularly because of the need to make political capital out of the State's inability to direct affairs, we can hardly allow 'ungovernability' to trouble us.

Secondly, it is difficult, but important, to avoid the trap of adopting an unreflecting view of oneself as 'on the left'. Leaving aside the libertarian ecologists, with their vague programme of action, the Greens, both in their view of themselves and in the positions they adopt in social conflicts, are on the left as long as they always also assess political alternatives according to two genuinely 'left-wing' standpoints: that of power and that of distribution. Accordingly, the diminution of power, or its restraint, and a distribution policy of equalising effect, of benefit to disadvantaged groups, rank as indispensable secondary goals. What these policies mean in practice is that one must at all events oppose measures that bring losses in terms of power and distribution.

In reality, however, within the framework of political conflict, something more than this is always implied when it is asserted that certain positions are 'on the left'. Additional, internal fuel for conflict arises from the fact that 'leftness' is ill-defined in relation to the preservation and emancipation postulates. Not infrequently, industrial methods of production and styles of life are declared a fit 'object' for preservation, although articulated social claims tend rather towards compromise with the other extreme, namely that of nature preservation. Occasionally, the preservation postulate is made to bend to the emphatic primacy of particular principles of order or socialisation (abolition of all markets, nationalisation as a pre-condition of ecological production, and so on). In line with this, one often finds a politically defensive, and therefore unsuccessful policy of unreflectingly giving precedence to theoretically derived (sup-posedly objective) interests, over the real claims and preferences of individuals. In the sense crudely delineated here, being consistently 'left' easily leads one into a circle of political impotence, the harder it is to bring institutional changes about, and the more urgently they are 'demanded'. The growing distance between the demand and ordinary thinking is not regarded as troubling, because that thinking is judged to be 'desperate'.

Indeed, the lack of definition of a purely 'left-wing' position indi-cates the urgent need for a concise statement of the standpoint of the Greens on the 'new' and 'old' conflicts. Suggestions that lifestyle should be vigorously championed as a new principle of political legitimacy [42] have to date elicited little response. Yet to produce continuity between particularised conflicts, to highlight the goal common to all movements and as a basis for attacks on the old allegiances, it is essential to establish a new principle of progress that is clearly recognisable (and not capable of confusion with socialist tradition). One is unlikely to find anything more fitting than the preservation–emancipation–lifestyle threesome.

Opponents

In a conflict with superior opponents direct attack can bring nothing but defeat. Only when the industrial society ceases to be seen simply as a structure ensuring a certain distribution of power and is viewed instead as a precarious balance between several conditions of exist-ence that cannot just be fulfilled without more ado but are 'prob-lematic' and 'self-contradictory'. Only when one includes this second perspective does it become possible to identify suitable start-ing-points for exerting systematic influence. Since this involves con-crete empirical knowledge of the political areas concerned, all that can be offered in what follows are pointers to fruitful exploratory strategies.

In the first place, the deficiencies (the 'ungovernability') of the established institutions, their abundance of internal problems (contradictory objectives, poor integration, social conflicts of interest), and their relative inability to shape or control social relations in conformity with their 'requirements' (lack of competence, knowledge, and resources. Also their involvement in precarious 'alliances', the conflicts of interest in their surroundings, etc.). In other words, the whole complex system of one particular social sector must be exploited politically. Making skilful use of the chances one comes upon means managing, with a relatively small input of energy, to 'co-determine' the thrust of the necessary adjustments. By pointing out to bureaucracies, party machines, and other organisations the 'escape routes' that are, consciously or unconsciously, 'made available' to them through unpredictable 'upheavals' in their environment (these include organising boycotts, delegitimising 'normal' political practice, impeding the exercise of specific functions), one will get closer to the goals that are unreachable by direct attack, namely the extension of individual and collective options for action.

Secondly, one should bear in mind that in a highly differentiated society, despite enormous resources and differences in power, there are fewer opposing forces – either apparent or of the kind that have clearly to be combated – than is commonly supposed. It is true that there is a high degree of resistance to any kind of design for change, and that repressive or ideological mechanisms of exclusion exist for dealing with professed 'system-changers'. However, as far as those involved in the particularised conflicts of the new social movements are concerned, the situation is as follows: they are not confronted with a well-knit state whose actions are purposeful and free from self-contradiction; nor is 'capital' participating in the proceedings as an entity following a unified plan and presenting a united front. Divergent interests, asynchronicity in the perception of problems, the fact that one can equally be affected individually or in a global physical way by conflict, all these features of real or apparent disintegration suggest that we should 'dispense with the assumption, widespread in the Marxist tradition, that social relations are undergoing de facto homogenisation'.[43]

It is therefore not just nonsensical to call on individuals to ignore the fact that they are largely dependent on the State for securing their existence, by issuing rallying cries like the one advocating a nonspecific 'hostility to the State'. In addition to this, it is easy to forgo the options for action that are still open to one if one succumbs to the temptation to define one's own identity, for the sake of ease, in terms of an opponent depicted as all-powerful ('the State'). The more obvious course is to help the social movements develop a more differentiated picture of the area of conflict and to combine a tactic of divide and isolate *vis-à-vis* the other side with a capacity for forming flexible alliances that extend beyond one's own camp. One will also have to be prepared to adopt a dispassionate approach to the intentions of one's opponents because, strictly speaking, these should matter only to the extent that they are realistic, i.e. truly capable of being realised.

In complex situations of conflict one constantly has to allow for the possibility that particular objectives aimed at by the social movements can be achieved only because the opposing side puts forward compromise solutions. These solutions, however, always come loaded with some of the opponent's interests. For example, where the prevailing causal relations are no longer firmly established or 'easily' determined or where different preferential orders are ranged against each other and each person rates his objectives according to different time-scales, one person is looking to secure short-term success, another is hoping to realise long-term interests. In this sort of situation there are numerous virtual areas of overlap of the varying aims, and there is also self-delusion about the 'best' way of realising one's own objectives in each case. For both these reasons, it makes no sense to reject compromise suggestions wholesale merely because one's opposite number believes they will be to his advantage (or even solely to his advantage). In cases where interests and knowledge of the social situation have reached different stages of development, there is always the possibility – and it is one that should be taken into account – that one side will manage to achieve its objective without the other side's having to tear its hair out. After all, many instances of conflict can, in certain circumstances, become non zero-sum games.[44]

If one makes use of a window of opportunity as a way out of the status quo and towards new options for action (options geared to preservation and emancipation), one will hardly be able to close one's eyes to the fact that there is currently no one spot in society that offers access to 'the system' as a whole or to an overall 'logic' just sitting there waiting, as it were, to be switched over or flicked off. Whether having to rely on paid employment for one's existence does determine one's opportunities in life is something that is often decided by factors outside the workplace and the labour market (e.g. whether one lives in a large conurbation or in the regions, whether one has access to a network of relatives and friends or is forced like many elderly people to cope on their own, whether one has to go through the 'learning process' of blaming oneself for unemployment or is self-confident enough to make 'the best' of it, and so on). When and whether existing nuclear power stations will be taken out of service is only secondarily dependent on the wishes of a small number of owners of capital. It depends primarily on political decisions about the structures that determine need and wastage, and about substitute methods of generation. Such decisions are most likely to be taken when 'the desire for ecological economy measures' amongst the population coincides with economic difficulties arising from current political practice. Whether finally work and working hours can steadily be redistributed to the benefit of the unemployed is something that will doubtless be decided (if at all) through industrial action. Such action (in favour of a non-egoistical goal of this kind) comes about only when those workers who themselves have employment consider that the additional leisure time gained represents a greater benefit than would the enhanced income which they could secure for the same amount of effort.

Hence, if one is looking for an area of society that can provide a 'breaking-point in the system', one should not ignore the potentially explosive material provided by unsatisfied demands in 'structurally problematic' areas of society. It is true that people's existing preferences do not at all 'fit in with' the idea of a global programme of social upheaval but only they can provide the 'initial material' for structural changes that will themselves form the basis of new and possibly wider-ranging preferences.

Competition and co-operation

Even if it has opportunities of exerting influence outside Parliament, a party involved in parliamentary activity is always judged by its electoral success and by the influence it is able to exert on everyday politics as a result of the seats it holds in Parliament. Because of the uncertainty about the long-term effects of any compromises struck today, there is currently considerable resistance among the Greens to any kind of down-to-earth strategic exploitation of its influence at this level. The aversions in this area do not all stem from the particular risks associated with party competition, but are also due in large measure to a general predilection for the supposed alternative of radical-cum-fundamental opposition (cf. Section II).[45]

It is no easy matter to work out whether the optimum realisable degree of influence can be achieved by the formula 'toleration without participation in government'. There are a number of arguments which lead one to believe that the mere 'threat' of a conditional coalition produces considerably higher dividends than the modest goal of toleration. When these two options are compared, far too crude a picture of the possible effects is often painted, both in terms of how 'the others' will react to offers of co-operation, and in terms of the repercussions of success or failure on the Greens. I propose here to deal briefly with one or two finer aspects.

(1)   The opportunity which the party sometimes has (because of the way the seats are divided) to participate in decision-making is without a doubt the most important lever it has on the political process, because the party is not identical with the social movements. There is, it is true, no reason to regard this as a source of real power, but the mere fact that there is a chance and need for co-operation which 'the others' are aware of and have to take account of in their behaviour opens up opportunities for exerting influence, often without its having to go as far as an agreement on co-operation. In general, it is the party most 'threatened' by voter-migration or by dependence on coalition partners that needs to react preventively. This need not always be the 'larger' partner; the Greens can also end up in this quandary.

Of course, the motive for the preventive accommodation – namely anxiety about competition – is 'external' to the issues over which the accommodation takes place. But even ill will cannot prevent certain 'material' effects from being achieved – thanks to acceptance of 'new' political issues or of ways of defining problems that had been rejected up to that point. This mechanism can be put to good use as a means of reinforcing one's own political aims, provided one subscribes to the premiss that political success in building up awareness of problems and alternatives is greatly dependent on access to 'published opinion'.

(2)   In reality, this lever is effective only as long as there is no claim to a monopoly on certain issues and problems. If particular questions (or answers) are represented as not being general or not being capable of generalisation (e.g. as demands that are only com-

prehensible within the framework of a 'green' view of the world), this produces a negative effect of self-isolation. It is then all the easier for the competitor-parties to confirm the particularised nature of the opposition's approach – which they have 'always found regrettable' – by continuing to refuse to discuss the issues put forward. There should therefore be as little party-political identity attached to the actual social claims and to generalisable perspectives on problems as possible. Political identity is not in any case endangered as quickly as is often suspected. First, because in most cases issues need to be stated emphatically and brought to a head, and this need, which is necessarily played down at the outset, is one that the 'accommodators' can scarcely satisfy of their own accord. Second, because in many cases only increased awareness of problems provides the conditions in which an understanding of systematic alternatives affecting the logic of social development can flourish.

(3)   This undoubtedly results in a counterposing pressure to conform on the party that is challenging the status quo. One has, after all, to be prepared to venture a little way out on to the opponent's territory so that the opponent registers the competition not merely as a flash in the pan but as a real threat. Every party (by no means just the Greens) concerns itself with issues of social development if only out of a desire to preserve its positions of influence. It is likely that not every way of presenting an issue will evoke the preventive action one is seeking. Thus ideas about opting out are hardly going to be an appropriate means of 'co-determining' the SPD from outside. This is more likely to be achieved by proposals that relate to real demands and can be presented in the form of an option for modernisation.[46]

(4)   The lever mechanism described above works, so to speak, as a catalyst (accommodations on the part of the opponent take place independently of any actual co-operation). The most hotly disputed issue at the moment, however, is the price of formally agreed toleration – both in positive terms, in respect of the value of possible concessions, and in negative terms, in respect of 'co-responsibility' for a political process that is largely beyond influence. There may be a fear that a party that is pursuing quite different objectives will appear corrupt in the eyes of its voters if, for tactical reasons, it agrees to toleration in exchange for only minimal concessions. However, one can start out on a more differentiated basis if at least two conditions are fulfilled, as they were in Hesse at the beginning of 1984. First, there must be a strong aversion among the voters to a

'status quo minus'. Which is what the 'grander' coalitions in each case are viewed as. Secondly, it must be necessary to demonstrate a readiness to co-operate in order to have any chance at all of acquiring the status of a negotiating partner capable of co-operation.

(5)   Account must be taken of the fact that deriving the greatest possible dividends from parliamentary co-operation depends to a large extent on the success of one's own preliminary political work. What is meant here is the ability to determine to a great degree (that is to say, to an extent that is disproportionately great in relation to the share of votes secured) the issues over which social disputes are conducted. If, on top of this, one can manage to rearrange the field of conflict according to one's own political perspective, by the way in which objectives and actions are formulated, the competition mechanism has the effect of boosting the quantitatively weaker party. It may therefore be assumed that increased skill in formulating social problems from the dual standpoint of (ecological) preservation and (social) emancipation will help one secure a degree of initiatory power whose benefits cannot be measured in percentages (of votes).

This too is ultimately a non-zero-sum game, one that is played beyond the level of numbers (be it numbers of seats in Parliament or budget entitlement). An effectively developed initiatory power will not, admittedly, cause any major upheavals in concrete terms. However, as a complement to extra-parliamentary conflicts it can give a vigorous shake to the technocratic monopoly on defining what is desirable and feasible. The main obstacle here lies not in the power of others but in one's own inability to formulate a type of politics that is geared to perceived problems and unsatisfied demands. This is undoubtedly where one of the reasons for the Greens' present lack of power to act is to be found, namely in the fact that there is a dearth of political ideas in the transitional area between highly generalised (and sometimes symbolically overloaded) demands such as the immediate shut-down of nuclear power stations, and minor, particularised consolatory steps such as special job-schemes or local measures relating to nature conservation.

Organisational culture
The multiplicity of specific issues, their unequal evolution and, most importantly, the heterogeneous social provenance of those engaged in political activity make practical pluralism an indispensable

precondition of existence for the Greens. In addition, there have been demands from various quarters that the organisation's boundaries should be open to initiatives, projects, protest groups, and indeed, other parties, so that discussion does not ossify in totally party-centred preoccupations. The imperative of internal pluralism and external openness is one thing, the preconditions which allow one to appreciate the political value of these features and to cope with the problems to which they may give rise, is another. This has a much greater bearing on the party's true problems than do all the best-intentioned recommendations in the world. The reason for this is that several factors contribute to the party's not being one integrated whole, pursuing a number of common objectives, and to its not being likely, in the near future, to transform itself into one entity with a single will.

Given this situation, the dilemma of radical majorities described above (Section II) results in some being driven towards the escape-hatch of radical rhetoric and the tendency to marginalisation, whilst others weigh up various alternative strategies of a religious or opportunistic nature. Reliance on socialist traditions and their myth of revolution produce centripetal as well as centrifugal tendencies, with the paradoxical result that currents of opinion that have no particular attitude to the 'new' conflictual typology may well end up at the centre of the organisation.[47] The upshot is that in the one area in which there are no forces deemed to be hostile – namely the area of organisation and communication – the Greens are unable to create anything and are not, so to speak, 'their own masters'.

Both the problem of integration and, to a greater extent, the need to produce a co-ordinated external impact make heavy demands on the internal discussion process in terms of ensuring that self-education and the determination of interests and priorities be organised in a rational and discursive manner. Yet lack of time and (personal) resources dictates that internal trials of strength are the preferred method of decision-making. The question of recruiting new members and of extending social support are largely left to chance, or to the whim of local conditions – that is, if they are not actually secretly exploited for particularist purposes.

Since there is no sign of any imminent strategy of self-transformation (within the framework of a more strongly integrated yet 'open' organisation), all one can do is helplessly point to the importance of the problem and warn against senseless 'apportioning of blame' by drawing attention to the fact that the Greens' internal differences are not brought about merely by ideological prejudices and divergences in strategic premises. What causes the trouble is the diverse and partially contradictory social demands which are produced by capitalist society and which struggle, sometimes in concert and sometimes against each other for recognition within the party.

Even if the fate of the party does not determine the success or failure of the social movements, the dynamic and continuity of those movements could none the less be given a boost by the political potency of the Greens. All the more so if it were possible to combine ecological/emancipatory politics with a strategy that was able to exploit as many options for action as possible because it had freed itself from ideas traditionally associated with movement-centred parties (cumulative attainment of a majority at one extreme, and centralist avant-garde organisation at the other).

V   Concluding remarks

The point of view proposed here, and the strategic approach that follows from it, run counter to a number of traditional strategic standpoints of reformist and revolutionary bent. Quite a few politically active individuals cling as passionately to the idea of an imminent (because necessary) revolution as to the aim of a society refashioned in ecological/emancipatory mould. But how important is it really, to have strategic approaches that are consonant with reality and non-utopian? Is it not conceivable that self-delusion about what is feasible, and an excessive degree of radicality, though irrational, are perhaps necessary conditions of success? There are counter-arguments to this. The first is that the theory which needed to make these kinds of immunising claims in regard to its realisation in practical political terms has now revealed that it has a number of structural faults (not only that it does not conform well to reality but also that it suffers from internal discrepancies). The second, on which I lay great emphasis here, is that there can be no criterion of optimum falsity when one is aiming to cultivate the habit of confident and purposeful action. If, however, there is no such thing as 'expedient' wrong thinking, the only course left is the quest for logical consistency and for the greatest proximity to reality, and a striving to avoid the perils of self-delusion.

Another important question is how great is the risk of adopting what may turn out to be a wrong strategy? Does one irretrievably lose some opportunities if one sets one's mind on multiple, complex conflicts involving varying, non-radical participants, instead of setting about convincing people, one after the other, of the necessity of 'the revolution'? The answer is simple, the approaches suggested here do not destroy any options, not even the option of revolution, should this exist. What they aim to do instead is to ensure the optimum use of real, existing opportunities. If these opportunities should include the possible emergence of a revolution (whatever that is taken to mean), then this would be brought to light precisely through the proposed strategy. Precisely because of this, a policy of extending the opportunities for action and the variety of approaches is superior to any campaign of radicalisation, however skilful its rhetoric.

There is a further problem. Can we really think only in terms of what is politically possible? Does this constraint not keep us unnecessarily bound up in the system? Everything that has been said up to now, in answer to this precise question, is intended to persuade that there are no paths to the transformation of society that do not exist in society itself. The politically possible is not one definite thing, not something that is fixed once and for all, it changes, in the form of an increasing or decreasing leeway, concomitantly with, and by virtue of, political action. But the opposite also exists, political impossibilities, that is to say, logically impossible things that one can think and express but cannot have or make. One example of something that is unrealisable in this sense is the desire for rapid radical upheaval (revolution), when it is articulated, because the preconditions of a hoped-for social change (and therefore also of the revolution) are absent. This is an instance of the recurrent confusion of two senses of the word 'necessary'. Is a change necessary (in the sense of inevitable) because the conditions for it have been fulfilled, because it is already 'mapped out in the system'? Or is it asserted to be necessary precisely because this is not the case, because desire finds no foothold in reality? This second variant is closely associated with the mythical hope in revolution.

Pointless striving to discover the preconditions of political action in its potential results amounts to a policy of wait-and-see. It is quite simply hoping for the advent of something unknown that will relieve one of the wearisome task of having to 'make politics'[48] with real, existing people, with their actual wishes and (partially contradictory) demands. However difficult this may be (and little has been said here about how to cope with these difficulties), it is the only opportunity available of taking one's own objectives seriously.

The more urgent a radical social change appears to be, the less one should ignore its preconditions. Hence this essay is ultimately simply a plea to respect the real starting-points for transition into a different logic of social development. These starting-points are multiple particularised conflicts, varying protagonists who are never 'totally radical', and, in particular, operation at a normative level of politics, where new, goal-related values take hold which help us to avoid the trap of exclusively economic thinking and to take the step from subjective desire to collective action. All this is not 'the incidental bit' that diverts us from the goal of 'radically reshaping' society. It is a starting-point and the first sizeable stretch along the path. We shall have to venture along that path if we want to find out how far it leads.

Notes

1   Rainer Trampert in his speech to the sixth Federal Assembly of the Greens, 18–20 Nov. 1983, as reported in *grüner basis-dienst,* 12 (1983), p. 11.

2   Interview with Winfried Kretschmann in *Moderne Zeiten,* 11 (1983), p. 26.

3   Rudolf Bahro as reported in the minutes of the 'Grüne Perspektiven' discussion–forum organised by *Kommune* and *Moderne Zeiten* on 15 Oct. 1983, p. 6.

4   Achim Bergmann, Gisela Erler, Wolf-Dieter Hasenclever, Ulrich Hausmann, Ernst Hoplitschek, Gerald Hübner, Hajo von Kracht, Winfried Kretschmann, Rudolf Leineweber, Boje Maaßen, Dieter Marcello, Thomas Schmid and Josef Schwab, 'Wider die Lust am Untergang', *Frankfurter Rundschau,* 268 18 Nov. (1983), p. 11.

5   The implication is not always that the Greens as a party would have to secure the majority of the votes. The requirement that the party should be able to command a majority is cited in a non-specific sense and thus relates to the totality of the new social movements or to the willingness to support a radical programme of reform through a number of very varied activities.

6   Cf. Bernd Guggenberger, *Bürgerinitiativen in der Parteiendemokratie* (Stuttgart: Verlag Kohlhammer, 1983), pp. 94 ff.

7   Cf. also Thomas Schmid, 'Über die Schwierigkeiten der Grünen in Gesellschaft zu leben und zu denken', *Freibeuter,* 15 (1983), pp. 44–58, this ref. p. 51.

8   Cf. Guggenberger, *Bürgerinitiativen,* pp. 107 ff.; Norbert Kostede,

'Mixtum compositum. Der Preis für Regierbarkeit', *Freibeuter*, 15 (1983), pp. 59–68.

9 Interview with Petra Kelly in *Der Spiegel*, 24 (14 June 1982), pp. 47–56, this ref. p. 53.

10 Cf. Norbert Seitz, 'Historische Anmerkungen zum Sinn einer parlamentarisch repräsentierten Fundamentalopposition', in Wolfgang Kraushaar (ed.), *Was sollen die Grünen im Parlament?* (Frankfurt/M.: Verlag Neu Kritik, 1983), pp. 113–19. On the SPD's pre-First World War view of itself as fundamentally opposing the system on principle, cf. Cora Stephan, ' "Grundsätzlich fundamental dagegen", Basis oder Demokratie?', in Matthias Horx, Albert Sellner and Cora Stephan (eds.), *Infrarot. Wider die Utopie des totalen Lebens* (Berlin: Rotbuch Verlag, 1983), pp. 35–58.

11 On this see Helmut Wiesenthal, 'Raumschiff Erde? Dilemmata des Ökologiekonflikts', in Georg Vobruba (ed.), *'Wir sitzen alle in einem Boot', Gemeinschaftsrhetorik in der Krise* (Frankfurt/M. and New York, 1983), pp. 59–79, this ref. pp. 65 ff.

12 There is no doubt that one can learn from failings and errors, but it is a grave contravention of logic to suppose that adverse experiences, failures, and defeats can constitute more than opportunities for learning, namely bases for action. It is this kind of misunderstanding which underlies the supposition that 'through political struggle and the struggle of the trade unions, the proletariat is led to the conclusion that it cannot change its situation radically by means of this struggle' (Rosa Luxemburg, 1899, in 'Sozialreform oder Revolution', as quoted in Luxemburg, *Politische Schriften*, I (Frankfurt/M.: Europäische Verlagsanstalt, 1966), p. 83). Thus it was hoped that the disappointments suffered in everyday conflict would produce positive effects in terms of lessons learned ('realisation', 'political maturity', 'class-consciousness'). But if failures can be predicted for the 'leadership', then they can in principle also be predicted for the 'led'; and if action is taken anyway, then other factors,and criteria for success and failure derived from those factors, become decisive. The logical error is therefore a double one. Firstly, 'learning from errors' can only be a non-intended by-product of action, and secondly, this learning effect is reason enough to avoid its repetition (on this see Jon Elster, 'States that are Essentially By-products', *Social Science Information*, 3 (1981), pp. 431–73, esp. pp. 452, 462.

13 Thomas Ebermann/Michael Stamm in an interview in *Moderne Zeiten*, 11 (1983), p. 32.

14 Stamm, *Moderne Zeiten*, p. 34.

15 Ibid.

16 Kretschmann, *Moderne Zeiten*, 11 (1983), p. 32.

17 Cf. Kurt Edler, 'Wie zum letzten Gefecht', *Moderne Zeiten*, 12 (1983), p. 15.

18 Bergmann *et al.*, 'Wider die Lust'.

19 Cf. Jon Elster, *Ulysses and the Sirens, Studies in Rationality and Irrationality* (Cambridge: Cambridge University Press, 1979).

20 For further references see Helmut Wiesenthal and Karl Hinrichs, 'An den Grenzen des Arbeiterbewußtseins. Argumente für eine erweiterte Per-

spektive', *Gewerkschaftliche Monatshefte*, 12 (1983), pp. 775–88.
  21 Cf. Ronald Inglehart, *The Silent Revolution* (Princeton: Princeton University Press, 1977). Also Kai Hildebrandt and Russell Dalton, 'Die neue Politik', *Politische Vierteljahresschrift*, 18 (1977), pp. 230–56.
  22 Incidentally (in regard to the discussion about the State's monopoly on power), what is particularly unpleasant about the State's monopoly on power as far as a radical opposition is concerned is not so much the nature of the monopoly as the general presumption of legitimacy when it is implemented, even in cases where it oversteps the bounds of legality. This means as a rule that the legitimacy of state power is discussed only after it has been applied (and had a deterrent effect), whereas the legitimacy of 'social power' (whatever shape this might take) is discussed, and thus called into question, by the protagonists themselves, as soon as there is the slightest chance of its manifesting itself – in other words, in advance. But presumptions of legitimacy are a decisive factor in determining the success of all manifestations of 'social power', because only the expressive (symbolic) character of that power can effect change, the institutional structures of society cannot be changed by physical/mechanical means.
  23 Cf. esp. Guggenberger, *Bürgerinitiativen*; Claus Offe, 'Konkurrenzpartei und kollektive politische Identität', in Roland Roth (ed.), *Parlamentarisches Ritual und politische Alternativen* (Frankfurt/M. and New York: Campus Verlag, 1980), pp. 26–42. Also Herbert Kitschelt, 'Parlamentarismus und ökologische Opposition', in Roth (ed.), *Parlamentarisches Ritual*, pp. 97–120; Claus Offe, 'New Social Movements: Challenging the Boundaries of Institutional Politics', *Social Research*, 52 (1985), pp. 817–68; Klaus P. Japp, 'Selbsterzeugung oder Fremdverschulden. Thesen zum Rationalismus in den Theorien sozialer Bewegungen', *Soziale Welt*, 3 (1984), pp. 313–29.
  24 Jürgen Habermas, *Theorie des kommunikativen Handens*, II (Frankfurt/M.: Suhrkamp, 1981), p. 576.
  25 Offe, 'New Social Movements', p. 43.
  26 *Ibid.*
  27 Joachim Hirsch, 'Alternativbewegung – eine politische Alternative?', in Roth (ed.), *Parlamentarisches Ritual*, pp. 12–46, this ref. p. 137.
  28 On the varied nature of actual social movements operating in the 'approaches' to the Greens, see Kitschelt, 'Parlamentarismus', and Angela Bolaffi and Otto Kallscheuer, 'Die Grünen: Farbenlehre eines politischen Paradoxes', *Prokla*, 51 (June 1983), pp. 62–105.
  29 Cf. Kitschelt, 'Parlamentarismus', pp. 116 ff.
  30 Offe, 'New Social Movements', p. 37.
  31 Unknown author, cited from memory.
  32 This is by no means a new observation. Cf., for example, Georges Sorel, *Die Auflösung des Marxismus* (Jena: Verlag Gustav Fischer, 1908), esp. pp. 52 and 65 ff.
  33 This aspect also figures in the 'minimum income' issue. The question of immediate individual independence from centralised political decision-making bodies is one that should at least not be viewed as unproblematic.
  34 Cf., for example, Walter Oswalt, 'Die politische Logik der

Sonnenblume', in Kraushaar (ed.), *Was sollen die Grünen?*, pp. 93–112.
Oswalt performs the miraculous feat of distilling some of the principles of
the party 'die Grünen' from water (e.g. p. 109).

35 Cf. Elster, *Ulysses*, pp. 9 ff.

36 Cf. Adam Przeworski, 'Material interests, class compromise, and the
transition to socialism', *Politics and Society*, 10: 2, (1980), pp. 125–53. It is
possible to reconstruct the same situation on the basis of power-theory. Only
when the less powerful side has exactly the same preferences as the powerful
side, in other words when both sides value or fear the same things, is the less
powerful side completely at the mercy of its extortioner.

37 For a detailed account, see Claus Offe, 'Griff nach der Notbremse', in
Kraushaar (ed.), *Was sollen die Grünen?*, pp. 85–92.

38 Examples of this are Oswalt, 'Die politische Logik der
Sonnenblume', and Manon Maren-Grisebach, *Philosophie der Grünen*
(Munich: Verlag Olzog, 1982).

39 As an example, see a paper by the author on the environmental issues
raised at this end of the preservation scale: Helmut Wiesenthal, 'Natürliche
Knappheit und die Zukunft des Kapitalismus', in *Alternative
Umweltpolitik*, Argument-Sonderband AS 56 (Berlin: Argument Verlag,
1981).

40 A particularly detailed exegesis of the thesis of the infringement of
aesthetic and communicative needs is given in Uwe Schimank,
Neoromantischer Protest im Spätkapitalismus (Bielefeld: AJZ-Verlag,
1983).

41 Cf. Petra Kelly, 'We want to make the Federal Republic governable
by renewing the content of politics and instituting a new political culture';
quoted from, 'Offener Brief an Willy Brandt', in Petra Kelly, *Um Hoffnung
kämpfen* (Bornheim-Merten: Lamuv Verlag, 1983), this ref. pp. 188 ff.

42 Cf. Claus Offe, 'Die Logik des kleineren Übels', *Die Zeit*, 46 (9 Nov.
1979), p. 76. Also Guggenberger, *Bürgerinitiativen*, p. 57. One cannot
disregard the fact, either, that the very broad *Prinzip Leben* (the title of a slim
volume published by Petra Kelly and Jo Leinen (Berlin: Olle & Wolter,
1982) has not up to now acquired any significance as an integrating factor
amongst the Greens.

43 Offe, 'Konkurrenzpartei', p. 37.

44 This is the case, for example, when one 'player' is pursuing an
economic objective (e.g. saving resources) and the other is looking to achieve
a qualitative change in the state of affairs (e.g. increased autonomy).

45 A strategy of radicalisation need not insist on following the all too
obvious maximalist route. Supposedly cleverer variants may try to remain
just beyond the putative area of compromise in each case, in order to be able
to give proof of 'incapacity for reform' to the negotiating partner. For a
critique of this strategy, see Joschka Fischer, 'Für einen grünen
Radikalreformismus', in Kraushaar (ed.), *Was sollen die Grünen?*, pp.
35–46.

46 Cf. Johannes Berger and Norbert Kostede, 'Fundamentalopposition
und Reformpolitik', in Kraushaar (ed.), *Was sollen die Grünen?*, pp. 13–27,
this ref. p. 26.

47   On the various colours of the Greens, see Bolaffi/Kallscheuer, 'Die Grünen', pp. 80 ff.

48   Lest any misunderstanding should arise at this late stage, it should be said that not all unsatisfied desires or social claims are suitable as fuel for productive conflicts over ecological/emancipatory values. Even a political approach intended to cope with extremely wide-ranging claims of this kind cannot avoid making some selections. Social movements are not *Volkspartei*.

2

Between identity and modernity
The new middle classes, social movements, and the crisis in the Greens*

I A new kind of voter

A spectre is haunting electoral campaign offices, the spectre of the 'new middle classes'. Not only do they constitute a steadily growing section of the electorate, but their social make-up and political attitudes also clearly distinguish them from the classic supporters of both social democracy and Christian democracy.[1] Their most striking characteristic, however, is their electoral behaviour. No other group of voters appears so obstinate and yet so flexible when it comes to casting its vote. These are voters for whom the act of voting signifies more than just an opportunity to declare allegiance to 'their' party. They want to influence the course of politics. One can say without exaggeration that the voters of the 'new middle classes' are the ones who decide the elections.

The electoral campaign managers of the *Volksparteien* are particularly unnerved by the behaviour of these new voters, given that they now make up about 40 per cent of the active electorate. On the one hand, they are 'rational' voters, not bound to a particular party and therefore receptive in principle to arguments, successful performance, and promises. On the other hand, they appear to threaten the autonomy of the parties, because they do not gear their conduct to their past electoral decisions but to their present interests and the state of the issues. These 'feckless' voters pursue their own goals and look for effective outcomes, whether these be lower taxes or more effective environmental protection measures. Nor do they suffer any identity complexes in 'lending' their vote to one party on one occasion and to another the next. Consequently, they see themselves not as seduced by party competition but as participating in it – actors

* co-authored by Tom Stryck

acting in their own interests, pursuing their own individual 'micro-strategies'. The reaction of professional politics is one of utter help-lessness. It labels those using the modest means at their disposal – namely, their vote – to 'do their own politicking', as 'floating voters'. It condemns their unpredictable behaviour as unprincipled.

Whilst electoral analysts identify 'trends towards decon-centration' and record a fragmentation in the traditional followings of the CDU/CSU (Christlich-Demokratische Union/Christlich Soziale Union) and SPD, party strategists ponder the question of appropriate longer-term responses. Given that the new voter-flexibility renders the classic instruments used to attract and integrate support useless. The growing instability in party preferences means that the rituals of pseudo-communication between the parties and their traditional voters have become mean-ingless. Abstract programmes, ideological image, and emphatic demarcation from rival parties are losing their effect. The new voter is undoubtedly not completely bereft of ideological needs and feel-ings of group identity. What he/she is chiefly concerned with is the proven or presumed competence of the parties in tackling problems. There is an increasing incidence of dichotomy between party preference and vote cast. The fact that there is also a great deal of scepticism in regard to the ability of the party system as a whole to do the job of representation is demonstrated by declining turnout.

At first, the growing proportion of rational floating voters seems to present a problem only to the big parties. Majorities seem in danger of 'tipping over', and presumed trends turn out to be mere wishful thinking. These direct effects benefit the Greens without any effort on their part. However, there is no guarantee (and rational voters are the least likely to provide a guarantee of stability!) that the newly-won voters will stay loyal to the Greens if the party merely commends itself as a 'lesser evil' in relation to the other parties. Stabilising the present favourable situation would be possible only if the Greens managed to foster that which is currently benefiting them. That the competition to win over the new voter cannot be conducted merely as a contest of slogans (like the CDU's 'Freedom in place of socialism', or the SPD's 'We in Nordrhein-Westfalen') has been demonstrated in the state elections that have taken place over the last few years. The voters have punished those – like the Greens in Hamburg and the SPD in Hessen – who have relied on mere sym-bolism, offering the electorate nothing more than the exposure of rivals (as did the Greens) or a simple unimaginative prolongation of government (as did the SPD).

Up to now the Greens have regarded it as unnecessary – indeed, as downright inappropriate – to engage in any analysis of the electoral spectrum or of the strategies of the established parties. In the early years the Greens presented themselves as an 'anti-party party' (Petra Kelly) and encouraged the voters to vote Green as a way of expressing their rejection of the merry-go-round of the established parties. But neither the voters nor the rival parties remained the same. The Greens operating in Parliament are the object of a different set of expectations than they were as a catch-all movement in its formative phase. Their rivals, who have become painfully aware, in the zero-sum contest for votes, of the cost of ignoring ecological issues, are beginning to 'learn'. They are adapting to the expanded agenda, either through practical incrementalism or in purely symbolic ways. Slowly and almost too late, the Greens are realising that the contest to present the arguments and win the votes must be geared not only to social democracy – i.e. the Greens' nearest rival, but to both the big parties. After all, the Greens too owe their political weight increasingly to the new voters. These are individuals who (once) regarded the SPD as the lesser evil but have become disillusioned, or who, equally illusionless and without the slightest sense of identification, vote CDU/CSU when there seems to be little difference between the latter and the 'old-fashioned' SPD on new issues which they regard as important (these range from women's issues to environmental policy). Or finally, those voters who gear their choice to considerations of competence and effectiveness and who tend to withhold their vote if there is no convincing alternative.

A sensitive and sober appraisal of the new voter, his expectations and readiness for involvement, is therefore indicated. Since the Greens do not wish to be a party that is content simply to be present in Parliament, it would be wrong to propose a mechanical adjustment to the changed voter-context. The Greens are still a party of the movements, albeit with waning intensity. None the less, closer inspection of the changed realm of the social movements is also called for. Here, as in the case of changed voter-intentions, a demy-thologised interpretation of the situation is called for. We shall begin by explaining why the new middle classes represent not a threat but a solid chance of development for the Greens (Section II). However, exploiting this opportunity necessitates a more open and productive relationship with the social movements (Section III), as well as a readiness to keep the Greens' own identity-related needs – as expressed in Green fundamentalism – in check (Section IV).

II On the political character of the new middle classes

One does not need the incentive of electoral tactics to examine the milieu, perceptions, political preferences, and degree of commitment associated with the 'new middle classes'. It is sufficient to recall that the 'new middle classes' are a product of the same processes of social and cultural change which gave rise to the Greens. Let us cast a backward glance. During their early years, the Greens served to a great degree as a joint 'spearhead' for numerous segmented areas of protest and oppositional forces. In so doing, they gradually added another, ecological (in the broadest sense of the term) line of conflict to the old German confessional and welfare state-based lines of conflict that had characterised politics up till then. The task of representing that new line of conflict was assumed by the Greens. It should not be forgotten that the emergence and gradual consolidation of the Greens is in no way the cause but rather an expression of the increasing willingness to call into question the 'sacred cow' of industrial growth and technological innovation and to make this a subject of public debate, and to adjust political action to this fundamentally critical stance. As the debate has advanced and the Greens' critical perspective has spread, they have found themselves confronted with an unforeseeen dilemma. On the one hand, they continue to be an alternative party, with an anti-institutional self-image and strong links with extra-parliamentary movements which, in accordance with the self-image they developed during the 1970s, seek to transform 'the whole of society' by means of 'radical' intervention. On the other hand, they have managed, through a political programme that is directed against the dominant patterns of growth, industry, and technolgy, to develop so much pressure for discourse and action that influential executive and administrative positions have ended up within their grasp. These positions now have to be secured if the Greens are not to give the lie to their own claims of the need for action and their own assiduous and well-founded mistrust of established politics.

In such a situation, there seem to be only two options for action. If the Greens bow to their 'traditional' supporters, who warn of an

inexorable adjustment to the 'logic' of bureaucracy and industrialism, then they may go down in history as far-sighted prophets of
impending catastrophes, but they will not be able to do anything to
change the course of things. If, on the other hand, they try to stop the
worst fears from being realised, they will probably succeed in
recruiting additional support and in chalking up some limited
material successes but will, in the process, violate 'radical' objectives
and disappoint their original followers. Are both these alternatives
equally real? The answer is to this question is no, because the
decision in favour of the steady transformation of 'radically'
motivated support into parliamentary and institutional influence has
already tacitly been taken. The green constituency has long since
ceased to be made up solely of adherents of a 'radical alternative
system', e.g. jobless young people, academic protest-voters, and
'alternatively minded' employees in the various branches of the
service economy. It also includes individuals who regard themselves
as admiring of, or dependent upon the latest economic and
technological developments. The Greens will probably never be able
to become the sole, or even the major representative of the 'new
middle classes'. The latter's fragmented nature and their growth,
encouraged by the economic-cum-technological dynamic, confronts
the Greens, as well as the other parties, with a political force that is
committed yet resolutely 'non-utopian'. Those who have long been
engaged in criticising 'the system' from within have some very concrete views as to how they would like to shape the course of events,
and the only way for the emotionalist green approach of uncom-
promising opposition to the system to survive these views is for the
positions of influence that have been gained to be vacated again.

The new middle classes are a multi-faceted phenomenon. Their
members bear all the hallmarks of the latest phase of social
modernisation. These are an increased level of education and
(material) well-being, transformation of economic and professional
structures (expanding service-sectors, increased percentage of white-
collar workers and civil/public servants), and urbanisation (decrease
in social ties, increase in geographic and social mobility). The values
associated with them correspond to the new flexibility and recep-
tivity to innovation that are demanded at the workplace. These seem
to boil down to a relatively stable set of social, political, and cultural
dispositions. Recognition for work done, success, professional
advancement, the gearing of conduct to the goal of extending per-

sonal competences and developing a 'self-determined' lifestyle whose chief features are material security, a high standard of living, individual opportunities to shape one's environment, areas of freedom, a high standard of education and an active concern to 'keep abreast of things', interest in political issues and developments, accompanied by scepticism in regard to ideological indoctrination, 'post-materialistic' preferences for environmental protection, social justice, and peaceful ways of resolving social conflicts, keen perception of Third World problems and high expectations in relation to 'state' guarantees – ranging from the rule of law to the provision of cultural amenities.

Corresponding to these interests, there is a remarkable readiness to become personally involved, not only in self-help intitiatives but also in political organisations (environmental associations, Third World groups, local citizens' initiatives, etc.). Participation occurs in all the forms of action which appear likely to influence living conditions or 'responsible' politicians. Since only a minority of the forms of participation are institutionally organised, the distinction between 'classical' social commitment and political action disappears. New forms of social and political participation are emerging which on the one hand aim to bring about certain social effects, and on the other hand confer 'meaningful' direction on the 'production' of the individual's own life.

This list of characteristics is necessarily simplistic. It has to wrestle with the difficulties which every formulation of theory has in representing social and individual realities in one and the same hypothesis. The multi-dimensionality and heterogeneity of social experience can, if at all, only be illustrated by succinct examples from one's own experience; thus you have the aged left-winger, overtaken by 'post-modern jollity', just about able, with the help of some strong red wine, to suppress his urge to participate in political activity, or the hard-bitten 'thirtysomething', still in the phase of highly aesthetisised but waning contempt for politics, the adaptable multi-role woman functionary, caught up in a relentless struggle with a daily fourteen-hour quota of researching institutions as a teacher, trade-union official, green supporter, and activist in citizens' initiatives, the skilled worker precipitated into the green circle and wearing down a lifetime's experience of conflict against the whetstone of theory-obsessed student functionaries, the high-tech female employee, who sees herself both spurred on and hamstrung by the competition of ecological and feminist issues, the jobless young person, whose alternative values are in painful contrast to his desire for social recognition and security, the finance official with an obsessive interest in nature conservation, no longer able simply to wipe away thirty years' experience of hierarchical organisations, and so on and so on.

The cognitive and normative differentiatedness of this cross-section of the 'new middle classes' reflects the overall complexity of socio-cultural development. Changes in modern industrial society, at the level of industry, technology, and political institutions, are occasioning, at the level of everyday action, changes in attitude, political expectations, and commitment which are both unconventional and individualistic. The motives may appear emotional and chaotic to the distant observer, and the politicians, also irritated, are wont to stigmatise them as inadequate or anomic and exclude them on the grounds that such motives are not consonant with the 'governability' of society.

Each individual sees his or her own life-story as a 'biographical novel' of a very mixed and multi-polar nature. In this individual biography, the high points of social, cultural, and political commitment count for just as much as the high points attained in the endeavour to secure success at work, or build up a particular image, or obtain erotic gratification. A 'complete' biography includes committed protest action, demonstrative 'breaks' with convention, and enthusiastic sallies into a sometimes self-engineered counter-publicity, care being taken not to lose sight of the limits of individual action and the personal costs of involvement. A complete inter-mingling of the private and the public, or withdrawal into privacy, with delegation of political interests, both these extremes of 'shifting involvements'[2] are accepted as part of normality. Although there is very little 'utopian thinking' and a lot of pragmatic down-to-earthness at work in the various patterns of action, the reference to the 'here and now' has nothing affirmative about it. There is a strong sense of reality, which does not allow itself to be overwhelmed by problems of identity, but is not mere strategic calculation either. The self-assuredness of the 'new' middle-class youth, brought up by 'critical' educationists to become critics of education, is combined with more sense of reality than was the self-assuredness of their parents, who took refuge from the normative certainties of the Adenauer era in the normative certainties of the student K-Gruppen

(Kommunistiche Gruppen) scene. Neither parents nor children need to be told how closely their own lives are interwoven with the calculus of economic efficiency. The interconnection between their own self-reproduction and the state of the international market has become a disagreeable but commonplace fact of social existence.

It should therefore come as no surprise if individuals do not regard the use of their labour, the 'exploitation' of their skills by capital, just as heteronomous, as a scandal *per se*. As rational owners of labour, not prone to any illusions, they accept the new technologies, the self-innovating components of the global dynamic of innovation, as incentives constantly to improve their qualifications. What at first appears to be merely a strategy for assuring one's own value through the improvement of individual qualifications is also experienced as a form of individual enrichment, and may even include some measure of 'inherent pleasure' in the constant accumulation of knowledge. Despite this, the resources which workers, in their own interests, invest in further education and training purposes are still structurally extorted; the link between the calculus of self-exploitation and the desire to forge one's identity in relation to the exploding multiplicity of options is an indissoluble one. As is well known, opportunities for individuals to keep pace with socio-technological change are not (yet) guaranteed by any institution within the welfare state but each person has to see to this themselves. Nothing would be more mistaken than to denounce the desire to participate in the modernisation process as *petit-bourgeois arrivisme*.

The conditions of reproduction of the new middle classes in the multicultural conurbations also determine their scope for political experience. They do so firstly to the extent that the manner in which the individual copes with the costs of reproduction, though distinguishable in analytic terms, cannot be separated in everyday terms from that which is described as satisfaction of needs. Consuming for the sake of one's reproduction as a source of labour, and being able to consume because of successful self-exploitation, is now only a rhetorical distinction in many areas. These are interchangeable perspectives on one and the same basic pattern of welfare state-based individualism. Individuals have a free choice within a zone of alternatives, of which 'opting out' is by far the most costly and risky. Between 'exit' into social marginality and oscillation between various modes of consumption, there lies the single third option of 'voice' or protest against the unsatisfactory make-up of this catalogue of individual opportunities. This is the logical starting-point for political commitment. There is a desire for an increase in the number and type of options, for a greater variety in possible combinations of the main focuses in life and work, for a decrease in the risks involved in experimenting with lifestyles, for easier transitions between social roles, in sum, for improved opportunities for adding 'fluidity' to one's life, and thus being able to respond to the social dynamic with self-assured discontinuity.

One of the historic achievements of social democracy in the 1960s and 1970s was to have fostered the 'depoliticisation' of workers in a *modus consumendi*, and to have nurtured confidence in the system. What is needed today is another collective protagonist to represent those parties that are rising up in protest at the consequences of the unreflecting satisfaction of 'raw' consumers' interests. Nor is the pattern of conflict any longer that of a struggle between labour and capital over distribution. Given that the potential risks engendered by industry grow out in all directions, there is no longer any area of life that remains 'unpoliticised' – housing, food, child-rearing, education, transport, leisure, health, and mass communications – the conflictual spheres and issues of the new protest movements are ubiquitous. The new middle classes are not infrequently to be found on both sides of the battle-lines. But the fact that they are multiply affected (on the one hand in their functional and professional roles, and on the other hand in their concrete living conditions) does not give rise to a classic sociological 'conflict of roles' which either paralyses its victim or drives him or her into the arms of the psychiatrist. This is due to another specifically new feature of the new protagonists: thanks to their high level of education and their key social positions, they quickly see that the problems that are agitating them have nothing to do with their own person but stem from the social set-up.

III Situational social movements

One odd feature of the new social movements that is often unjustly ignored in theoretical accounts is the degree to which they are state-oriented. In adopting this stance, those involved in new forms of political action are acknowledging the functional transition that has taken place from industry to the modern industrial State. The State has become an indispensable piece of regulatory machinery, which strives to offer individuals a minimum of 'assured' conditions of reproduction. It stems the flow of risks from the 'wage–labour' wellhead and tempers the problems associated with wage–labour dependent reproduction. In West Germany (the Federal Republic) at least, the attempt by neo-liberals of the most varied hue to 'revoke' the position of the State and have it merely perform functions of institutional goal-formation and administration seems to have failed. The State has become indispensable in providing an extensive, though seldom effective, means of tackling the economic and material consequences of modernisation. Its 'resources', however, are only of modest size. The State's capacity for action always represents a residuum of economic resources, since income from taxes promises to continue to bubble forth only as long as businesses know they are free to shift part of their costs (air pollution, the wearing-out of manpower, the laying-off of workers, etc.) beyond the market-place. The massive clear-up operation conducted by the State is lagging ever further behind its causes. Official policy has been unable to prevent the most prominent symbols of industrial modernisation (nuclear power plants and reprocessing facilities; aircraft runways, car-test tracks, and urban motorways; high-tech paradises, arms pools, and chemical products) from encroaching on the sphere of individual experience, with traumatic effects. What was intended by politics as a gesture to satisfy business was seen by individuals as a stream of dangerous and disruptive events. A substantial number of people considered that their needs in regard to continuity and security had been gravely violated.

Serious attempts to explain the phenomenon of the 'new social movements' operate – with good reason – on the assumption of the unlikeliness of collective action. Individualism, passivity, and ignorance are taken as the norm, optimistic commitment and successful collective action are exceptions that require explanation. Yet one should avoid taking academic scepticism as the starting-point in assessing forces of action for political purposes. One would then note an 'improvement' in the possibility both of perceiving sources of danger in all the different spheres of life and of realising the ineffectiveness of the usual techniques of evasion and avoidance. The death of the forests and the pollution of water, transport chaos, and polluted foodstuffs, the greenhouse effect, allergies, Sandoz and Chernobyl, the accumulation of missiles here and death from starvation in the Third World, these indicative chains of events give the lie to any automatic repressive response along the lines of 'this will all blow over as well'. The sources seem reliable, the information correct. The discrepancy with popular definitions of normality is manifest. Despite great differences in social experience, despite individualisation and the collapse of traditional identifications (with Church, party, or union), no patterns for assimilating this experience are emerging which inevitably evoke apathy, passivity, and privatistic resignation as a response.

On the contrary, the disillusionment can easily reach a level at which the current events can be 'assimilated' only by means of modified interpretations or new interpretive schemata. This was the case when the 'that's enough!' logic of the new peace movement emerged in opposition to missile modernisation, or when, 'after Chernobyl', young mothers stood up against the indifference of those in charge of energy policy in Germany. Striking incidents prompted a new interpretation of the complexity of world events, and a definition of that complexity as something that could be changed through one's own activity. Although there were still some gratifying experiences in terms of collective forms of action – e.g. the actions around the autumn of the missiles in 1983, or the 'after Chernobyl' movement of 1986 – a change in the paradigms underlying the individual conception of politics was also possible. This occurred all the more easily, the more stable the new-found interpretive framework seemed and the more attractive the milieu associated with the new world-view appeared.

When political participation is suddenly felt to be meaningful, the guises it may take are manifold, corresponding in range to the variety in cultural milieu. There is nothing automatic either about the paths that lead to participation, or about the causal connection between political interest, level of information, distrust of institutions, and the degree of readiness to become involved. The spectrum ranges from cynical commentary on the 'political farce', with an increased level of consumption of current affairs, through participation in petitions, demonstrations, and political rallies, right up to joining environmental associations, women's groups, Third World or citizens' initiatives, from initially 'non-committal' collaboration in actions, strikes, traffic blockades, refusal to pay taxes, occupations of town halls, to the assumption of office within a group and continuous involvement in the work of a party. Whether these alternatives become a scale of increasing or of decreasing involvement depends on internal (biographical) and external (social and political) circumstances. The forms in which influence is exerted, the scope of expected changes, the struggles that have to be gone through, the degree of commitment and sacrifice – all this varies with the political climate, the density of the communications network, and the subjective criteria of success. The traditional collective identities (based on region, religion, and profession) have lost too much of their force to supply answers to these kind of questions about participation.

The Greens' attempt to adjust to this pattern of motives and these forms of action has been inadequate. The myth of global resistance through varying campaigns, propagated after Chernobyl and during the census boycott, negates people's real motives for involvement and offers little prospect of any institutional results. Green organisational policy shows itself ignorant *vis-à-vis* forms of participation that are spontaneously selected in line with personal lifestyle and are considered subjectively to be appropriate. To the extent that the Greens are able to exert any influence at all on the development of social movements, they are not 'open' enough towards them. Their reservations prevent them from helping to mobilise a protest force that goes way beyond the spectrum of left-wing-cum-alternative subcultures, while people are developing forms of protest that put official politics under pressure because these types of protest do not fit into any known ideological mould. The green organisational élite is busy cultivating its belief in a cumulative 'growth in awareness', in a linear escalation of motives for action, and in the myth of an offensive against 'the whole system'. The habit which the new middle classes have of 'rationally' gearing themselves to 'local' prospects of success is an asset that should not be squandered in naïve 'global scenarios'. The green 'headquarters', trapped in its false conception of the avant-garde, may find it difficult to accept that people are capable of judging for themselves which forms of action promise to be effective and what risks must be taken into consideration if society's regulatory system is forced into a process of self-transformation.

It would seem useful to take a closer look at the relationship – by no means a straightforward one – between Greens and social movements. Since each side believes it knows exactly 'what' the other form of action consists in, and 'how' it works, myth and self-misunderstanding are mutually dependent here. Despite the varieties and ramifications of the various forms of 'new social movements' in the Federal Republic, the Greens tend to acknowledge only a section of these as 'their' interlocutor, namely those that see themselves as organisers of actionistic and expressive forms of politics. The protean variants of the alternative and ecological movements, of Third World projects and 'eco-centres', of self-managed businesses and alternative culture, which have long since become a country-wide phenomenon, are either disparagingly dismissed as politically naïve ('self-helpers'), or paternalistically assumed to be sure-fire Green voters. This overlooks not only the potential which this section of the movement has to offer in terms of experience, but also its function as a guarantor of continuity and as an interface between the differing motives for action. Wherever the strength needed for spontaneous self-organisation has been preserved during unpropitious political periods, whenever political commitment has managed to unshackle itself from contemporary fashions and specific spurs to protest, this has been due to the solid co-operative networks of the 'scene'. They made it possible for critical thinking to retain a practical side and to be transmitted over cultural barriers to younger people and people with different values.

Yet the political thinking of the 'leading' green functionaries is much less influenced by the real culture of the movements than is supposed by outsiders. The experiences of the alternative economy have not been incorporated into the manifesto debates about decentralisation, ecological innovation, or self-management.[3] Nor were any lessons learned, in respect of political mobilisation, from the successful communications practices of the socio-cultural movement – which by then had penetrated even to the remotest provincial town. The Greens still select representatives who gear themselves exclusively to the historic paradigm of the disruptive mass-movements of the 1970s. But the latter-day adherents of these mass-movements are labouring under a double delusion.

In the first place, the unreflecting recourse to history glosses over the fact that it was experience of impotence amongst the very strong movements of the late 1970s which provided the motives for the foundation of alternative slates and green parties. Both the 'German autumn' of 1977 – which culminated in a hysterical outbreak of suspicion and witch-hunting out of all (reasonable) proportion to the true threat of terrorism – and, most importantly, the various battles against nuclear power during the same year (at Malville, Brokdorf, Kalkar, Grohnde, and Wyhl) signal an important lesson. The 'return of the protagonist'[4] to a process of modernisation that has seemingly become subjectless can no longer be thought of in terms of involving the State in a conflict in which state force must be overcome. Given that the State can bring its machinery of force into action without any wrangles over legitimation, what is needed to transform post-industrial society is a post-socialist notion of social movements. Since the State no longer embodies absolutist rule, conflicts may be decentralised and shifted out into all functional areas of society as a whole, not just of the State. All institutional systems of regulation in society, the decision-making processes in businesses and schools, in fiscal departments and local councils, in interest groups and trade unions, can be made into arenas for the conduct of disputes that have acquired a more specific character. Nowhere is 'everything' at stake, but at every instant 'the whole' is in question. A dispassionate consideration of the realities shows that there is no other way – if one is aiming to achieve the maximum in terms of possible effects and does not wish to become the victim of inappropriate methods.

Secondly, the Greens find it difficult to reconcile their functions as a party that is closely linked to the movements with the operational logic of non-party-dependent movements. People ignore the fact that the relation of harmony to disharmony is a poor indicator of the political benefits of co-operation. Why? At times when both forms of action (party and movement), or indeed only one of these, are successful, the relationship between them necessarily becomes strained and stressful for both sides. 'Strong' movements distance themselves more sharply from parties the more supporters they attract from amongst the followers of all the parties. The fact that in so doing they dispute the claim of individual parties to act as parliamentary spokespersons of the movement should come as no surprise. This is after all a precondition for ensuring that the political gains of a broad-based mobilisation are given trans-party ratification in Parliament. A similar tension – one that can develop into open conflict – also arises when the party that is closely linked to the movements – i.e. the Greens – secures parliamentary influence. The party's dependence on voters who are not participants in the movement or, in certain cases, circumspection in regard to a coalition partner, compel the party to moderation in its public pronouncements. The universal rhetoric of the movement, with its 'utopian' statement of goals, then has to be replaced with tactical circumspection and a strategic policy of information (including deception, promise, and threat). Where the mobilisatory force of both party and movements is on the increase, a 'natural disharmony' therefore results. The anti-missile campaign and the latest anti-nuclear movement provide ample proof of this. These proofs point not to any deficiency in the Greens' relationship to the movements, but to the unavoidable 'costs' of a politically productive con-figuration.

Parodoxically, the Green Party and the social movements get on best when things are going badly for both of them. This is currently the case, now that the post-Chernobyl protest movement has waned. Both forms of action are reacting to the loss of support in society by making their discourses more radical. The movements are attempt-ing to hold their drastically diminished following together through intensive communication and symbolic-cum-expressive action. However, in the struggle to safeguard identity, sensitivity to the greater part of the movement's natural public goes by the board. Hence the movement's thoughts once again turn to the party with which it is linked which, experiencing the same sort of weakness, presents itself as an ally and interlocutor for 'radical' movements. The new-found harmony strengthens the position of those groups within the party which were unable, in any case, to gain anything from parliamentary influence and which prefer the model of a small, vociferous protest-party. Unfortunately, the new-found harmony between party and movements disguises the real drawback inherent in the situation. The mutually reinforced idiosyncracy becomes a trap, the world-view nurtured in isolation in accordance with the formula 'We are right because we agree' provides no way out of the crisis. The agreement between the two odd sisters is actually an indication of their common weakness. In such a situation, a rational protagonist – as is well known, the Greens are a less than perfect example of the latter – should check to see whether cherished tradi-tions do actually still serve the common interest. He should express scepticism in regard to opportunistic rhetoric which would like to make its own black-and-white thinking the touchstone of parlia-mentary politics as well, and which registers every adoption of green issues by politicians from other parties as a loss of identity for itself. It is problems of this type that form the basic pattern of the factional dispute that is going on between the pragmatists around Joschka Fischer on the one hand, the eco-socialists round Thomas Ebermann and the radical ecologists round Jutta Ditfurth on the other.

A more sober view of the social movements must take account of their peculiar operational logic. Social movements are forms of action that require incentives and are dependent on general trends. An important part of their effectiveness lies in the fact that they can start unexpectedly and grow unpredictably. They are a kind of 'societal self-management by exception', in that they draw attention to neglected problems and to new ways of looking at situations. They set traditional distinctions between what is important and what is unimportant on their heads and, when successful, they ensure that the formerly inconceivable becomes articulable, and the articulated realisable. This is their strength – but also their weakness, since more than this is required for success. Firstly, succinct incentives, secondly precise definitions of success, and thirdly an attitude of expectation which I shall define here as 'capacity for disappointment'. All three features imply changes which will mean that, in future, social movements will either be less important or have a different character than in the past.

(1) Whereas up to now social movements have found their incentives in a range of one-off catastrophes and scandals, this pattern no longer seems to hold good for the future. In future, one should expect increasingly broadly scattered risks, implying the break-up of the pattern of geographically and materially concentrated impact. Multi-causal, synergetic, and 'extensive' forms of impact will become the norm. The materially and chronologically specific incentive, such as was embodied in the infrastructure measures planned in the 1960s and implemented until the 1980s (construction of roads, airports, and power stations), is becoming the exception. The dangers of the 'risk society'[5] are everywhere and everyone's. Their effects can be identified only in statistical terms – e.g. as a fall in average life-expectancy. We must assume that such a change in the structure of events will mean a diminution in the number of succcinct incentives to mobilisation based on adverse personal experience of the effect concerned.

(2) For one-off mobilisation, the decisive criteria of success were prevention of the impending events or the containment of defined risks. Typically, large-scale demonstrations and occupations took place at the showplaces of technocratic arrogance only when 'construction' (of the nuclear power station, the nuclear reprocessing plant, or the missile base) had been announced or had just begun. But if the nuclear machinery has already been set in motion, if the launch-pads have already been erected, all those affected can do is

hope that it will not turn out as badly as they feared. Once threatened risks become irreversible, the goal of warding off the dangers can no longer be the motive for participation in social movements.

(3) One of the things that fosters willingness to become involved is the fact that the opponent or opponents in the conflict could have planned or acted differently. Only against the background of an 'optimistic' alternative is disappointment, or rage and anger, possible. And at the same time one sees to whom one should address the demand that a certain activity be stopped. Without an identifiable addressee at whom one's disappointment may be directed, any protest remains ineffective. One ought therefore to ask how long the potential for disappointment will be maintained. If it is likely that in future, 'acting differently' is going to be a rarer practice on the part of governments and investors, if we end up with insidious adaptation to higher levels of risk, or if the notion of systemic interdependences, convincing in terms of social theory, extends to the realm of policy formulation and evaluation, then there is a danger that the moral sources of commitment will dry up.

Changes of this kind place great responsibility on the Greens as far as their handling of the demands and authentic views of spontaneous movements is concerned. The fundamentalist wing is highly sceptical in regard to isolated movements and narrowly-defined practical goals. It thought the 'Mothers after Chernobyl' initiatives that were started up in many places too apolitical, and spontaneous occupations of town halls an inappropriate means of promoting the idea of radical changes to energy policy. But in what other forms could the hoped-for transformation of social values have got under way? As far as the fundamentalists are concerned, spontaneous movements make sense only when they promise to be a preparatory stage for 'system-shattering' actions of a kind that include the possibility of violence. Since militant participants in movements, and their identifying watchword ('We are fighting the State'), are regarded as politically progressive, those concerned have to hope that sometime and somehow the tiny sect will turn into a self-assured mass-movement. As to the green postulate of non-violence, they would like to think of this as being intended merely as a tactical measure, and would like it best if the state monopoly on force were countered with a kind of pluralism of violence.[6]

To this illusory concept of a 'spiral of revolution' two objections may be raised. Not only does it ignore the way in which violent actions develop their own dynamic and become oblivious to the original goal (not to mention the State's superior instruments of force and justificatory grounds). It is also based on a crude misjudgement of the motives of those participating in movements, mistakenly believing such people to be like members of 1920s political task-forces. Inclusive movements open to self-selected commitment are no longer to be had without the concomitant of a plurality of world-views and the postulate of non-violence. The Greens will therefore also have to address themselves to the forms of expression and action of those sections of the population whose socialisation did not occur in the milieu of left-wing or alternative subcultures. Furthermore, in view of the less favourable structure of incentives that will apply for future movements, the Greens should have ready various organisational aids for spontaneous initiatives (whatever their concern!). They could, after a rough verification of the objectives, provide movements actually involved in action with generous support in the form of information and resources, without simply calculating what advantage there was in it for the party, or making the willingness to provide some sort of 'return services' a precondition of this help. By so doing, they would probably attract the hostility of the other parties, but they would also acquire an 'interface' to society's perception of problems, a perception from which they are in danger of gradually becoming alienated.

IV Pragmatic politics and the trap of fundamentalism

Eight years after their foundation, the Greens currently find themselves in a period of discouragement. But the state of the party is not an indicator of the mood of society in regard to policies of reform. Whatever a term as woolly as that of 'environmental awareness' may mean, the fact is that more and more people want to live an 'environmentally aware' life, and support systematic ecological reforms in many different areas of life. There is no ground for resignation, we are not living through the era of the great ecological 'turn-around', but we are not living in a 'nuclear state' either. Why do the Greens find it so difficult to see themselves as a protagonist whose own action and lack of action have an important influence on the development of his own operational sphere and the pace and alternatives of social change? Having discussed some of the important changes in the Greens' external environment, in the electorate and in the social movements, we shall now attempt to throw some light on the 'internal' causes of the green crisis. Our thesis is the following: in their excessive concentration on the question 'Who are we?', the Greens are missing most of the opportunities open to them to influence society.

Attentive observers of the Greens since their foundation have noted that they are an extremely heterogeneous party, an alliance of expediency between groups with different orientations who share one prime goal, namely the survival of the party. In an allusion to the minimum percentage of votes required for entry into Parliament, the Greens may aptly be described as an 'artefact of the 5 per cent clause'.[7] None the less, the question of whether they may after all still manage to knit themselves into an organic unit remains an open one. From the modest beginnings of a productive pluralism, there could develop a 'post-industrial framework-party',[8] in which groups with differing orientations would be able to co-operate on the achievement of almost all concrete goals. Or does the fact that the Greens are still a conglomerate of traditional left-wing, pragamatic ecological, and radical life-style-reforming philosophies only allow of a pessimistic prognosis? No one can comment reliably on this at present. Since we are not indifferent to this question, and would like to think of the Greens being a collective 'left-wing/ecological' protagonist with a proper sense of reality and a capacity for strategic operation, we shall begin by explaining our scepticism *vis-à-vis* the natural desire for reconciliation within the party, and shall then indicate a few of the elements which, in our view, form part of a realistic referential framework.

According to a view that is widespread amongst green party members and in the media, the Greens would do well finally to sort out an ideological compromise between their different wings. They should, it is said, plot a middle course between the objectives of 'fundamentalism' and 'pragmatism' and recognise the varying approaches as having equal status. However commendable the motives of this proposal of compromise, its realisation would be fatal. The party has for a long time already owed its continued existence to the (still present) will to compromise on issues vital to party survival. At the same time, however, one cannot overlook the fact that formal compromises on programme and strategy cause commitment to flag and make the Greens appear increasingly less attractive. In order to become capable of action once again, the

Greens must set themselves the task of making a critical assessment of their 'intellectual tools', and of acknowledging the weaknesses of both their philosophies, which have now each developed along separate and opposing lines.

The fundamentalist and pragmatic discourses differ fundamentally from one another in their attitude to reality. Whereas the fundamentalist discourse is self-referential, oriented to the past, and confident in its world-view, the pragmatic discourse is geared to results, oriented to the future, but uncertain of its identity. Only in one respect is there any similarity, each engages in a logic of circular reference, excludes central elements of the other discourse, and conveys feelings of group nostalgia. Fundamentalist reasoning feeds on resolute and unnuanced criticism of opponents and of certain structural concepts styled as opponents (e.g. 'capital' or 'technology'), just as rival organisations (e.g. the Social Democratic Party) and macro-structures (e.g. the capitalist economy) may still be characterised in terms of earlier 'deeds', the crimes of the early period of industrialisation, for example, or the suppression of workers' revolts, so it seems necessary for the fundamentalists to assert their own identity through loyalty to earlier modes of thought. The continuity of their own system of attitudes and values is regarded as an important precondition of political success – and this even when the social environment, including their opponents, have undergone considerable change. Strictly speaking, fundamentalist action is not result-oriented (consequentialist) but expressive, in other words geared to self-portrayal and/or avowal of belief.

Criticism of green fundamentalism must not make things too easy for itself. The idea of producing a political effect through the avowal of identity is by no means absurd. In the peasant wars of the late Middle Ages, in the early civil struggles for individual rights and political freedoms (particularly the securing of the universal franchise), in the struggles of the workers' movement for social rights and the recognition of their collective organisation, simply stating who one was precluded all possible misunderstanding as to the object of the dispute and the objectives one was pursuing. The social conditions were clear-cut enough to allow this. Only with the development of modern society, with its multiply differentiated functional spheres, have the conditions become ambiguous and 'hard of hearing'. As far as the effects of fundamentalist thinking and expressive politics today are concerned, it is difficult to believe that antagonistic definitions of opponents, linear notions of causality, and a concept of conflict geared exclusively to the zero-sum game are sufficient to provide an adequate analysis of social reality and to identify an opponent with great powers of decision who would none the less allow himself to be forced into the arena.

Sometimes it also seems as if fundamentalism is appealing to an ethical centre of society, or is relying on the moral competence of its opponents; radical criticism and resolute rejection are displayed as if there were well-defined addressees who would be moved by this to cast off their 'wicked' character. Is it expected that radical and distancing criticism, in which differences of opinion are portrayed as hostilities, should act as a 'self-destroying prophecy'? This kind of consequentialist understanding of fundamentalism is misleading. Fundamentalist reasoning may make use of consequentialist semantics, but its purport is normative, its function expressive. One should not count on society's reacting positively to a theologically presented critique. Modern society is somewhat worse than fundamentalism supposes it to be. Its 'structures' are not only cold and insensitive, they are also unsuitable as a subject of moral commentary. They reproduce themselves in processes that are not only highly interdependent and complex but also contribute in extremely varied ways to their own maintenance. Reactions to unexpected events are not fixed and are too unpredictable for one to be able to set a trap for 'the system' (these characteristics, incidentally, provide scope for successful interventions). The fundamentalist discourse may meet with a rather favourable response in the media, but the decision-making processes, which are always specialised, remain untouched by its abstract generality. It is well known that the degree to which political dissension, along with every kind of eccentricity and Bohemian behaviour, is tolerated is greater in democratic societies than anywhere else. In such a context, even a forced discourse about identity fails to provoke anyone. A self-assured opposition must seek out other ways of achieving the changes it desires.

And what of pragmatic politics? At first glance, the pragmatic discourse seems less dogmatic and more pluralist than its fundamentalist counterpart. There is even a slight degree of self-referentiality along the lines of 'We are to blame for this.' A 'pure' logic of doing and effecting would, after all, be impossible. Goals are constantly at issue, the ultimate justification for which is normative in character and touches on the protagonists' self-image. But the central element of this discourse is something different, namely the assessment of reality as amenable to change (i.e. the political calculus is explicitly geared to the future). This sometimes gives rise to over-optimistic expectations, as were observable in the debates about the benefits of red–green governmental coalitions. At the same time, the orientation towards the future indicates the existence of a cognitive gap that rebounds to the advantage of fundamentalism. Pragmatic reasoning necessarily seeks its justifications in assumptions about the effects of future action, in other words through recourse to realities that are merely envisaged, not yet realised. There is a lack of certainty in knowledge and action. Whether the assumptions made by prag-matic politics turn out correct or incorrect is something that lies only to a limited extent within its own power. It addresses itself to a strategic field in which other actors with other intentions figure. An honest politics of reform, which is concerned to ensure rationality and transparency, must confess this uncertainty as part of the basis of knowledge on which it operates.

Given that neither type of discourse offers much in the way of instructions for action, some auxiliary constructions are required to enable distinctions to be drawn between 'correct' and 'incorrect' actions. In case of doubt, the path of least resistance is opted for, political successes are measured in terms of the pace of individual careers, and when justifications are called for, recourse is had to the hackneyed rhetoric about the 'natural' links between small steps and long-term goals, with the small steps always leading (of course) 'in the right direction'. There is also talk of 'bit by bit' progress towards utopian goals – as if this were a roadway made up of Lego blocks. Neither appreciation of reality nor the capacity for strategic thinking are encouraged either by the fact that connotational elements from the one discourse are mixed with similar elements from the other. This is because there is a clear asymmetry operating in favour of fundamentalism. Pragmatic interventions in the institutional system are difficult and uncertain, and when they succeed this too reinforces fundamentalism's actional basis. A different situation obtains in the case of the fundamentalist assertions of identity. They are easily interpreted by the public as signs of a deficient sense of reality, and they discourage voters who have pragmatic expectations. Although this effect is noted from within the fundamentalist attitudinal framework, it is not judged to be something negative. It confirms what one always knew, namely that 'the capitalist system is not amenable to reform'.

So what objection could there still be to the view that the green factional dispute should finally be resolved through a comprehensive programme of reform, through a plan for the gradual transformation of the 'whole of society' to which everyone could assent? That this idea only finds favour with those inside the party and not with the voters may well be due to people's inertia and is not worthy of complaint. But the situation is different in regard to the doubts concerning the feasibility of comprehensive programmes. These doubts need to be examined. If they seem well founded, one should start looking out for a better strategic approach. Three perspectives on the problem may clarify what is meant here.

(1)   Complex strategies of reform which reach far into the future are handicapped by the fact that the formation of individual expectations is asynchronous. Whereas some people lower their demands out of disappointment, others tend to raise them. For this reason alone, the idea of a cumulative radicalisation of the population is unrealistic. The rhythms of personal biographies, the distribution of opportunities dictated by social structure, and the demographic make-up of the population preclude the development of identical experiences and concurrent priorities. Consequently, a democratic consensus in favour of the initiation of a comprehensive, long-term programme of reform is also unlikely. Concurrent intersubjective perceptions would be an important precondition in ensuring that people agreed on their interpretations throughout all the phases of the process. If there were dissension about the particular stage reached, conflicts about distribution would break out between individuals who laid claim to enjoyment of the target-benefit too early and individuals who were prepared to continue to endure sacrifices in order to see the ultimate objective realised. In addition, the question arises as to how one deals with those who abandon the collectively selected goal 'mid-way', because they no longer consider it attractive enough, or because it appears inferior to certain new objectives. How does one prevent the changes in preference of some people from infecting others? And how can one get people who did not participate in determining a particular goal – because they were too young, or indeed were not even born – to pledge themselves to that goal? If we wish to avoid setting up an 'eco-dictatorship', and if we treasure the legitimacy and productivity of democratic pro-

cedures, we shall have to exchange the idea of a scheme of comprehensive reform for schemes based on a well-considered incrementalism that displays a capacity for learning.

(2) If it is true that important goals can be realised only in a step-by-step manner, one must take care to avoid dangerous errors in the choice of one's means. Thus, for example, Jon Elster[9] has pointed out that a social innovation that has only partially been implemented does not itself convey a picture of the effects which it would have if it were applied wholesale. For instance, self-managed enterprises operating in a market economy in which businesses belong mainly to private owners or shareholders can constitute a valuable addition to the collection of variants of possible business objectives and definitions of profitability. This in itself would be sufficient ground to grant them public privileges. However, many factors (including the practical experience of the Yugoslavian economy of self-management) militate against the idea of aiming for a universalisation of the 'self-managed enterprise'. What we would observe would be, not the realisation of a magic recipe, but at best a change in the structures supporting the egoistic calculus. This points indirectly to a host of innovations which one should not postpone until one has opportuntities of exerting 'global' influence.

(3) Other concepts of reform function only when all the preconditions for them are completely fulfilled. If only some of the conditions for success are guaranteed, one has to reckon not just on a 'second best' result but on negative consequences. Were one, for example, to introduce a guaranteed minimum income at a time when levels of unemployment were high, and at the same time strike compromises on financial levels such that the amount produced was less than a living wage, and if professional qualifications and opportunities on the job market remained as unequally distributed as they are today, the result would be fatal. The benefits claimed by the advocates of a minimum income would not materialise. Instead of offering workers support so that in cases of doubt they could reject poor wages and unhealthy working conditions, we should have a re-enactment of phenomena from the time of early industrial policy on poor relief (e.g. the Speenhamland System). A guaranteed basic income would constitute a social gain only if the conditions for its success – including an adequate level of payment – were fully guaranteed.[10] If the 'correct' instrument is in danger of being perverted because the preconditions for its realisation are incomplete,

then one must wait, or look for alternatives.

These examples of the kinds of basic problems associated with complex strategies of reform compel one to give more consideration to manageable measures that remain capable of adjustment and make no claim to provide any instant and eternally valid recipe for success. At the same time, a committed policy of reform of the kind one expects from the Greens must be geared to take advantage of unexpected opportunities, exploiting them to bring about the implementation of pre-planned measures. Reacting to Chernobyl with a 'we want it all and we want it right now' demand for the shut-down of nuclear power stations, instead of putting forward a scheme for the conversion of the energy industry that could have commanded a consensus, was an avoidable error. If the Greens stick to the former style, there is a danger that they will involuntarily help to perpetuate the process of problem-generation.

It is time to concede that there has been a clear diminution in importance of the discussion about the green programme of action. The sort of technical solutions that may be envisaged for coping with the endless list of ecological and social problems are already largely familiar, or else can be determined by a process of analogical inference. We need qualitatively different, quantitatively reduced procedures for converting materials, in order to limit the burdens placed on air, water, and soil. We also need moratoriums on, and rules of cessation for the use of high-risk technologies. We need solidarity and tolerance in order to contain social injustice. But the completeness of our catalogue of measures does not constitute a political argument. Precisely in the instance where these measures are 'comprehensive', there remains a gap. It is not clear what will be done if it turns out that every individual measure has some cost or disadvantage attached to it which will affect almost everyone, even though he or she will also experience the advantages of cleaner air or healthier food. What will happen if the disadvantages accumulate amongst particular social groups? What sort of guarantee of subsistence do we offer to those who lose their jobs when ecologically harmful production-lines are closed down? How do we safeguard the productivity and profitablity of those businesses from whose profits labour-intensive sectors and ecological improvements must be subsidised? What sources of income and kind of lifestyle do we offer to young men who sacrifice their career-goals to the (well-founded) quota-principle of jobs for women?

To state the problem in exaggerated form. What is our response to the fact of general dependence on a functioning industrial capitalism, which means that a sizeable proportion of the negative aspects of our conditions of life (environmental destruction, poverty, and social inequality) stand in a causal relation to the pleasant sides of life – freedom of consumption, comfort, prestige? It is quite understandable when people refuse to stop the bad out of fear of something worse.

We have no instant recipe for success but are arguing for a 'package' made up of the ability to intervene politically, a resolute awareness of risks, and a sincere willingness to learn. The Greens' left-wing-cum-ecological image also commits us to developing institutions which reduce society's dependence on economic constraints, and to extending social safeguards against every kind of relationship of dependency based on blackmail, whether on the job-market, in social policy, in industry and academic institutions, but also in marriage and the family.

We shall have achieved a productive balance between our ecological and social goals when managers and entrepreneurs can no longer avoid critical discussion of their decision-making practices. Also, when they begin to take the criteria of a reasonable lifestyle as a reference not just in their marketing strategies but also in the goals set for research and development. At the same time, workers must be able to rely on the fact that ecological policy-makers will fulfil their social responsibilities in a more satisfactory manner than do current economic and social policies, with their dearth of ecological interest. However, we should not cherish any false illusions about harmony. There is no saturation-point for material consumption, nor is there a level of income, however high, which guarantees a total transformation of materialist into post-materialist values.[11] Competition for status and possessions remains one of the driving forces of industrialism and as natural resources become scarcer, the competition for positional goods will, as Fred Hirsch has pointed out,[12] become more intense. Criticism of flagrant inequalities and selfishness must therefore remain on the agenda of ecological politics. Patterns of distribution are one of the few variable parameters in the dilemma whereby modern industrial society always functions both in and against the interests of the individuals who depend on it. A party such as the Greens must take account of this complexity both in its structures and in its forms of action. The collective protagonist

100 *Between identity and modernity*

should be able to perceive and act in no less complex a manner than the individuals whom he represents and whose support he seeks.

Notes

1 Cf. Ute Kort-Krieger, 'Der realistische Wähler', *Politische Vierteljahresschrift*, 27 (1986), pp. 290–310, and Max Kaase and Wolfgang G. Gibowski, 'Die Landtagswahlen 1987/88', *Aus Politik und Zeitgeschichte*, B30–31 (1988), pp. 3–18.

2 Cf. Albert O. Hirschman, *Shifting Involvements: Private Interest and Public Action* (Princeton, NJ: Princeton University Press, 1982).

3 On the contrary, relevant experiences were often belittled as 'self-exploitation' and dismissed.

4 On the links between political–empirical and theoretical changes in the field of the social movements, see Alain Touraine, *Return of the Actor* (Minneapolis: University of Minnesota, Minnesota Press, 1988).

5 Cf. Ulrich Beck, *Risikogesellschaft* (Frankfurt/M.: Suhrkamp, 1986).

6 A more sensible response to the misuse of the state monopoly on force is to define the conditions of its emergence more strictly and to draw fine distinctions between the forms of its application, and to subject these to thorough legal inspection.

7 Cf. Detlef Murphy and Roland Roth, 'In viele Richtungen zugleich: Die GRÜNEN – ein Artefakt der Fünfprozent-Klausel?', in Roland Roth and Dieter Rucht (eds.), *Neue soziale Bewegungen in der Bundesrepublik Deutschland* (Frankfurt/M. and New York: Campus Verlag, 1987), pp. 303–24.

8 Cf. Joachim Raschke, 'Soziale Konflikte und Parteiensytem in der Bundesrepublik', *Aus Politik und Zeitgeschichte*, B49 (1985), pp. 22–39.

9 Cf. Jon Elster, 'The Possibility of Rational Politics', *Archives Européennes de Sociologie*, 28 (1987), pp. 67–103.

10 A figure of at least DM1,000 per month would probably be needed for this, rather than an initial amount in the region of DM500, as suggested recently by Ralph Dahrendorf.

11 Cf. Ronald Inglehart, *Culture Shift in Advanced Industrial Society* (Lawrenceville: Princeton University Press, 1990).

12 Cf. Fred Hirsch, *Social Limits to Growth* (London: Routledge Kegan Paul, 1978).

3

The Greens and the decline of the social movements
Radical-left church or rival for the centre ground?

The influence of the Greens on West German society is beyond dispute. The Greens are not only an unprecedentedly successful new creation in a party-system that had supposedly cut itself off and developed a dynamic of its own. Their success as a 'party of the movements' has also given interest in matters ecological a boost that is unknown in other industrial countries, or is only just starting up. But past success is no protection against future error. Like the SPD during its period in government, the (non-governing) Greens are currently demonstrating that blanket trust in their politics is unjustified. Successful efforts by organisations to safeguard their existence are not the same thing as the realisation of the goals which people have in mind when they give support to 'their' organisations. Even the green party is not immune to self-perpetuating tendencies.

Intended and unintended effects

The presence of green parliamentarians in town councils and state parliaments encouraged the 'established' parties to take notice of problems and political alternatives to which they were unlikely to have given serious and prolonged consideration unless prompted by competition. Issues such as alternative energy policy, 'nuclear-weapon-free' parishes, environmentally friendly rubbish disposal, cycle-way construction and traffic abatement, support for women's refuges and positive discrimination for women in filling job vacancies, action in support of asylum-seekers and against hostility to foreigners, as well as a general uninhibited lifting of the lid on social and ecological ills have now become common property, though they do not have an easy passage into the political routine. In cases where proposals dealing with these or similar concerns are merely referred to commissions or end up at best as subject-matter for expert reports, those responsible for the shirking find themselves in danger of losing votes. This is the most familiar, but not the only, effect of the green presence. Three further effects deserve our attention.

In the first place, the advent of a large number of young, bureaucratically inexperienced spare-time politicians who have not yet worn themselves out 'tackling a real job or two' has led to an unexpected extension of political fields of action. A good many green proposals and schemes attracted attention because they were brought into the debate in a very uninhibited way, regardless of all the possible obstacles, opposed views, and other priorities. The effect was paradoxical, as a rule, the Greens were obliged to adjust their expectations 'downwards'. To the astonishment of political 'old stagers' and frustrated left-wingers, there was suddenly 'more' in prospect in the way of opportunities for change than is comfortable for those who plead pressure of circumstance. The field of political possibilities has been extended because with the Greens, optimism about reform and the willingness to take political risks have come back into play.

Secondly, the Greens – not always deliberately and in many cases contrary to the intentions of their fundamentalist camp – have contributed to the enhancement of the status of Parliament: the parliamentary party has distinguished itself not just by irreconcilable disputes but by an unaccustomed diligence. A host of legislative initiatives and a drastically increased use of the instruments of control provided by (written and oral) parliamentary questions and commissions of inquiry have meant that conservative government policy has had to operate under an unusually bright glare of public criticism and has had to defend itself against almost every possible argument in favour of the marginalised, be these recipients of social benefits or peoples of the Third World. The Greens are 'partly to blame' for the fact that the conservative turnaround did not just proceed quietly along the cynical lines pursued by the Thatcher government in Britain and that it only very rarely produced the results expected of it by Bavaria's chief minister.

The third and final feature to note is the shift in power within the party spectrum occasioned by green electoral successes. In the federal elections of 1987, the Greens' constituency had extended to cover considerable numbers of (younger) skilled workers, as well as white-collar workers and civil servants, including those employed in the high-tech sector.[1] Since votes are won primarily at the expense of another party, namely the SPD, the latter's chances now no longer depend solely on implementing successful mobilisation ploys (e.g. the social-democratic 'togetherness' feeling) in the competition with the CDU/CSU. The SPD also depends on its persuasive power as a left-wing party of reform that now finds itself under pressure of competition. Voters with aspirations to ecological and social reform have found an alternative in the Greens. This has meant a radical transformation in the social democratic field of action. SPD majorities could be expected only in those areas where the Greens looked weak and unattractive. Elsewhere, 'red' participation in government appeared to be possible only in alliance with the Greens or, as an emergency measure, within the framework of a Grand Coalition. As long as the FDP affects an exclusively liberalist economic stance and feels obligated to the new conservative course, the Greens will be (were?) able to help determine the SPD's chances of governing and thus also the course of its development. If they managed to resist the fundamentalist temptation, they would not even have to fear a pairing-up of the two larger parties and they would be sure of gaining a considerable number of votes and these might furnish the SPD with the basis for making self-assured alternative proposals. Thus, despite the fact that the Greens have regarded themselves modestly as a mouthpiece for social movements and as someone to 'point the finger in the House',[2] in fact they play a key role in the party system, even though they sometimes shy away from the burden of this responsibility.

A problematic environment for the environmental party

Because of the increased uncertainty about future political majorities, the Greens were at first viewed as troublemakers by their competitors. It was hoped their rise would follow the same pattern as that of the NPD (Nationaldemokratische Partei Deutschlands) during the 1960s, being unexpected, unmerited, and short-lived. Their motley character meant they could be discredited either as a tardy product of the student revolution, or as a cluster of conservative-cum-ecological tendencies, or even as a 'breeding-ground for right-wing authoritarian forces'.[3] What, apart from the environmental issue, might constitute their own particular profile, distinct from that of the other parties, remained unclear. Prominent greens and well-meaning intellectuals attempted to establish a green identity, as an 'anti-party party' opposed to the system (Petra Kelly), as a quasi-religious 'movement for a fresh start in the cities'.[4] Or somewhat more realistically, as a 'new type' of party that would articulate the experiences of those whose vital interests had been infringed.[5] In practice, however, the Greens' 'image' was determined to a greater extent than was that of other parties by a tendency to moralising criticism and a radical programme that was often far removed from concrete action. No sooner had a package of measures comprising left-wing ecological reform of the economy, egalitarian social policy, and emancipatory anti-authoritarian (later feminist) goals been tied up than it began to be called into question from within the party. In the interests of realising green objectives, the Greens could not avoid accommodating themselves to existing circumstances and opportunities for action.

Radical democratic principles such as the requirement that official functions be rotated, that mandates be of an imperative nature, or that decisions be unanimous (the consensus principle) bolstered the Greens' claim to be practising morally superior (democratic grass-roots) forms of politics, but these principles proved to be an obstacle to continuous, effective, self-monitored action. Enforced rotation was circumvented very early on by the institution of informal cartels, which occupied places on the party list and posts on the committee in a kind of game of tag. Equally, because of the varied opinions and objectives, neither the imperative mandate nor the principle of consensus had the hoped-for effects. They were incompatible with the ubiquitous need for discussion and the necessity of taking decisions under pressure of time. Hence even the Greens were obliged to rationalise themselves organisationally with the result that they now began to record the same problems amongst their supporters as did the 'established' parties – stagnating membership numbers, declining willingness to undertake unpaid work, and ill-informed grass-roots decision-making.

The fact that the Greens also eventually experienced widespread 'problems at the grass roots' was due to another process of accommodation as well, one that was noticed only at a later stage. This was the calm expectation that the autonomous movements and initiatives of the 1970s and 1980s would continue to act as an inexhaustible source of energy for the Greens. Instead, a 'decline in political activity by the new social movements'[6] has been observable for quite a time now; anti-nuclear, peace, and other groups have shrunk to that nucleus of stalwarts which seems immune to frustration because it has mastered the technique of putting group identity above political objectives. The only thing left to counter-balance this documented development is a vague hope that the autumnal decline of the social movements will be followed by a new spring.

Yet such hope is deceptive. In the first place, the Greens' own success at getting ecological issues on the agenda and abolishing misplaced confidence in progress has led to changes in their voters' expectations of them. The call now is not just for awareness of problems but for solutions as well. Secondly, the flagging support must also be blamed on the obvious gulf between 'real' fear of catastrophe and radical 'utopian' recipes. Many people doubt that they can create a 'completely different society' when it is not even possible to convert energy production to methods that are defensible in the long term. In addition there is the realisation that repeated exposés act like a dangerous tranquilliser if they do not lead to a discussion about practical alternatives. They give the appearance of action but do not even cure the symptoms, let alone tackle the causes.[7] If the notion of a movement-based party is adhered to despite changing social experiences, the process of erosion currently affecting the movements will eventually extend to the Greens' membership and to their political influence.

Catalogues of measures as a means to identity?

Given their varied origins in the environmental and anti-nuclear movement, in citizens' initiatives, and in remnants of the student-based 'K-Gruppen' 'parties', the Greens were not bound together by any single world-view or consensus over positive objectives during the first few years of their existence. They were united only over what they did not want. Namely the continuation of a development that was blind to environmental factors, to the effects of technology and to people's needs, whether because of the pressures of the capitalist market or under the dictates of an authoritarian state bureaucracy.[8] As a 'post-industrial framework-party'[9] of pluralist composition, the Greens chugged along happily in this negative coalition as long as all that was needed was to criticise the competition. 'Green' stood for ecology, alternative ways of living, and an egalitarian distribution of resources, etc. However, when the effects of the green presence were reflected in an ecologisation of the programmes of the other parties (particularly the SPD), the Greens themselves came under increasing pressure to provide answers to 'how ?' questions. They suddenly found themselves at a crossroads in terms of party profile. In one direction lay the more arduous route of developing a programme of action consonant with their own, as yet unformulated, interpretation of reality. In the other direction lay the easier course of confining themselves to drawing together the demands made by the social movements and shunting them further on.

As demands and objectives were hammered out, the federal party and a number of regional branches opted for the second course. The issues 'generated by the movements' were added together, and in any doubtful cases, an approach of maximum verbal radicalness was determined on. In reply to each individual problem, an abstract negation of that problem was offered as an ad-hoc remedy. Since then, the wide-ranging catalogue of calamities has been swollen through a process of 'encyclopaedic compromise', in other words the demands of movements whose concerns are inadequately represented are simply added on to the list. Consideration of the overall contexts in which issues arise and of ecological and economic interactions gets short shrift in all this. Whether such programmes still have any readership outside the party is debatable. In any case they lack priorities, chronological perspective, and a guiding theme.[10]

Sociological analyses make clear why the Greens' insistence on the primacy of the movements is leading them into a cul-de-sac rather than bringing them an upturn in their fortunes.[11] Movements that group themselves around prominent individual social problems are assured of continued (temporary) existence only if, in addition to all other purposes, they act as a communicative framework which confers a certain identity and in which the membership constantly sees its self-image reinforced. Social movements now also perform this function because there has been a break-up in the traditional social milieu in which individuals formerly developed their identities as participants in stable collective interpretations of society (interpretations which in certain circumstances could also provide the basis for solidary action). Since that break-up, groups and organisations with voluntary memberships have had, in addition to anything else, to help in the tasks of giving meaning and confirming identity. The fundamental social change that has occurred particularly over the last four decades has led not just to the disappearance of the experiential basis of the class-based (workers') party but also to excessive strain being placed on the organisational frameworks which, like the social movements, have taken that party's place. In order to ensure their continued existence despite the differing experiences and conditions of life of their members, they have to reinforce even the smallest overlaps in their members' perceptions of the sense of things, and, in cases where doubt arises, forgo any analysis or criticism of the content of those perceptions.

In terms of its world-view and political programme, the Green party is based primarily on social movements, and because of this it ends up as a medium through which the quest for meaning is pursued and through which a self-referential type of communication is conducted. The party talks mainly about itself and loses its capacity for sober perception of reality.[12] The identity question ('Who are we?'), which every organisation founded on solidarity must answer, here becomes an all-purpose tool with which all other questions are prised off and jettisoned as impermissible. Debates that ought to take place about goals and options for action ('What shall we do?') do not occur, self-portrayal dominates the objectives and projected effects of action.

As long as the social movements themselves 'admit' enough reality in that they try to secure influence within society, the party profits from their knowledge, from the authenticity of their demands, and from the commitment of their participants. But when there is a multiplicity of weak, contradictory groups (e.g. the autonomous anti-nuclear movement and the 'post-Chernobyl' mothers' initiatives), the party is faced with the task of harmonising differing views and itself elaborating a defensible programme of action. This task is all the more urgent in that the demands made in less 'animated' times are heavily influenced by the disappointment experienced by the activists in the movements. These demands turn out more radical and more implacable, with the result that they remain largely incomprehensible. This makes it all the more unlikely that there will be any consideration of 'second-order solutions'. That is to say ways of coping with the effects of proposed solutions to probems.[13]

How orientation to social movements can produce immobility was demonstrated inter alia by the Greens' habit of drawing up a catalogue of demands long in advance of election-dates (in other words, without knowing the result of the election or the negotiating situation) with a view to co-operation with the SPD. This kind of refusal merely to act as a majority-maker fulfilled an important function in the Greens' early years. It was intended to correct the widespread notion that smaller parties are automatically looking to form a coalition with the party of government and that they are willing to forgo their own goals to achieve this. This the Greens were not, and are not, willing to do. Paradoxically, however, this prior stipulation of conditions carried on being made even when the Greens' exacting claims and their aversion to participating in government at any price were well known. Comprehensive packages of demands were directed at the SPD even when the latter had long since clearly indicated its refusal and had begun to seek its 'own' majority or a different partner. Voters who might have supported the Greens had no choice but to interpret the catalogue of demands either as a refusal to co-operate in any way or as proof of green self-centredness and detachment from reality.

The conflict between the identity of the movements and the direction of policy lies at the root not only of the wearisome 'Realo versus Fundi' dispute but also of the 'violence question' that is constantly being directed at the Greens. The Greens are certainly not characterised by any tendency to violent confrontations or fantasies of civil war, as conservative politicians are fond of suggesting. Yet the issue regularly surfaces when prominent Greens call the constitutional principle of the State's monopoly on force into question with emphatic gestures, in an attempt to confirm their identity through encapsulations of hostility, for example, *vis-à-vis* the State.[14] More serious than the 'violence' fetish, however, are the effects which the dominant orientation to social movements has on the political profile and creativity of the party.

Innovation and regression

In the early 1980s, when the conflict between identity-related needs and political objectives was still latent and the 'established' parties' attempts at slander welded the Greens together from outside, the sense of a new breakthrough captured imaginations far beyond the party membership. Everywhere, green work-groups discussed the 'cyclical ecological economy', 'new social policy', the transformation of science and education, women's work and technological development. The Greens were the driving force, target, discussion forum, and pool of ideas for proposals designed to bring about a 'new politics'. Academics (abroad as well as at home) who were working on ecological and social questions made reference to the Greens and to the chances of reform which they might open up.

It is from this period of creativity, up to about 1984, that the Greens' most important contributions to a number of currently widely discussed issues date were made. Issues such as the conversion of socially unacceptable types of production (e.g. arms conversion), the reform of the tax system along ecological, employment-oriented lines (e.g. wealth-creation tax), acknowledgement of the work done by carers and the provision of security for them, the redistribution of paid work to the unemployed and to all involuntarily jobless women, comprehensive reductions in working hours (with a graduated offset in wages), the gearing of flexible working hours to the needs of employees, and universal basic social security. Many of these proposals have now become common property; thus in its Irsee draft programme, the SPD took up a good many ideas from the green discussion. This should still be regarded as a positive development, despite doubts as to whether a people's party can actually undertake concrete steps to realise such intentions without pressure from a small but persistent coalition partner.

Nowadays, the prospering of green areas of debate – as evinced even in the dispute about the proposals for redistribution of work put forward by Oskar Lafontaine – contrasts oddly with the sterile, prejudice-laden, and uncreative mood prevailing amongst the Greens themselves. From being effective policy-innovators, they have become a feeble amplification system for conflictual rhetoric, without thereby gaining any mobilising capacity or persuasive force. In more recent times, the only issues on which they have achieved anything exemplary have been those relating to policy on women, where they have introduced a draft law to combat discrimination and have consistently applied the quota-principle to all party posts and mandates. In all other areas of policy, issues of identity predominate over the question of the suitability of proposed reforms and the nature of their likely effects.

As a result, the chances which are open to the Greens thanks to their left-wing ecological image and the attention they attract are fast disappearing. Instead of viewing themselves as a focal point for debates about how we ourselves can shape an ecologically aware society, and instead of looking for solutions that hold out the promise of reduced dependence on the exploitation of capital in line with the needs of the world market, they content themselves with ways of thinking dating back to the nineteenth-century labour movement. In those days, however (but not now), one could assume (a) that the abolition of market-based and capital-based conditions would not claim any significant victims, because it involved direct social benefits (in the sense of 'enhanced productive forces'), and (b) that nature provided an inexhaustible basis for life, in accordance with the old saying 'Time is a great healer.' By opting for the simplest interpretations, the party is doing the same thing as naïve sociological research which 'loves to overestimate the expressive-cum-symbolic possibilities of the new movements'.[15] The 'Greens and trade unionists' work-groups are an example of this. They have provided many disillusioned trade-union activists from the SPD and 'K-Gruppen' with a new home where they can dream of the revival of the workers' movement and where every wage-dispute is misconstrued as a 'labour versus capital' showdown. This appraisal, with its hefty dose of working-class ethic, is also reflected in the contributions of green trade-unionists to the party's economic programme, for which they claim a sort of experts' monopoly. The response of a number of the Greens' major decision-making bodies to Oskar Lafontaine's proposals on labour policy and policy on working-hours follows the same regressive mode of thinking. Instead of submitting their own proposals for avoiding unnecessary casualties. In other words, for guaranteeing new jobs and thus advancing the discussion that had at last got under way about redistributing work in a way that is advantageous to the unemployed, the Greens promptly denied the claims contained in their own programme in regard to graduated compensation and the institution of shorter working-hours.

Faced with the pressing ecological and social problems to which they 'owe' their rise and whose recognition is less and less tied to membership of a particular party or to electoral behaviour, the Greens appear to be engaged in developing a unique kind of 'left-wing conservatism'. Their new self-image, oversimplified and based on emotive definitions of the opposing forces, has led to self-castration at the level of new ideas. Their politics presupposes a much simpler social environment than that which currently exists. Capitalist enterprises, business associations, and rival parties often come up against systematic barriers resulting from informational factors or complexity and are thus prevented from recognising their long-term interests or from realising these in the optimum way. In this situation a rejection of 'green' concepts by one's opponents can no longer serve as proof of the correctness of one's own choice, as is often supposed. In the complex system that is modern capitalism, where reforms can succeed only if that system's vital (supply) operations are not jeopardised but are respected and safeguarded with a view to effecting their transformation, the nature of reformist political intervention cannot be decided according to individual whim or on the basis of rhetorical considerations.

Opportunities and risks

At present, however, it is not just the Greens but also the people's parties – SPD and CDU/CSU – who have worries about finding suitable ideas for mobilising support and about the changing electoral base. The parties' traditional 'typical' voters are becoming fewer. Everyone is busily trying to discover what moves the new middle classes, the only thing that really seems to be known about them is that they hardly have any lasting ties to particular parties any longer. Voting this way on one occasion and that way the next, with a view to achieving very specific effects on the composition of the government or on policy objectives. The Greens cannot draw any comfort from the uncertain situation in which the 'big' parties find themselves. Their fate also hangs on the decisions of this same group of voters, which does not consist entirely of egocentric Yuppies and Dinkies.[16] The disappearance of the typical SPD or CDU voter has a counterpart amongst the Greens, since the alternative scene has also been subject to a fraying-away and this has made itself felt on the party. They also have increasing difficulty in remaining meaningful to younger voters, for whom the alternative scene's ethos of political/cultural protest is something alien. Young people have not experienced the anti-liberal, anti-communist fustiness of the Cold War era, nor the passion for technocratic surveillance evinced by previous governments (including social democratic-cum-liberal coalitions). The Greens' 'youth gap' and their very low membership give serious grounds for concern that there is a 'petrification of conditions under way within the party'.[17]

The success of the drive to ecological awareness, the universalisation of 'green' themes, and the disintegration taking place in the alternative scene mean that fewer and fewer voters can be motivated purely by the kind of informational approach the Greens offer, or by the image they project. Why should anyone vote green if the Greens are not willing to take risks? The party's ability to intervene has become the precondition for its survival. Though what its next chance of doing this will be is as yet unclear. But showing willingness in regard to coalitions with the SPD, as is expected by a majority of green voters, is not in itself a sufficient condition for a politics of ecological reform. Majorities must reflect reality, partners in co-operation must genuinely want to do what they are doing. In spring 1987 the Red–Green coalition in Hesse came to an end because of irreconcilable differences between the yardsticks by which the SPD and the Greens felt success should be measured. The successful co-operation of the two parties, which included exposing mismanagement in the nuclear industry in Hanau, foundered on the antagonism between social democratic reluctance to take risks (only the newly elected CDU/CSU administration had the gumption – albeit half-hearted – to resort to shut-down decrees) and the green objective of a complete opting-out of the nuclear business. In Hamburg, the gap between the SPD and the Green Alternative List proved, for the third time, to be so great that neither side was able to support the idea of serious talks on co-operation. In this case, what had a clear adverse effect on the Greens' future opportunities of exerting influence was the rediscovery of the FDP as a coalition partner. If one measures their options merely on the one-dimensional left–right scale, the Greens appear to be cast in the role of dummy or 'place-holder' at the left-hand edge and have very little room for manoeuvre. Either they join up with the SPD or they confine themselves to a role of protest and opposition. In contrast, an SPD that opened itself up in a rightward direction again, with the pain of adjustment gradually subsiding, and had the choice between the Greens and the FDP as possible majority-makers would have considerably increased its scope for action. The fact that the Greens relate exclusively to one partner for co-operation and discussion makes them vulnerable to blackmail.

The fate not only of the Greens but of an ecologically motivated politics of reform depends on the right decisions being taken in this ticklish situation. The objective pressure of problems and the change in voters' motives mean that essentially only two combinations are possible, both of them risky. One is to try to replace the love–hate relationship with the SPD with a dispassionate appraisal of the options, and at the same time to establish a stronger rapport with the liberal sections of Christian democracy, a rapport that is critical but nuanced in its approach to different issues. This latter step should be taken not in order to prepare the way to an agreement on coalition for which bases do not exist, but as a means of exerting influence on the discussions conducted in those circles and of loosening the bulkheads that prevent majorities being formed on particular issues across parliamentary-party boundaries. Secondly, the Greens' own ecological-cum-social values – rather than just the dictates of demarcation from one's opponents – must be given a look-in again. How urgent this is has been demonstrated by Joachim Raschke in an imaginary look back at the current crippling linkage of the capitalist and ecological issues. Unless it proves possible to move beyond this green package deal we shall probably be able to say in the future that 'Anyone who opted for (socially responsible) capitalism was not able to articulate the importance he attached to the ecological question, and anyone who supported radicalism in dealing with the ecological issue could not differentiate this adequately from a socialist programme of change.'[18]

The political opportunities which are open to the Greens can now only be exploited at great risk to the current perception which they have of their own identity. The Greens should acknowledge the differentiated nature of the society which they want to change and shape, so that voters who are interested more in effects than in identity are prepared to become involved in the party. That the Greens are still capable of learning is indicated not only by the frequent self-critical modifications of course that are instituted after elections, but also by the great degree of 'openness' which persists *vis-à-vis* grass-roots initiatives. It is true that the Greens now function just as much as a training-ground for demagogic talents as do other parties, but a lot of uncertainty still clings to the party's decisions, because they 'come up from the grass roots' rather than being steered by the leadership. This feature may promote a repoliticisation of the party of the movements. However, this does not justify hopes that the Greens may develop into that centre of social and political creativity which many once dreamed of. Nowa-

days parties are neither conferers of purpose nor centres of innovation. It would already be a great help if they were relieved of the
burden of unrealisable expectations and were thus set free to
organise productive debates about which paths to take to attain a
future that is worth living.

Notes

1   The Greens obtained 7 per cent of the votes among skilled workers,
and as much as 8 per cent among trade-union members. Their share of the
vote amongst (lower-ranking and middle-ranking) white-collar workers
was 10 per cent. Cf. Ursula Feist and Hubert Krieger, 'Alte und neue
Scheidelinien des politischen Verhaltens', *Aus Politik und Zeitgeschichte,*
B12 (1987), pp. 33–47, this ref. pp. 40 ff. Slightly higher percentages are
quoted in Forschungsgruppe Wahlen, 'Die Konsolidierung der Wende. Eine
Analyse der Bundestagswahl 1987', *Zeitschrift für Parlamentsfragen,* 2
(June 1987), pp. 253–84.
2   This (in German, Ankläger im Hohen Haus) is the title of a book by
Dirk Cornelsen (Essen: Klartext Verlag, 1986).
3   This is the title of an article, authorised by J. Rau, which appeared in J.
R. Mettke (ed.), *Die Grünen, Regierungspartner von morgen?* (Reinbek:
Rowohlt, 1982).
4   Rudolf Bahro, Wer kann die Apokalypse aufhalten?, in Bahro,
Wahnsinn mit Methode (Berlin: Olle & Wolker, 1982), p. 21.
5   Cf. Claus Offe, 'Konkurrenzpartei und kollektive politische Identität',
in Roland Roth (ed.), *Parlamentarisches Ritual und Politische Alternativen*
(Frankfurt/M. and New York: Campus Vertag, 1980), pp. 26–42.
6   Bodo Zeuner, 'Parlamentarisierung der Grünen', in *Prokla,* 61 (Dec.
1985), pp. 5–22, this ref. p. 5.
7   Cf. A. Stolzenwaldt, 'Hanau: Selters statt Sekt', *Links,* 208 (Apr.
1988), pp. 8 ff.
8   One should recall here the much maligned motto 'Neither left, nor
right, but forward.' Those who supported it, however, were not proclaiming
their neutrality in the conflict over the distribution of resources, etc., but
were making it known that they distanced themselves from the traditional
utopias of both Right and Left.
9   Joachim Raschke, 'Jenseits der Volkspartei', *Argument,* 137 (Jan./
Feb. 1983), pp. 54–65.
10   The first parliamentary party of the Greens did, however, sup-
plement the cumulative programme with an integrated scheme for environmental and social policy which was discussed under the rubric 'Reconstruction Programme' and was adopted by the party before the 1987
elections.
11   The argument that follows is taken from Andreas Brandhorst,
Klassenpartei und Bewegungspartei, dissertation, University of Bielefeld
(Faculty of Sociology), 1988.
12   Cf. esp. Niklas Luhmann, *Ökologische Kommunikation* (Opladen:

Westdeutscher Verlag, 1986).

13 This applies, inter alia, to the link between hazardous industrial production and the lack of employment options. Cf. Claus Offe, 'Zwischen Bewegung und Partei. Die Grünen in der politischen "Adoleszenzkrise"?', in Otto Kallscheuer (ed.), *Die Grünen – Letzte Wahl?* (Berlin: Rotbuch Verlag, 1986), pp. 40–60, this ref. p. 53.

14 The fact that this spoils the chances of conducting a public discussion about the legitimacy of the State's use of force, the conditions that trigger it, and the (much too low) threshold set for it, is a result of purely expressive action which, though unintended, must still be answered for politically.

15 Klaus von Beyme, 'Neue soziale Bewegungen und politische Parteien, *Aus Politik und Zeitgeschichte,* B44 (1986), pp. 30–9 (this ref. p. 30). Cf. also Tom Stryck and Helmut Wiesenthal, 'Between identity and modernity', Chapter 2 of this volume.

17 Joachim Raschke, 'Die Grünen zwischen Bewegungs- und Parlamentspartei', *Gegenwartskunde,* 2 (1987), pp. 171–84 this ref. p. 178.

18 Raschke, 'Die Grünen', pp. 182 ff.

PART II

4

Issue piracy

The distorted conflict over flexible working-hours

If it is true that the industrial societies of the capitalist world are currently undergoing transformations that involve important structural changes, then, at least in the case of West Germany, working-hours will probably be one of those hinges which is unlikely to swing back into its former position once it has been set, groaning and creaking, into motion.

A whole series of more or less promising endeavours are currently centred round the issue of changes in working-hours. IG Metall and other trade unions are mobilising support for their demand for a 35-hour week. A group of five trade unions around IG Chemie are staking their hopes on reductions in working-hours. The SPD and CDU/CSU have put forward bills for new legislation on working-hours. The ruling coalition hopes to deflect workers' interest in a shorter working-week with its law on early retirement . . . the list could easily be lengthened by adding other, less important steps. In all this, one particular issue is attracting a great deal of attention because in almost all the schemes for change it is either canvassed along with other measures, or is directly promoted, or is strictly rejected. That issue is flexible working-hours.

Flexible working-hours do not only figure as point number one on the counter-offer made by the employers' associations to IG Metall; they are also the common goal of the various bills on working-hours drafted by the big parties, including the SPD, although – unlike the CDU/CSU – it sets the 5-day/40-hour week as a standard, having a separate clause that allows for seasonal deviations with no upper limit. It seems as if capital's logic of constraint has suddenly invaded the heads of politicians and federation bureaucrats: nothing can be done any more without 'flexibility'.

At a time of 'surplus supply' of manpower, when even a drastic reduction in the supply of work, e.g. through the introduction of the 35-hour week is nowhere near sufficient to put an end to unemployment, it seems that what we have is not a quantitative but a qualitative time problem. It almost looks as if up to now the companies have not been able to achieve what they wanted, namely the 'correct' amount of work in terms of duration at the right point in time.

But that which now constitutes the countervailing position adopted by businesses to combat the introduction of a shorter working-week, and which also enjoys the support of a Grand Coalition comprising the SPD, CDU/CSU, and FDP, is not by any means originally or exclusively a 'business issue'. It became possible to play off the greater flexibility in working-hours against the unions (as an 'alternative' to shorter working-hours) only after the latter had unequivocally declined to champion employees' demands for a kind of flexibility that was geared to the wishes of the workforce. If this issue now appears merely as a dubious excrescence of the capitalist logic of rationalisation, then this is only half the truth. The other half is a piece of strategic history in the conflict between labour and capital whose lessons – rich in implications – must, little by little, be absorbed.

Since the start, in the mid-1960s, of the current discussion about working-hours, 'flexible working-hours' has meant diverging from rigidity to rules that organise working-hours in a way that seems sensible in regard to particular considerations. One such consideration, for example, was the rational use of transport, recreational, and training facilities, in accordance with the notion that having chronologically extended use is more sensible than expanding capacity to cope with short-lived peak demand. Naturally, the extension of shift-work and shop-hours was also considered here. And by no means every kind of non-standard time of work or use would have brought social advances for employees. However, given various definite limits, for example in regard to use of space or available resources – organisational alternatives to the constant expansion of infrastructure appeared definitely open to discussion (and is probably still open today).

A second consideration was that of individual thinking on the use of time. This consideration found expression in the thoroughly plausible assumption that employees might be keen on an arrangement of working-hours that takes into account personal wishes in regard to the use of time. The concept of 'sovereignty over time' embraced a whole gamut of possibilities for individual choice in the matter of the duration and location of working-hours (these ranged from voluntary temporary part-time work to extended holidays or 'sabbaticals'). Although these kinds of ideas were quite a bit in advance of the actual needs articulated by workers, they none the less formed part of a trend of changes in values which also affects attitudes to work in which the automatic acceptance of performance, obedience to authority, and renunciation ('for their own sake') makes way for a greater consideration of personal and social goals. But this is no 'turn-around'; it is more of a creeping tendency which embraces mainly younger generations and the workers, as well as marginalised groups, with better training-opportunities.

Both these angles on a more rational ordering of time evoked only a modest response, and one that was negligible in terms of practical politics. 'More sensible' ways of structuring time were of no particular interest either to employers or to trade unions, because they were expressly intended to be an alternative to investments, investments which meant growth and jobs. Also troubling for both sides was the idea that self-confident workers might come along with a host of unreconcilable requests in regard to working-hours and thus disrupt the ordered progress of production and administration, or that, they might make agreement on the unions' goal of a collective reduction in working-hours more difficult.

The proponents of workforce-oriented flexibility can certainly not be exonerated of all the blame for their failure. There was an all too credulous assumption that individual time-patterns could be reconciled with the protective functions of collective agreements (such as wage-settlements and industrial-relations arrangements). Only very rarely was any distinction made between real existing part-time work, with its obvious disadvantages for the women-workers involved, and an individual work-time that could be chosen as an alternative to full-time work. There was a naïve failure to appreciate the employers' interest in cheap – because largely unprotected and easily rearrangeable – part-time work, and it was occasionally assumed that all that was needed to create 'more' and 'better' part-time jobs was trade-union initiative leading to an industrial agreement.

A job-sharing model imported by the employers of the chemical industry and the CDU remained practically without effect despite enormous publicity. It was at that point, if not before, that the truth began to emerge, that the persistently evoked possibility of smoothly 'reconciling' the workers' interests in regard to autonomy over time with the companies' profitability requirements was a pipe-dream. The 'value' of flexible working-hours does after all lie in the matching up of very concrete time-packages (which are temporally fixed both in their size and in their placing) with equally specific demands or interests. But when capital is aiming at working-hours that fit into the production process with optimum flexibility, whilst the workforce is wanting to fulfil desires for self-determination that are geared to social needs, then the objectives each of the two sides has in mind are not just different, they are contrary to one another. That objective in each case is to organise time to a greater extent than before in line with that side's own interests.

Whether because of the illusory hopes about harmonisation, or because of the short-sighted and undiscriminating treatment of the flexibility issue by the unions, the damage that has now been done is considerable. A dynamic of negation of demands was set in motion which does far more than merely reject inappropriate and currently unrealisable proposals. Instead of being acknowledged as universalisable and legitimate, the tentatively articulated interest in self-determination in regard to life's most precious good was repudiated and, not infrequently, slandered. Those involved overlooked the fact that, when expressed in concrete terms, the indisputably universal interest in autonomy always manifests itself in individually differentiated forms. This is ensured by the great variety in people's biographies and personal conditions of life.

A double price must now be paid for the tactical organisational decision to declare oneself incompetent to champion a 'new' social demand (even if only by 'preserving' it for better times). On the one hand, a not insignificant potential for a redistribution of working-hours between the employed and unemployed has been written off. The realisation of this potential (involving about 400,000 extra jobs, as is also generally conceded) would be clearly beneficial in employment terms, though not exactly a simple undertaking. But every step towards realisation, for example in the form of demands for temporary or partial exemption from full-time work could contribute to the reduction of unemployment and thus also to the improvement of the workers' position on the job-market. On the other hand, and this is the worst aspect of all, the wholesale rejection of the claim to more autonomy over time (I am not talking about a reasoned rejection of this or that way of realising the claim) drives those advancing the claims to the other side of the battle-line between labour and capital. The universal applause won by Oskar Negt's Sprockhövel speech, in which, amongst other things, he appropriated those motives for the implementation of the 35-hour week which up to then had practically been fought against, does nothing to change this. All that remains for us to do is note the failure to organise existing aspirations in support of the demand for a workers' right to 'reduced working', a demand that could have provided a much more effective counter (in employment terms) to the employers' 'traditional' demand for more work than does the bald 'No more overtime' approach, which is always directed against those who do more work.

Until the beginning of 1983, employers introduced the subject of flexible working-hours into discussions only in a tentative and half-hearted manner. Employers' associations went round businesses plugging the idea of 'more part-time work' as if it were acidified beer, pungent but without effect. Company demand for part-time work had long been satisfied. Only after IG Metall and other unions decided to press for a 35-hour week did Gesamtmetall – and shortly after it the BDA – get down to business. 'Flexible working-hours', long suspected by the employers of being a Trojan horse which would merely introduce tiresome desires for autonomy into the ordered process of production, now became the sheepskin disguising various rationalisation schemes relating to the organisation of time.

In spring 1983 Volkswagen unveiled the new ideas. 'Yearly agreements on working-hours' with weekly quotas of hours varying in accordance with the state of the order-books, 'alternative shifts' for part-time workers, these were the new contents of the concept of 'flexible working-hours'. Apart from in the well-worn area of part-time work these have not yet become a reality. But it seems certain that the hijack has been successful and that there is no need to fear any significant social opposition if the ideas tested out by Volkswagen, Siemens, and other companies in the public arena are implemented.

Before most employers and personnel managers have even grasped what large-scale companies and employers' associations have managed to secure for them simply by reaching out and grabbing a neglected issue, the question of 'flexible working-hours' has already been transformed into a multi-purpose weapon for use against schemes for the collective reduction of working-hours. In the first place, employers can exploit the 'homeless' social demand for autonomy over time. As long as the workers' desires in regard to this idea have not been completely disappointed. Secondly, they can be used to open up new areas of rationalisation. This is new to the extent that even two years ago a system of organising time that runs counter to the self-evident needs of the workers, e.g. 50-hour weeks in spring, 30-hour weeks in autumn, when orders are slack, would never have been considered acceptable. Thirdly, the employers can make flexible working-hours into a formula for compromise in the dispute over the 35-hour week which means, paradoxically, using the workers' interests in regard to the quality of their time as a means of blackmailing the unions. This is possible because neither union members nor the public are able immediately to spot the snag in (what sound like 'sensible') 'flexible' solutions. Fourthly, the employers are managing to do what the unions found it very difficult to do in relation to the demand for a 35-hour week, set an objective which makes social sense at the personal level, over and above objective and economic rationality (the improvement of the job situation). What was once expressed in formulas like 'A fair day's pay for a fair day's work' and 'On Saturdays daddy's all mine' nowadays marks a 'slot' in the mobilisation for the struggle for shorter working-hours. There is a lack of ideas of a good or proper life and counter-arguments which could set limits to the validity of purely economic considerations. Ideas which might, amongst other things, develop in line with ecological issues or the demand for self-fulfilment.

Up to now fights over structural changes have never been won without the rallying force of a social vision or of a normative justification of the goal. Anyone who points to the problems which a careful handling of new social demands would have caused the unions is not out of the woods. What he has to do is show how refusing to treat such demands enables the unions to make a better job of tackling impending conflicts and helps them avoid pressure to change. In other words how they could end up more successful. This is probably no easy task.

5

Alternative technology

Small is beautiful, soft technology is ecological, craft-based production saves energy and capital. In small-scale workshops the dichotomy between manual and intellectual work, between work and leisure, is removed, and everything can at last be decided democratically. The most difficult problems have in fact already been resolved, since what is being produced, and how it is produced, can be understood by everyone. It is qualitatively beyond reproach, lasts longer, is easy to repair, is enjoyable to make, fits in with the natural and cultural environment, and facilitates self-sufficiency and independence. In a word, one can enjoy alternative technology with a carefree heart. This, in only slightly exaggerated form, is the message contained in a concept that has left its mark on alternative literature. The concept of a technology which is, in its own words, alternative, radical, small-scale, and neighbourhood-based.

So much good must have more than one source. At least three strands of the modern critique of technology have come together here. The oldest and sturdiest is probably that of 'intermediate technology for developing countries'. Just as it was hoped that technology which was 'appropriate' to local conditions would create a large number of jobs that would foster self-sufficiency, similar effects appeared to be possible in the industrialised countries. A reduction in the division of labour, jobs that were economical on capital, independence from supraregional markets. In short, a little bit of local autarky. From quite a different geographic quarter came the idea that alternative technology was a precondition of individual self-emancipation. It was the countercultural youth-movement of North America which sought to realise its 'Californian dream' of an alternative lifestyle in a series of rural communes. Do-it-yourself technologies were to open up the way to a holistic and autonomous life, in systematic opposition to the spiritual and cultural impoverishment experienced by people living in the industrial conurbations.

The third source is the standpoint associated with nature conservation and environmental protection, with its critical attitude to growth. Dwindling resources, the risks associated with energy production, the disruption of nature, and the destruction of the countryside, all the various aspects of the ecological-cum-economic issue became arguments in favour of non-industrial provision, craft-based do-it-yourself, and a more modest way of life. Whereas appropriate technology was defined primarily as being small-scale, simple, and cheap, and the principal characteristic of counterculturally defined technology was alternativeness, all the proposals for a different kind of technology here converged in the imperative that a more sparing use should be made of nature.

Technological critique now operates under a different banner: it has become 'positive'. Even just a few years ago, appraisal of the effects of technology on society was predominantly negative. Social philosophers engaged in the critique of civilisation (Gehlen, Adorno, Horkheimer, Marcuse, and others) did not consider that modern technology's drive to conquest would lead to the realisation of progress or would provide a route to greater individual freedom and a 'sensibly' organised society. They pointed to the 'costs' of technology, so readily overlooked. Increasing alienation, the irrationality of the whole process, and many other, specific factors. Nowadays when technology is assigned a 'decisive' role, it is once again a positive effect that is often being assumed. Thus alternative technology is seen as a lever that can help bring about a better, 'humane' society.

Proposals for technical solutions on a sensible scale (E. F. Schumacher – 'small is beautiful';[1] I. Illich – 'self-limitation'),[2] the desire for a holistic life, and, finally, the various ingredients of the discussion about 'limits to growth' are the basis from which the new scenario of a reform of society through technology has evolved. Hosts of solar houses and windmills in a natural environment that is largely untouched, free and happy individuals, all producing their own food, maintaining social relations based on solidarity, and no longer delegating the resolution of political issues to vague central institutions but deciding for themselves competently and with gusto.

Technology as a bringer of happiness?

Despite all this, trying to capture the 'essence' of alternative technology in the concrete proposals that are made in regard to processes
and products is a hopeless undertaking. Wind-powered generators,
methane plants, compost toilets, solar heating, greenhouses, clay-
building techniques, these examples, neither individually nor taken
together denote anything definitively 'alternative'. The concrete
examples of alternative technology seem to be the aspects least suited
to advancing the idea behind the concept. If one takes them, and the
objectives referred to at the outset, literally, one runs up against some
long-suspected impossibilities. Even very modest consumer
requirements in this society cannot be satisfied using craft-based
skills alone. Craft-based productivity is too low to feed 'everyone', or
to produce enough goods for exchange. In addition, the level of
technical knowledge needed in order to get rid of the division of
labour is still too high to be attained voluntarily by most people. And
in any case, the achievement of community spirit and grass-roots
democracy cannot be guaranteed 'by technological means',
especially not by technologies that are labour-intensive and time-
consuming. Decentralisation may indeed increase the political
autonomy of 'small units', but it does not increase the security of
their supply and reserves at times of uncertainty. It is also ques-
tionable whether there is really a saving of resources when supply
systems are decentralised on principle. In the field of energy, for
example, reasonable pooling of energy production would be cheaper
and more reliable than a rigorously decentralised system.

Anyone expecting to find in alternative technology a doctrine of
technology as the bringer of happiness actually finds only 'paper
heroes'.[3] None of the technological proposals that have been propagated has, 'in and of itself', any socially innovative significance.
And the list of proposals as a whole turns out to be a catalogue of
desires and contradictions. So should we say good riddance? Should
we call a halt to 'promises and illusions', as one plea, by O. Renn,[4]
against the 'soft revolution' was entitled? To do this would probably
be to fundamentallty misunderstand twenty years of technological
critique. Between simplistic designs on the one hand, and blithely
utopian goals on the other, there lie two further elements. Firstly, an
explanation of the contradications in alternative technology.
Secondly, the value, in terms of knowledge gained, of attempting to

further the critique of technology through positive arguments and examples.

However one assesses the contributions of the pioneers of alternative ideas,[5] alternative technology is not so much a theory as the programme of a social movement. But what we are talking about here is not a movement unified in space, time, or the kinds of people it involves. It is a small, international, and very fragmented, in other words actually decentralised, movement of withdrawal that is looking for ways out of the unreasonable demands of highly technologised industrial society. The movement was backed by people who saw more sense in the argument 'Change yourself to bring about change' than in the widespread habit of critically but passively 'waiting and seeing' whether it would be the prophets of doom or the prophets of breakthrough who were proved right by future events. 'Of course' they were mainly people of a certain educational standard and belonging to the middle class. What had understandably prompted them was usually the disappointment of certain traditional hopes, in regard to their careers, for happiness in relationships, for social progress, or for socialist revolution. And all the relevant experiments expressed not only long-term goals but also the desire for very immediate satisfaction. For the experience of creativity and of nearness to nature. Also of pride at what one has produced, and a sense of community. Social opposition movements constantly come up against the problem of excessive expectations. Expectations which are by no means wilfully produced by those movements themselves but are brought to them from outside, by people who have a positive desire for something other than the options which this society has 'on offer'.

Thus the much-evoked but highly contradictory goals of alternative technology are, in the first place, nothing other than a catalogue of the concrete deficits of the industrial society. In other words the lack of options for a life with technology but without environmental damage, wastage of energy, high capital-requirements, job-stress and unemployment, intensive division of labour and specialisation, etc. It is incorrect to assume that all these unfulfilled demands are important to all people at the same time and to the same degree. Our society is markedly differentiated not only in its production-system but also in social conditions of life. Fewer people than ever before share the same experiences, and therefore the same objectives. They do not seek the same path to the much sought after goal of an autonomous lifestyle that is based on solidarity and is in harmony with nature.

What alternative technology offers in the way of a description of technology is thus no more and no less than a few selected offers designed to accommodate specialised needs in regard to opting-out. If you are bothered by your dependence on poor quality, industrially produced food, then try to grow your own fruit and vegetables or breed your own fish. If you do not want to contribute to the 'need' for large-scale power-stations, then set up your own energy-supply, etc. One may quite rightly criticise the individualistic character of these kinds of answers to social problems, but there is one respect in which they are 'political': they express a different order of values, one in which particular – positive and negative – effects of the application of technology are held to be highly significant. In simple terms the message would be that we want a technology that is environmentally and socially acceptable, even if it is not the cheapest. We would rather do without a certain amount of comfort and free time than be dependent on continued industrial wastage and destruction. Better to live more simply but more naturally than to work oneself to death in a blighted environment just to have a perfect home. Strictly speaking, therefore, we are not talking about a utopian goal. What is at issue here is rather a concrete desire for 'kinds of work and technology that are geared to values and ethics, instead of being bound purely by the dictates of economic exploitation'.[6]

Not every problem has a technological solution

Alternative technology's blueprint for society is a counter-vision to the rather gloomy pictures of progress associated with industrial capitalism and state socialism. However, in addition to the somewhat naïve reversal of technological determinism (in line with the slogan 'good technology creates a humane society'), one comes across some very dubious reasoning in the debate about alternative technology.

We have long since lost control over technological development

This means two things. Firstly, there is no force within society that is capable of directing the further development of technology in a way that is to its own long-term advantage. Even 'capital' seems incapable of safeguarding the bases of industrial-capitalist production (in particular, natural resources, markets, and 'appropriate' human motives) against the repercussions of 'its own' technology. Secondly, however, the social conflicts over technological issues do not seem to guarantee any 'reasonable' end-results either. This is because the growth in complexity of socio-technological systems has no counterpart in the form of a growing social ability to master complexity.

At the level of knowledge alone, so many specialist areas have developed that individual heads are no longer able to contain all the relevant angles on problems (or even the logic of the controlling systems). Knowledge of how something functions (functional knowledge) is by no means the 'normal' starting-point for technical innovations. Such knowledge often lags quite a way behind knowledge about design and production. Knowledge about upkeep and repair (maintenance knowledge) is systematically split off from the kind of knowledge about practical use which those working or using the devices have. And that which one could describe as effectual knowledge, that is to say knowledge about intended and unintended effects, besides becoming the critical factor, has been curiously split off and 'removed' from that which planners and designers think about.

Alternative technology demands that the various divorced dimensions of knowledge be brought together again in the heads of 'normal' people, and not just in the heads of a few generalists. Since this is not possible at every level of technological development, the degree of complexity that has been reached must, in order to ensure democratic direction, be diminished. On no account are there to be any further increases in complexity. Such increases would 'surely' widen the gap between technological development and attempts at political regulation or control. And this gap or time-lag between the generation of problems and awareness of them is the most dangerous aspect of the whole process. It provides the leeway in which more complexity is created 'at the front line of development'. And the less able the powerful members of this society are to direct developments in their own interests, the more emphatically they will reject social demands for control by pointing to the already dangerously high level of complexity.

Technology is far more than just a 'tool'

If one thinks only of tangible objects and physical effects, one has already lost the battle. Technology is an aspect of all social institutions, even the most private, indeed, it is the 'hardest' aspect. Technological rules and structures channel and 'order' people's dealings with each other, and they do so in a way that makes it easier for people to adapt their desires and interests to these very tough structures than to undertake to change them. In other words, to go beyond the limits of current options for action. Contrary to what was implied by the old belief in progress, technological innovations often destroy more opportunities than they create. For example, once the 'radical monopoly' of private transport has established itself, people's social contacts and dependencies inevitably become distributed over a considerably extended catchment-area.[7] This means that the pedestrian 'system' of transport can no longer perform the same functions if motor traffic collapses.

As a social institution, technology now bears more resemblance to language than to objects (a point established by D. Dickson),[8] and the effects it has via extensive causal chains (extensive in concrete, temporal, and social terms) can no longer be traced back to intentional means-and-ends relationships. To this extent, alternative technology is right when it defines as progress every step that leads back towards as clear a means–ends relationship as is possible. Unless we are willing to engage in a kind of 'opting-out' into less technologised forms of living, we shall not be able to halt the technological self-colonisation of society. 'Going back' here means taking into account more factors than just immediate effectiveness and efficiency, and this includes, notably, helping establish ethical, participatory, communicative, aesthetic, and other criteria.

Not every problem has a technological solution

By the device of trying to see how the technological means required for living can be kept to a minimum, alternative technology attempts to avoid the trap of 'thinking exclusively technologically'. It 'knows' that the draw towards technological solutions to social problems (the so-called 'technological fix') is due less to an irrational love of technology than to a general dependence on properly functioning job, product, and service markets. To this extent, alternative technology is doubly 'anti-capitalist'. In the first place, it voices the general doubt as to whether a particular concrete problem can really be solved by technological means alone. Thus, for example, electronic surveillance-systems, which are a 'measure' of an actual need experienced by old people living on their own (if the toilet door has not moved for a time, for example, an alarm is set off) are not an acceptable alternative to the organisation of self-determined styles of communal living. In the second place, the whole concept of alternative technology is underpinned by the notion of 'demarketisation', i.e. as many products and services as possible should be made or peformed by people themselves instead of being produced and sold as goods. Not least, it is assumed, because organising one's own work can be more satisfying than consuming a lot of things that one has bought with one's wages. The criteria which it is suggested should inform decision-making are therefore things like dispensability, the possibility of renunciation at a later date (reversibility), and, possibly, alternative (non-technological) ways of satisfying demands.

New criteria for technological choice

In alternative technology, the idea of a simpler way of life forms the basis for the choice of 'appropriate' technologies. Because there is no single idea of a good and 'sensible' life that is valid for all people, the criterion of choosability, the desire for a 'technology geared to autonomy' plays a highly important role.[9] The issues here are those of the degree of freedom to organise oneself and the opening-up of options for action that were formerly inaccessible. And this applies not only in the 'initial' choice of technological facilities, but 'permanently', in their application. Since the actual uses to which the technology will be put are not to be decided once and for all, but are to remain open to variation, there is a curious leaning either towards very simple (e.g. handicraft) tools or else towards very modern machines (e.g. multi-purpose computer-aided machines).

There is a tendency to rush to label criteria such as 'social usefulness', 'conviviality', or 'autonomy' as springing from subjective whimsy. And indeed, it is not easy to discern the socially innovative impulse at work in small, isolated projects, be it running your own energy-production plant or having a greenhouse in your back yard. The impression one often gets is rather one of resignation

and withdrawal. Nevertheless, the importance of an alternative technology embodied in practical measures must not be underestimated.
It is in such measures that the much-evoked changes in social goals
and values take concrete form. Anyone who merely bemoans the
disunity of the experiments, the lack of 'objective' criteria of
usefulness, or the low efficiency, is actually only demonstrating that
there is indeed a conflict of values at work here. Within the
framework of which order of values should rationality be defined?
What counts as profit, what as loss? From the point of view of the
'techno-rebels', the economic calculus of efficiency is no less woolly
or irrational. It takes for granted areas that can be exploited without
putting anything back in economically (natural resources, quality of
the environment, cultural assets, job-motivation), and it is unable to
justify the extreme short-sightedness of usual calculations of cost-
effectiveness.

What criteria?

What may be learned from the collection of ideas that make up
alternative technology? Beginning with the familiar catalogues of
features, one could make these politically practicable by 'elaborating' them, for example as a list of criteria for technological choice.
'Elaborating' could mean: beginning by distancing oneself from
assertions that are extremely ill-founded or all-too-blithely taken for
granted (e.g. 'Alternative Technology functions in any age . . .
abolishes the distinction between work and leisure . . . increases
efficiency by being limited in scope . . . is safe against misuse . . . is
democratic . . .'). A second step could be to identify the most important features as varying dimensions of complexity, and to do so in
such a way as to bring out the differences between technologies that
'master' and those that 'can be mastered'. A third and final step
would be to classify what remains, on the one hand according to
criteria of ecological appropriateness, and on the other hand as a
collection of examples of the application of additional, non-
economic criteria for decision-making. Although a list that has been
reduced and systematised in this way, and has had one or two extra
aspects added to it (like that of reversibility – see Table 1) provides a
picture of the state of the debate about technological alternatives, it
hardly constitutes adequate promotional literature for the historic
idea of an alternative technology.

Notes

1 Schumacher, *Small is Beautiful.*
2 Illich, *Tools for Conviviality.*
3 Rybczynski, *Paper Heroes.*
4 Renn, *Verheißung und Illusion.*
5 See, for example, Schumacher, *Small is Beautiful*; Illich, *Tools for Conviviality*; Morris and Hess, *Neighbourhood Power*; Dickson, *Alternative Technology*; Boyle and Harper, *Radical Technology*; and Bookchin, *Towards an Ecological Society.*
6 Hallerbach and Mez, 'Keine Kritik ohne Technikkritik'.
7 Illich, *Tools for Conviviality*, pp. 46–84.
8 Löw-Beer, *Industrie und Glück.*

References

AGAT (Arbeitsgruppe für angepaßte Technologie) (ed.), *Technik für Menschen* (Frankfurt: Fischer Taschenbuch Verlag, 1982).

Bookchin, M., *Towards an Ecological Society* (Montreal: Black Rose Books, 1981).

Bossel, H., *Bürgerinitiativen entwerfen die Zukunft* (Frankfurt: Fischer Taschenbuch Verlag, 1978).

Boyle, G. and Harper, P., *Radical Technology* (London: Wildwood House, 1976).

Dickson, D., *Alternative Technology and the Politics of Technical Change* (London: Fontana, 1974 (German version Munich: Trikont Verlag, 1980).

Hallerbach, J. and Mez, L., 'Keine Kritik ohne Technikkritik', *kritik.* 8: 25, (1980).

Illich, I., *Tools for Conviviality* (London and New York: Calder Boyars, 1973 (German version Reinbeck: Rowohlt, 1980)).

Löw-Beer, P., *Industrie und Gluck* (Berlin: Wagenbach, 1981).

Morris, D., and Hess, K., *Neighbourhood Power. The New Localism* (Washington: 1975 (German version Frankfurt: Fischer Taschenbuch Verlag, 1980).

Renn, O., *Verheißung und Illusion*, (Frankfurt, Berlin and Vienna: Ullstein Verlag, 1982).

Rybczynski, W., *Paper Heroes. A Review of Appropriate Technology*, (Garden City and New York: Anchor, 1980).

Schumacher, E. F., *Small is Beautiful: A Study of Economics as if People Mattered* (London: Abacus, 1973).

Wiesenthal, H., 'Alternative Technologie und gesellschaftliche Alternativen', *Technik und Gesellschaft. Jahrbuch 1* (Frankfurt and New York: Campus Verlag, 1982.

TABLE 1
Alternative technology
Major criteria and objectives in contrast to those of traditional technology

'Alternative' means:	Instead of:
ecologically appropriate	*ecologically destructive:*
• low energy-requirement	• high energy-requirement
• no pollution	• heavy pollution
• reuse of materials	• one-way use of materials
• protective of other forms of life	• threatening to other forms of life
• preserving natural variety	• diminishing natural variety
controllable complexity:	*uncontrollable complexity:*
• little specialisation of knowledge or skills. i.e. tending towards general comprehensibility of functions and effects, low level of division of labour, side-effects mostly predictable, low risk of accident	• high level of specialisation of knowledge in relation to research and development, production, functioning, application, and surveillance, without consequent unpredictability of effects and unknown risks
• long time-scale	• short time-scale
• changes remain reversible	• irreversible changes
• differentiated and pluralistic solutions to problems	• solutions to problems are generalised and monistic
several social rationales are valid:	*the economic rationale prevails:*
• the goal = the preservation of social systems and life-chances	• the goal = growth in production-systems and economic values
• the means = distribution of goods independently of work, satisfaction as the motive for work	• the means = the job-market as the mechanism for distributing conditions of life, need for income as the motive for work
• efficiency = the ratio of total social good to total social cost, measured against social yardsticks (profit and loss account + ecological books + social balance-sheet are all required)	• efficiency = ratio of individual company profits to individual company costs, measured in the relevant market-prices (only profit and loss account required)
• rationalisation = reduction in job stress, increase in job-satisfaction, shorter working-hours	• rationalisation = replacement of manpower by capital, greater adjustment of work to fit in with the way production is organised.
• social structure = determined by production-groups working in co-operation and by neighbourhood groupings	• social structure = determined by isolated small-scale families and individuals in an urban environment

- tendencies = craft-based production to satisfy local and regional needs, possibility of extensive self-sufficiency, decentralisation of resources and decision-making (universal democratic participation), revival of styles of living based on solidarity and local culture, increased willingness tohelp shape social life)

- tendencies = mass production for the world market, world-wide relationships of dependence, centralisation of resources and decision-making, market-style relations replace norms based on solidarity, increasing alienation between people, and between people and society

6

Deer at the world market
Left-wing economic policy and its problematic world-view

Economic reform is the key concept of left-wing politics, its aim being to refashion society in accordance with certain social and ecological criteria. The concept itself, and its protagonists, have for some years been experiencing an insidious decline in credibility and in the power to command attention. The programmes of action of classical socialist economic policy, founded on planning and control, nationalisation and state employment, the creaming-off of profits and control on the movement of capital, now seem of little value, not just here at home and not because there is no need for an alternative economic policy. The phenomenon is a world-wide and cross-bloc one, and it has emerged despite the challenge of the neo-liberal programme of deregulation, despite awareness of the ecological crisis and of the unknown risks of biological and genetic engineering.

The reason for this development is obvious, but the one-time partisans of a total renewal of society through economics find it difficult to accept the facts. It is not the capitalist economy's proneness to crises, nor the unfair distribution of surplus production in wage gains and net investments, nor the alien nature of work and feelings of impotence at the workplace, nor pollution and the craters in the lignite-mining areas, nor contaminated baby seals in the North Sea, nor the misery in over-indebted Third World countries. It is not any of these painfully familiar 'by-products' of modern capitalism that determines the attitude of the wage-dependent to the issue of economic reform. It is a simple but omnipresent piece of calculus, namely that capitalism is a non-zero-sum game, not only in terms of economic growth, but as a global incentive-structure engendering productive efficiency, needs, and innovations, not only in terms of increased output, increased consumption, and increased risks, but also in terms of an increased ability to learn and capacity to react *vis-à-vis* self-created risks. The chances of ecologising production do, it is true, seem slim overall, but they appear relatively favourable where competitive democracy and market competition occur together.

The consequences, however, appear paradoxical. In the Soviet Union, even the leadership's conservative majority has to bank on 'Perestroika', because, despite years of propagating enemy images, of patriotic emotionalism, and of a political process cut off from the outside world, they have not managed to uncouple the population's consumer desires ideas on lifestyle from the Western 'paradigms'. At every point in the West where some need for modernisation is still deemed to exist, whether this be in France, Italy, Portugal, or Spain, left-wing parties have long since developed their own programmes of deregulation, in accordance with the motto 'First produce more profitably, then you can distribute more equitably.'[1]

If there is a tendency at odd points in the Federal Republic, in certain sections of the SPD, the unions, and the Greens, to 'rest on laurels' and adhere to what is left of the socialist economic programme. This is due to two all too readily repressed facts. First, that the economy of the Federal Republic (the third strongest industrial nation in the global economy) is largely free of worries about modernisation. Secondly, that in order to ensure the proper functioning of a functionally differentiated society, it is perfectly sufficient if only those who are able to exercise real influence on things − bankers, managers, wage-negotiators, mechanical engineers, car-workers, and so on − pay close attention to what is happening.

Incitements to left-wing politicians to indulge in a luxuriant misinterpretation of the global economic framework for action are nowhere as great as in the Federal Republic. If this remains so, it is unlikely that left-wing political demands (ranging from the Greens' Reconstruction Programme to the SPD's Irsee draft manifesto) will have any significant, let alone desirable influence on the process of economic change. In future, the questions at issue will not be practical ones such as 'What sort of measures must be taken to counter soil-pollution?', which up to now have been used to disguise the lack of any guiding concepts. The central question will be one relating to reform policy. Namely, how is an intentional reshaping of society possible when one knows that most acute situations of danger are the unintended products of deliberate actions, whether short-sighted and egoistic or well-intentioned and idealistic?

The range of measures which the material situation imposes on us in regard to our handling of air, water, soil, and waste stands in need of expansion and clarification, and this will have to be done mainly by experts. The protagonists of reform, meanwhile, having for several years acted as forums for environmental issues and citizens' initiatives, will now once again be confronted with the problems relating to their own sphere of action. Notably that of how what is acknowledged to be necessary can be translated into reality, and what order of priorities is necessary to performing that translation. The old economic world-views provide no answers here. The advice offered by supposed specialists, professional moral philosophers, 'new age' sermonisers, welfare-state technocrats, or crisis-exploiters, who have all made their proclamations of impending economic crisis into cornerstones of their own identity, contain all sorts of what would be 'true' hypotheses if only one single approach prevailed. They offer no clues about how to deal with a plurality of contradictory doctrines of salvation.

'Economics' is a universal theme, about which no one can say everything. This paper too has its lacunae, it does not provide an instant recipe for an economic boom in the Ruhr. It contains no proclamation of the true principles of ecological production, and the author is not about to reveal what form of business enterprise, joint-stock company, co-operative, mining association, small business, state-owned concern, or self-managed collective he considers to be the finest. There are experts whose task it is to settle questions of this kind, experts whose jobs must not be wantonly put in jeopardy – actionists, aesthetes, preachers, and mystics.

Visions of capital

If one does not wish to follow the traditional line of rhetoric which begins by stating that economic power is the nucleus of all evil but goes on to say that it can only be overcome 'historically', not politically, a conceptual clarification is called for. Namely, differences in economic power should be viewed as unequal opportunities to counter unwanted effects, effects generated by risky action taken through and in a complex partial system of society, that is to say 'the economy'. That system's complexity is as 'great' as it is *inter alia* because the choice of types of intervention (within the national framework) is disproportionately small in comparison with the global range of effects which those acting can produce and on which they must reckon. This complexity can be understood correctly only when one realises that 'everything' for the sake of which change is being sought. Namely, our social and cultural conditions of life depend on the continued functioning of the system which is to be subjected to pressure for change. As far as our conditions of life, and what happens to them, are concerned, 'capital' does indeed play a central and 'powerful' role. It does this not so much by prescribing what is to be done, but by its ability to react extremely sensitively and disagreeably to any schemes for change.

The relationship between economy and society may be described by means of three different concepts of capital. Capital as the steamroller, which flattens everything before it. Capital as the 'chronically sick father, to whom all members of the family must show special consideration'.[2] Finally, capital as a shy deer. As far as highly-developed industrial societies are concerned, the first concept of capital lost all meaning decades ago. These societies have been thoroughly capitalised. Only the world-view underlying traditional concepts of reform is still completely geared to it, with its tools of dynamite and anti-tank blockades. The preconditions for using these tools have disappeared. There are no forms of existence independent of capital which could be used as a base from which to initiate a promising defence, let alone an attack. Even agriculture has now put its pre-industrial phase behind it. Capitalist conditions of production unfortunately no longer constitute a constraint on, but are rather a condition of the material and social satisfaction of needs.

Nowadays, economic policy must be elaborated within the interpretive framework set by the two other concepts of capital, in other words, the sick father and the shy deer. Each dislikes the other. The latter wants to graze only where there is no whiff of the moribund, and roast venison is not the speciality of the house. To the extent that it has to strike a balance between ailing, moribund structures and 'new' structures, economic policy is like a prayer to the gods to send a lot of rain (e.g. innovations) but on no account to send a flood. What economic policy must first do, therefore, before setting any material or social goals, is to adjust itself to two underlying conditions. Firstly, the dependence of the whole of society on the proper functioning of capital investment as a system of employment and a source of taxable income. Secondly, the varied nature of businesses and branches of industry, a variety that must be deemed to be much greater than the terminology which the social sciences (and in particular industrial sociology) offer as a means of describing them. That terminology comes nowhere near embracing the extensive differentiation that may be observed in economic phenomena, in terms of size, organisational structure, management styles, strategies of innovation, types of product, production techniques, market-power on buying- and selling-markets, manpower requirements, dependence on the world market, and so on. The terminology which we commonly use is appropriate to the level of differentiation and industrialisation of the 1950s. What we call the economy or capitalism today has outstripped the yardsticks of the Erhardt era, not only in regard to the degree of interweaving and the problems this brings, but also in regard to sensitivity and the ability to adjust.

Mutual dependencies have become universal and telephonically swift. The economy must now be thought of as a system, which means no longer counting on the reversibility of causes, since there is no longer any stable linear causal chain. Systematic removal of causes would, in most cases, lead to a worsening of effects, and anyone attempting to 'claw back' the (temporary) advantages derived by capital from unemployment would cause more unemployment. The question of whether state employment programmes are feasible and effective, whether companies can be attracted to invest in Leer rather than in Rosenheim, no longer depends only on the rate of inflation or demand 'on site'. It also depends on interest rates in the USA, on the trade policy of corporations in Japan, on the extent of the Strategic Defence Initiative programme, and on the development of consumer demands that can be satisfied at favourable cost only by the electronics industry of the Far East.[3] Such dependencies cannot be dealt with by shutting one's eyes to them or by wishful thinking and utopian fantasies.

When reality no longer fits into one's familiar world-view, it may be emotionally satisfying to seek a radical 'solution' in the making of 'demands'. Capitalism, however, is much less anodyne than it is depicted as being by those who believe that it is the appropriate addressee for 'critical demands' and that, given the 'correct' awareness, it can be 'got over' in either step-by-step or long-jump fashion. Moreover, 'it' is not a spine-chilling cellar but an indispensable heating system that warms and at the same time threatens to explode. 'It' is not a course of development that one has to pace out, but a yardstick of development that stands in need of replacement. The dependencies that are created in and by it are so tough that those who are familiar with them, be they managers, politicians, or simply share-owners, look with amusement on any frontal attacks made on them. Titles to capital interests may change their owners as a result of stock-market crashes or expropriation, but anti-system rhetoric has no effect on the systemic links that bind them together. Such rhetoric demonstrates that there is no danger of any change, because those seeking change merely reveal their ignorance when they propose goals such as increased income from taxes, increased borrowing, full employment with higher unit wage-costs, or ecological production through the diminution of the capacity for innovation.

Worn-out fetishes

In comparison with the explosive mixture of power and complexity which constitutes the economic system, the terms 'market' and 'State' (or 'organisation') appear decidedly under-complex. At best they are idealising abstractions. The use of market mechanisms, in the sense of the weighing-up of alternative costs and profits, is common practice throughout the real world, even within organised structures. Equally, successful market operations are inconceivable without organisational preconditions, without techniques of risk-limitation and provision for innovation. If price-bargaining on spot-markets were the wisest thing going, companies would not hesitate to refound themselves every week, with new employees and different machines, and on different sites. However, because market operation and organisational operation each involve too great risks in regard to efficiency, and very high informational and transactional costs, one finds them occurring either as mutual preconditions or as a systematic mixture. 'In themselves' they are neither good nor bad, neither 'industrial' nor 'ecological'. Their social effects depend on underlying political conditions and on the nature of their links with social institutions (education system, job market, social security).

Anyone who considers the differences between operation on market principles and operation on organisational principles to be decisive should try to imagine where the sources of the respective guiding rationales which he assumes lie behind these are located. In the case of the market, there is a constant process of adjustment of economic action to ambient conditions (prices and quantities), which are no more than 'snapshots' of the aggregate effects of various operations. This might mean prices, as determined by the impotence of the unions in South Korea and the correspondingly low unit wage-costs there, or it might be the level of oil output currently opted for by Saudi Arabia as a compromise between budget, and cartel-related considerations. Whether such ambient conditions are regarded as 'reasonable', either in respect of their origins or of the uses to which they are put, as a yardstick for action, action for which the company alone must answer, is an empirical question, not a question of principle. In the case of the organisation mechanism (including state regulation), the 'reasonableness' of the results is determined by political negotiation. This depends on the interests, scope for action, and cognitive faculties of those involved. Do they have sufficient understanding of their own interests, of the social and economic environment, and of changes in the latter to be able to bring about intended results? Are they able to fall back on other alternatives for action which do not call for co-ordination and which thus put them in a position of 'power' *vis-à-vis* those partners who are dependent on co-operation? Whether market-based or organisationally-based interventions are 'better' for tackling a particular problem is always solely a practical question, the answer to which must embrace much more than mere economic circumstances and consideration of principles.

In the type of politics that is geared to decision-making (rather than being purely rhetorical), 'market' and 'State' have long since ceased to be real alternatives. They have become mere ciphers, used by protagonists as a way of assigning themselves and others to categories based on opposing economic world-views. In this symbolic sense, 'market' means that indispensable intervention in the economic process occurs in the knowledge of the importance of market competition and of the autonomy of individual businesses. The market's efficiency in allocation and its motive force in innovation are to be guaranteed. The decisive feature, however, is that a champion of the market who is conducting economic policy is viewed by investors as being 'self-controlled'. It is assumed that he knows when and where to desist from political intervention. This is what gives liberals and conservatives their advantage in economic politics, not the receipt of slush money or the pledging of personal capital but the well-founded expectation that the signals that warn against or block too great a degree of interventionism will be read correctly and in good time. An economy completely free of state involvement, in line with the textbook principles of neo-classical market-doctrine, is by no means the vision preferred by business. Though the traditional world-view, which was geared to the 'patriotic' national economy and regarded external trade as a secondary factor, is currently being replaced by an awareness of global economic interactions and of the dependence of individual businesses on the fate of world markets. This only implies a shift in the level of arrangements (e.g. from 'national capital' to local conditions for businesses financed from whatever source), it does not imply a shift in the status of any principles (for example, from 'State' to 'market').

The 'state' cipher, on the other hand, signifies recognition of the social costs that arise when monetary calculus takes priority, when 'non-goods' such as nature and manpower are subordinated to market conditions. Consistently with this, political will aims at setting up framework arrangements that limit and compensate for these tendencies. No matter how many well-intentioned pro-market protestations accompany this action, investors assume that once interventionists (e.g. in the SPD and the Greens) have set foot on the path of intervention, they will, if they feel they are being successful, continue along it. One should note that in a non-linear system such as the economy, ascribing success in a causal manner, and concluding that duplication is possible, are indeed problematic approaches. There is some truth in the assumption that anyone who has adopted intervention as a principle has misunderstood his own position and will be inclined to intervene more frequently, more radically, and more daringly the more successes he ascribes to himself. In the world-view of the investors, state intervention is seen as a drug, whose use by its addicts they frown on. Hence, only those who spot the warning-signals and limits can count on any kind of understanding for intervention. Liberals could do more than they want, whereas to have to not do what one really wants to do in order to be successful is the classic dilemma which social democratic economic policy always has to face.

That something as complex as the economy continues to be debated in such simplistic terms as 'market' and 'State', despite the fact that any intervention carried out in strict accordance with the relevant principles would provoke an economic disaster, is an indication of the highly developed functional division of society, and also of the way in which discourses that are meaningful (and help establish group identity) become detached from real problems and functional relations. Politics and economics, and science and politics are much less closely related than their protagonists make them out to be, and furthermore they are fragmented into numerous self-referential discussions. This may be demonstrated by two simple observations. First, there is the continuing misconception that the external dependence of an open economy can be measured largely by the actual flow of trade over its borders, without taking into account how much more of a threat imports would constitute to internally consumed production if that production were not also generated in large measure in a way that comes up to the standards of the world market. In other words, in an internationally competitive manner. Secondly, demands are made, and presented as instant remedies, for things like drastic reductions in working hours or the imposition of taxes on resources, without its being noticed that the desired effects in terms of influencing the course of things would be accompanied by massive structural effects on a scale that would relegate the protests of the Rheinhausen steelworkers to the 'News in Brief' column.

Problems with protagonists

When left-wing attempts at intervention fail, or else are not undertaken at all for fear of failure, this is generally due to two unrelated factors. Firstly, the great sensitivity and resistance of businesses to any attempts at direction. Secondly, the inherent limits of the political capacity to direct.

(1)   The resistance of the economy to attempts at direction does have to do with power, but not in the sense that left-wing politics is too frightened to issue orders or establish incentives (as if it did not know how much the State needs tax-income and a high level of employment). It is more that flourishing businesses which are a rich source of jobs and taxes generally have several alternatives open to them in regard to their future development and choose between these according to ambient political conditions as well.[4] In fact, it is only economically weak businesses struggling at the edge of competitivity which are obliged to respond to political intervention, because they suffer from a lack of capacity for investment and innovation. Innovative, internationally competitive businesses which determine,

rather than suffer structural change can afford to ignore the aims of political intervention. They initially simply pay the higher interest-rates or taxes (which may be the price for subsidising areas of business that are in trouble), whilst planning their next tax or labour-saving investment-programme, their next takeovers or mergers, their next relocation or transfer of capital. They do this in the knowledge that politics can only act for so long in a manner that runs counter to those demands and expectations of the voters which can only be satisfied by internationally competitive production. The superior power of 'powerful' businesses rests primarily on the asymmetrical dependence of society on a flourishing economy, and not on corruption and bribery (though the latter may help reconcile politicians to their sorry role). If politicians wish to manipulate the dependence of the State on the economy in particular directions, they must ensure that there are sufficient profitable areas from which to cream off the money needed to finance that manipulation.

(2)   The inability of politics to engage in directive action on a long-term rational basis is due to more than just the resistance of businesses to direction. Internal problems relating to function and co-ordination prevent parties, trade unions, and social movements from developing programmes of action that are both attractive and appropriate to reality. In functionally differentiated society, with its multiplicity of self-referential discourses, organisations that are dependent on voluntary membership face almost insurmountable problems in terms of being simultaneously large and effective as well as integrated and intelligent, and capable both of survival and of strategy. If their programmes of action did justice to the true complexity of society, they would no longer be suitable as slogans for securing approval and support. The political protagonists of the present are, without exception, internally incapable of strategy in the strict sense of the term. The most they can do is point to attractive destinations, but in the interests of self-preservation they must refrain from calling on people to make the journey there. Because none of the pressing problems in the areas of work, social security, and ecology can be solved without difficult structural and institutional changes, and these changes in some cases involve increased costs and risks. The big *Volksparteien* are incapable of putting any strategies of reform into practice. In the battle to secure votes they tend either to make the position of the government out to be better than it is, or if they are in opposition, to promise the impossible.[5]

The problems faced by trade unions and social movements are much the same. But they are made even worse by the fact that the effectiveness of such bodies depends directly on the action of the members themselves, on their readiness to engage in strikes or demonstrations. This presupposes a minimum level of commonality in the interpretation of situations, in other words a collective consciousness that is all the more unlikely to emerge the more variation there is in people's social conditions, experiences, and world-views. One consequence of such variation is, for example, the ability of trade unions to chalk up such ambivalent 'successes' as the reduction of working-hours through the sacrifice of flexible working-time. Or the habit of styling the objectives of social struggles as 'goals in themselves' (e.g. 'immediate opting out'), which may result in the temporary preservation of group identity and by tinting all glasses the same colour. Another sorry piece of evidence is the reaction to the (inadequately worked-out) proposals put forward by Oskar Lafontaine (leader of the SPD). In order to distract attention from the question of how more unemployed people could be provided with jobs through reductions in working-hours, a question that is currently a source of stress and provocation to the unions, a popular front was finally formed, stretching from Rappe to Ebermann.

Using the rhetoric of radical class-conflict, this front succeeded in retranslating the unions' (comprehensible) self-imposed decision to represent only those interests that were capable of strike action (in other words those in work) into a struggle on behalf of 'the unemployed', thereby managing to get the 'two-thirds society' organised from the left. ('Two-thirds society' is a term coined by left-wing social democrats to describe the results of conservative social and economic policy, which they see as marginalising one-third of society.) Instead of there finally being a move to start up the debate about what social policies might be introduced to replace patchy wage-bargaining solidarity, the unemployed were cynically referred to the 'solidary contribution of the employers',[6] in other words, to the adversary in the conflict.

If, despite this, one forces oneself to take a dispassionate view, and approaches the issue from a different perspective, one sees that 'left-wing' thought has inherited two tendencies from the socialist tradition of the workers' movement which may have gone together in former times but no longer do so. The first is to identify and seek to achieve that which, in the light of a careful analysis of the situation, appears to be realisable. The second is to 'demand' that which the collective consciousness deems to be just. Until the world became thoroughly capitalised, these two things were one and the same, namely political recognition, democratic freedom, social security, and the shared utopia that was the goal of socialism. Nowadays, a decision in favour of realistic strategies signifies the rejection of old interpretive models, although such models may still function as symbols of left-wing group-identity. The traditional combinations of programme and identity are no use as a potential for action or for threat. They are no more than tokens of the tribalisation of left-wing politics. Yet the realisation that left-wing models of interpretation were once in conformity with reality, before that conformity disappeared, does perhaps contain an element of hope. There could once again be something in the nature of a correspondence between the diagnosis of reality and the aspirations of society in regard to shaping itself, provided social change were not too stormy, and also that loyalties to the nineteenth century could be limited and the intellectual clear-up operation accelerated. In such a case, the following observations could be read as a kind of investment contribution.

Myths about control

It appears to have become established practice, in the review sections of newspapers, to see the survival of society as dependent on changes in values or on increasing 'new age' consciousness. In other words, on the straightforward replacement of older generations by younger ones. If this is the the case it is merely one variant of a subcultural misconception, namely that one's own thinking foreshadows the way in which 'everyone' will, sooner or later, also have to to think. Where so many different interpretations of reality exist side by side without prejudice to each other, new ways of thinking do not spread like wildfire. They find their niche, and that is that. Society has long since adapted to variation in ways of thinking and is able to offer almost every kind of 'otherness' – an adequate space somewhere between the health-food co-op and Harrods. What is lacking is not appeals to think 'differently', but the underlying conditions needed to be able to act 'differently', namely obvious individual and collective advantages in adopting ecological methods of production and life styles that can be practised, standardised, reproduced, and exported with the accent on whatever way of life one chooses.

Finding a way to organise this is the peculiar problem of 'systemic' strategies of reform.

However, the agenda for debates about reform are being determined by other issues, the importance of which seems greatly overestimated. Thus a number of people besides green 'reconstruction' experts are expecting far too great a degree of benefit from the spread of 'open' decision-making processes,in reconstruction committees, ecological councils, economic and social councils, and so on. There are plans to extend corporate-style negotiating bodies, of which ample use is already being made, by the addition of representatives of affected groups. But however homely the motley picture of the student, knitting-needles in hand, sitting next to the chain-smoking female worker, the class-conscious union official, the anxious capitalist, the representative of a pharmacists' association, and the wildlife boffin may seem, one has to assume that such a set-up will lead to a great damping-down of responsibility and motivation. In a situation where no one is forced, by common working ties, to understand the interests of the others, each will try to hitch a free ride, deriving some profit for himself in return for as little input as possible. Any kind of confrontation between supporters of opposing but mutually dependent interests is more fruitful.

Mutually dependent interests may give rise to co-operation, but this alone cannot guarantee outcomes that seem reasonable to concerned outsiders as well. The fact that the *de facto* growth-based coalition (or better still, co-productivity) of labour and capital has had disastrous ecological consequences is due not to the co-operation aspect but to the lack of fall-back options. In other words, to the specific vulnerability of the work-force to blackmail, because it has no alternative to paid labour. The crux of the discourses inspired by verbal radicalism lies in the fact that the alternatives of an egalitarian distribution policy, of a guaranteed basic income, or of a collective employment fund (to help those who suffer as a result of the structural changes in industry) degenerate into objects of aesthetic appraisal, of emotional self-confirmation, and of the expression of identity. All within the framework of a strictly conflictual semantics, of course.

The advantages of global participation, meanwhile, are quite different. Firstly, they make it possible to block specific issues, because it is relatively easy to create an *ad hoc* negative coalition in order to counter disagreeable proposals. Secondly, they make it possible to put off decisions, for example, in order to reduce social complexity by slowing down the rate of social change. These are therefore primarily recipes for stabilising a worthwhile status quo in a far-off time when things are finally running 'as they should be'.[7]

Too much hope is also placed on the possibility of extending the range of economic organisations by the addition of a few more or less agreeable forms of organisation, such as self-managed enterprises, co-operatives, and nationalised branches of industry. A change in ownership gives no indication of whether the business concerned will help reduce the dependence of producers on the market, or devote its profits to the creation of a future 'moral economy', in which the social costs of production will be included in the calculations. Yet these are the requirements which should be met by every applicant for state subsidies, whatever the structure of ownership may be.

Kicking the habit

A capitalist economy on which all conditions of existence and forms of security depend should be viewed as a severe form of addiction. Sudden withdrawal is just as likely to lead to demise as is the unbridled continuation of the habit. Gradual weaning is the only option, with many types of substitute drugs being called for. Instead of starting off from the idea of redesigning 'society' in accordance with the 'correct' principles, or of recommending past utopias to future generations, what we need are mechanisms which generate self-motivated social change and keep that change in motion. For this, one should, all due reservations having been made in regard to risky analogies, imagine a kind of social evolution. If choices are to be made with a view to conforming to social and ecological requirements, we should begin by ensuring that there is greater variety in the relevant phenomena. Given the right circumstances, a positive selection may then be made (i.e. the right production policy) in order to ensure that particular things are produced in particular ways. In the main, however, the selection, given that it needs variety as a basis, must be restricted to excluding the undesirable. The third evolutionary mechanism, namely preservation, would then mean enabling the organisations that make up the economy to engage in rapid and efficient self-corrective procedures, with the proviso that these organisations would be compelled to act, once they had realised which criteria of ecological and social acceptability they were infringing. On this point, I should like to make six further observations.

(1)   It is better to tolerate the *de facto* independence of the economy from politics rather than to try to replace it with direct control, which would be highly risky. This is the 'systemic' reasoning behind a further decoupling of income distribution from the employment system, for example, by means of a guaranteed basic income. In this way, politics would also attain greater autonomy *vis-à-vis* the economy and would be able to intervene without being hamstrung, as it is today, by the whole employment issue. If it were left up to businesses to decide how to satisfy ecological requirements, one could expect politics to react more rapidly to new knowledge about problems, and businesses to be more ready to adapt than if employment issues and obligations in regard to production processes were involved. The variety of types of business, branches of industry, economic climate, and strategies of innovation could be exploited to facilitate adaptation, instead of operating as a barrier, as they do in the case of highly generalised strategies of intervention.

(2)   The guiding principle would thus be a politics of 'management by exception', which avoids being caught in a spiralling need for intervention brought about by intervention itself. The criterion of success for such a politics would be that it caused businesses to internalise, in ways that are appropriate and differ from case to case, the social costs to which they contribute, without unnecessarily jeopardising their position on the markets. Besides being implementable at any time, a series of specific regulations would also galvanise the framework of expectations of the businesses themselves. They would know 'for certain' that in future, environmental criteria would count for more and more. Taking correct decisions would then mean being able to reckon on fewer and fewer opportunities for externalisation and, in the interests of the company, turning designers and marketing strategists into agents for the ecologisation of production.

(3)   Like natural evolution, this economic strategy would justify itself not in terms of some supposed 'ultimate goal' but in terms of the adaptability and simultaneity of a number of different routes. One motive factor would be the exploitation of favourable opportunities, the ability to 'take off'. Incentives would be set which encouraged adaptability rather than rigidity, the ability to (un)learn

rather than traditionalism, sensitivity rather than impregnability, flexibility rather than intransigence. One cannot yet assess what intellectual innovations and practical opportunities would result from such a shift in political perspective. One test-case would be, for example, the use of the next energy-price increase to move over to an infrastructure based on energy-saving.

(4) A purposeful approach to system complexity implies that problems as a rule are not solved at the point at which they arise, nor even at the point at which they are identified, but rather at the point where they are amenable to treatment. This means that not every economic problem can be solved economically. Where the existence of businesses is tied more to the global economic situation than to regional requirements, solutions will increasingly have to be sought in the realm of social policy.

It also means that tracing things back along causal chains will lead to solutions only in lucky circumstances, that is to say where the rare case of reversibility applies. This is the reason why, for example, the causative principle is inappropriate as a reaction to the many 'synergetic' problems related to the environment. Whereas a drastic extension of liability (in particular the principle of strict liability) promises to be effective in that it links risks back from the area of their conceivable occurrence to their potential originators, and shifts the latter's self-interest in the direction of avoiding incalculable risks (a feature that would be thwarted, for example, by a generalised obligation to insure, given the 'free ride' motive).

(5) At the same time, one should do away with the expectation that solutions to large and complex problems must be equally 'large' and complex. Such assumptions spring more from our instincts than from the capacity for abstract analysis which, to be sure, is one cause of the whole mess but which should not be got rid of until we have made good some of the damage caused. Of course, ecologising production methods and lifestyles involves the undogmatic use of the whole overrated range of tools associated with an ecologically-based economy, from the decrees and prohibitions beloved of the left to the right's favoured instrument of putting a price on air and waste, as much more attention must be paid to the effect these tools have on the adaptability and capacity for innovation of the 'objects of control' as to their direct ecological consequences. Whether one likes it or not, the most creative forms of organisation by far in this society are market-dependent enterprises, not political parties, ministries, or

research institutes. Steering these enterprises' capacity for self-direction on to a socially desirable course means investigating and testing out alternatives for production precisely at those points where avoidance of damage, as well as the shifting-back of risks, is economically profitable and where an intimate knowledge of the technical/functional alternatives coincides with a capacity for innovation. The task of politics would then be to fix responsibility, target-requirements, and timetables. Leaving companies to choose the way in which they can adapt is unfortunately regarded by many a moral aesthete as too simple a mechanism. For complex problems they prefer complex solutions.

(6)   Another set of approaches that is suspected of not being complex enough to be recognised as system-transcendent is that involving the securing of certain rights for workers who wish to talk about risks associated with company operations without jeopardising their jobs, the right to raise an issue, to register an objection, or to withhold labour. Such measures would make possible the proper settlement of conflicts over ecological and health risks which would otherwise remain hidden under the cloak of workplace 'togetherness', since at present it is the worker who considers his own health interests or the risks to everyone in general who is regarded as the daft one. The same dilemma over the collective good is at work here as in the case of motorway speeding in foggy weather. A single individual wanting to be 'sensible' and driving at 30 miles per hour while the juggernaut pilots whizz along behind him at 100, is endangering himself and others. In contrast, safeguards in regard to 'publicising' awareness of the risks involved in company operations might set a process in motion whereby the criteria for assessing 'correct' economic management would tighten up, as it were, of themselves. The logic of a weaning strategy based on 'learning about the system' does not fit in with the classical understanding of reform, which is a product of 'steamroller' capitalism and knows only about armour-piercing weapons and euthanasia. The steamroller has now stopped rolling, having flattened the very last corner of society. Capital, that ailing father looking for nourishment and mothering, has left no legacy out of which we might fashion something better. As for keeping deer at the world market whilst avoiding 'venison addiction', the old left-wing recipes, for their part, are about as useful as a collection of drunken drovers.

Post-capitalism?

What is generally an unconscious choice of world-view in economic policy determines the chances of success of attempts to 'ecologise' the economy and society. Ecologically-based economic policy will get under way only when it works up its own momentum. There are too many essential starting-points and important decisions for central co-ordination and direction to work. What is important is that there soon be some practical successes which provoke certain demands, with these demands in their turn providing the yardsticks for politically determined goals and, as such, helping to fix the framework of action of the economic protagonists. Such a spiral of demand depends on the existence of economic organisations that learn through experience and are competent to adjust their own course. The change would acquire dynamism in that the expectation of further change according to the same criteria would become part of the normal social process. The fact that most taxpayers fill in their tax-returns truthfully, or that teachers take care to ensure their pupils' success (although they are not on piece-rates, as are, for example, doctors), this kind of thing does not depend on controls and the threat of penalties, but on norms that have become accepted as self-evident and established as a 'group ethic'. The idea of investing radical political commitment in, of all things, the establishment of 'normality' may at first sight appear absurd. Such a move would, however, draw a hopeful lesson from an almost hopeless situation, one that has long since developed immunity to traditional antidotes.

Let us imagine that over the next ten years some wheeling and dealing among political parties, backed up by joint blockades and protests by environmental groups and social movements, might lead to the weaving together of a security net made up of extended workers' rights, employment funds, and a guaranteed basic income, as well as a few material and moral successes in the field of environmental commitment. Then the play for a self-fashioned society could begin in earnest. With this in view, should we not confidently leave it to the historians of the future to decide in which year they think the term 'capitalism' ceased to be appropriate as a characterisation of events?

Notes

1 This is why, for example, the Italian communists are in favour of flexible working-hours that fit in with company requirements.

2 Uwe Schimank, *Neoromantischer Protest im Spätkapitalismus* (Bielefeld: AJZ-Verlag, 1983), p. 14.

3 Fritz W. Scharpf, *Sozialdemokratische Krisenpolitik in Europa* (Frankfurt/M. and New York: Campus Verlag, 1987).

4 The strategic environment in which companies find themselves, characterised as it is by uncertainty, contradicts the assumption of classical Marxist economics according to which, in relation to the exploitation of capital, there is only one route leading to maximum advantage, and that this route will inevitably be followed by brainless puppets until they eventually fall into a political trap.

5 Until the Greens' regressive and narrow-minded turn-around, it was believed that this was where the strategic advantage lay for a small party, since such a party has a greater capacity for analysis and for the development of new ideas that the 'bigger' parties, and knows how to exploit the latters's power calculations in order to secure a disproportionate degree of political influence.

6 IG Metall, 'Was die Metall Oskar Lafontaine vorrechnet und vorhält – Das Positionspapier der Gewerkschaft', *Frankfurter Rundschau* (6 and 7 Apr. 1988).

7 An excellent example of this is the corporatist Concerted Action in the health service, if looked at from the 'appropriate' angle, i.e. that of doctors and industry.

Editorial note

The following sociological texts have informed the argument developed here, although they are not specifically referred to in the text of the article. J.F.

Ulrich Beck, *Risikogesellschaft* (Frankfurt/M.: Suhrkamp, 1986).

Kurt Biedenkopf, *Die neue Sicht der Dinge* (Munich: Piper, 1985).

Niklas Luhmann, *Soziale Systeme* (Frankfurt: Suhrkamp, 1984).

Claus Offe, 'Die Utopie der Null-Option' in Johannes Berger (ed.), *Die Moderne: Kontinuitäten und Zäsuren* (Göttingen: Verlag Otto Schwarz, 1986).

Helmut Wiesenthal, *Strategie und Illusion* (Frankfurt/M. and New York: Campus Verlag, 1987).

7

Ecological consumption
A generalised interest with no mobilising force?

At the start of the 1970s, when there began to be talk about the 'limits to growth', awareness of ecological problems was restricted to a small number of experts. Now, twenty years on, there is an incomparably greater, socially universalised sensitivity to the dangers that menace the bases of our life.[1] Just as striking as this process of learning is the increase that has simultaneously taken place in the extent of the ecological problem, that is to say, the growth in pollution of water, soil, and air, far-reaching in its effects, and in many cases already irreversible. There have been changes in climatic factors and in the atmosphere (for example, depletion of the ozone layer) which were produced a considerable time ago but only became 'noticeable' after a long time-lag. There has been a loss of variety in natural species. There are new dangers involving genetic variation and experimentation. These problems combine with our feelings of loss of various aesthetic qualities associated with nature. Ecological awareness lags behind its causes. The discrepancy between the action that would 'really' be required for a prompt prevention of damage and actual readiness to act is still increasing. Or, to put it 'positively': only after the loss of further guarantees of life and of pleasure in life will the gap between the need for action and intention to act be closed. And this will be not so much because of what one hopes will be a better-developed ecological awareness, but because the number of actions that are still worth undertaking is rapidly declining on account of the irreversible nature of many ecological changes.

If one does not wish to confine oneself to describing trends and painting scenarios of catastrophes, whether realistic or not, but would like instead to find ways of preventing the prognosis from coming true, one has to decide in advance to avoid the ever popular question of the causes of the ecological crisis. Not only lack of time but also the complexity of the problems make it plain that we should steer political and scientific action towards the quite different question of the remaining options society has for 'ecological learning' – options that are perhaps underestimated. The former question may spring from a well-founded curiosity, but as soon as one decides, in view of knowledge about the interdependence of ecological data, to analyse industrial society as a system, it loses its political (i.e. action-oriented) point. The system-based perspective seems superior to the way of looking at things in which ecological problems appear as end-points in causal chains which one merely has to work one's way back up in order to eliminate the 'root' of the evil.[2] Working on a basis of systemic connections is advisable not just because social theorists recommend it, but because something which relies on very specific 'good' and 'bad' factors to the extent that industrial society does is indeed a system. Low costs of living are won at the expense of an industrialised landscape, with all the fatal consequences this implies. Mass consumption of high-tech products is possible because paid labour is subject to conditions imposed by global markets. Moreover the overall reduction in directability of the 'industrial system' is a result of its excessive capacity for innovation. In such circumstances, the options for deliberate changes in the system are not to be found in historical 'causes' that have long since become irreversible. Anyone looking for the potential, and as yet unactuated 'causes' of an ecologically appropriate society ends up considering actors and actions that are not 'responsible' for the ecological crisis, either in the causal or in the normative sense. Their distinguishing feature is that they are not available for immediate action. It is with this in mind that the following chapter pleads for an upgrading of the 'consumer'.

Other factors also militate in favour of an upgrading of the consumer, notably the inadequacy of other protagonists. Thus, although the State's capacity for reform and direction *vis-à-vis* the economy is by no means exhausted (but should not be overestimated).[3] Even if all the appropriate and practicable 'instruments' used in the ecologically-based economy and in directing innovation were brought into play, their effects would remain limited because of the obstacle of interest in high wages, secure employment, and internationally competitive consumer goods. Moreover, one has to bear in mind the 'internal' hindrances of the political system in regard to innovation,[4] namely the self-referential way in which the resources of law and money are handled – the self-contained logic of party competition for votes and the narrow horizons as regards consideration of the consequences of political action and non-action.

It is also time to take stock not just of state policy but of moral rigorism as well and to admit that the latter is politically powerless. Political education, appeals and radical criticism, 'new age' consciousness and 'the communication of fear' should be regarded as indicators of the gulf between the need for action and the actual action taken, but not as a bridge across that gulf. Why this is so is clear from certain social facts which contemporary social theoretists identify as the functional differentiation and self-referential nature of the partial-systems (sub-systems) that make up (the social system) society.[5] These block any prospect of the spread of universal perspectives and guarantee that thought and action in the political, educational, economic, and legal systems in each case follow their own logic rather than expressing 'solidarity' with society 'as a whole'. In any case, moral appeals ignore the fact that all individual forms of expression of altered thinking (that is to say, believing, wanting, complaining, and indeed even 'autonomous' individual action) remain far below the level of institutional direction, which is dependent on the combined action of bureaucratic organisations rather than merely being the result of erroneous decision-making.[6] Abstract descriptive formulas such as the widespread 'eco-eco' imagery of the 'contradiction between economics and ecology' are an indicator of this gap rather than a means of helping to 'eliminate' it.

However, there are also positive arguments in favour of giving careful consideration to the sphere of consumption and opportunities consumers have of exerting influence. After all, developments in the market and quantitative and qualitative data relating to demand constitute the factors which companies gear themselves to in order to make profits and secure their existence. Changed conditions of demand are the things to which companies point when they introduce innovations in products or procedures, or when they try out new strategies (e.g. by introducing more flexible use of manpower). In addition, 'environmental awareness' seems to accord better with the consumer role, which is characterised by (at least in theory) freedom of choice, rather than with the wage-earner role, with its typical features of abstraction of purpose and alienation.

Handicaps of consumer politics

The prospect of securing relatively good opportunities of influencing companies at the selling end fades rapidly when one asks what would be the preconditions for exploiting such opportunities. However elegant the idea is of latching on to companies' self-interested ecological sensibilities, the results achieved up to now by consumer politics have been dubious. The findings of consumer research, which reached its most recent high-point during the 1970s, are also sobering. Consumer interests are 'problematic' on at least three counts:

(1) They come into being in an operational sphere that is delimited, structured, and has its development determined by the interests of production. In other words, in an objectively dependent operational sphere.[7] Because of the prior decisions of producers and suppliers, consumer behaviour is subject to pressure to conform to one-sided data. It is the object of strategies of suppression, in that instrumental needs (e.g. driving a car in order to get from A to B) become 'ends in themselves' (e.g. being able to drive as comfortably, exclusively, and quickly as possible). It is subject to insidious alignment to the yardsticks of industrial production,[8] and is discriminated against by, amongst other things, the fact that activities associated with consumption are much less highly rated by society than those associated with production.

(2) Consumer interests manifest themselves only *ex post facto*, that is to say they are at a chronological disadvantage compared with the supply side.[9] They are largely reactive, rather than innovative or prescriptive.[10]

(3) Consumer interests are socially diffuse, they are held by all, in other words, by no one in particular. Indeed, every consumer also has a range of other interests relating to other operational spheres and factors (as employees, members of a profession, bringers-up of children, taxpayers, supporters of reform, etc.).

The consequence of all this is straightforward and disenchanting. The more generally and comprehensively 'consumer interest' is formulated, as compared with the highly differentiated supply-side and the multiplicity of social roles, the less amenable it becomes to organisation. The more one goes into detail as to the causes, timing, and location of differentiated consumer-problems, the more specific, the more dependent on circumstance, and the 'smaller' any kind of viable interest-grouping will be.[11]

Given this inferiority of consumer politics and consumer education, there is no reason to doubt the classic thesis which posits a systematic inferiority of consumer interest. However, organisation, of a kind that specialises[12] in consumer interests, and is representative of the variously manifested consumer interests, and moreover is also strong enough to act as a countervailing power, is an essential precondition if influence is to be exerted on the production side. Only through associative organisation would it be possible to co-ordinate politically or economically effective consumer action, namely in the form of boycott operations. Only a representative organisation could protest successfully against unecological products and interpret decreases in sales as the result of a deliberately critical shift away by customers.[13]

Paradoxically, however, the establishment of a strong consumer organisation is hindered by precisely the kinds of goal-related considerations which make it appear particularly useful. This is because the individual contributions to the creation of such a purpose-designed instrument for championing common interests are also calculated purposively. This happens roughly as follows: I know that a large number of individual contributions are needed to bring about the intended (economic or political) influence, which, in turn, will be of benefit to everyone, including those who have not contributed. I myself am quite prepared to make my contribution, but I have to reckon on the fact that others will decide differently and will forgo any action. Hence my sacrifice is in vain if not enough other people join in. Furthermore, I know that the effect of my contribution is much too small to be decisive in securing success. Thus if a lot of other people join in, my contribution does not matter.

Now if all those involved arrive, by this kind of rational thought-process, at the conclusion that their contribution is either pointless or superfluous, and that they cannot do anything about this the result is not solidarity but 'rational passivity'.[14] No one has demonstrated this more clearly than Mancur Olson.[15] The result of 'rational analysis' does not, however, mean that organisations such as 'consumer protection associations', 'consumer councils' or similar bodies have no chance of survival. But it does signal the improbability of strong associations that are able to influence their members' action in such a way as to build up boycotting power for an effective consumer politics. Of course, we can have any of the things that already exist, namely weak and fragmented organisations, umbrella organisations (with other associations as members), and organisations with different purposes (e.g. the provision of no-obligation information to consumers), or, in the most extreme case, acting as a lobby for the interests of industry.

Would it not be rational, in such unpropitious circumstances, to throw all rational calculations overboard and look for alternatives?

Unsatisfactory alternatives

One possible alternative is to obey the unilateralist imperative (i.e. to follow unconditionally the appeal that 'each should begin with himself'), instead of waiting on the good example of others or on solutions to the difficult question of organisation. There are two observations that must be made in regard to this suggestion, which is one that crops up in almost every 'ecological discussion'. First, the ineffectiveness of this approach is confirmed with striking regularity wherever it occurs. It is precisely the failure of such appeals that compels us to hunt for ways and means that promise 'surer' results. Secondly, there are doubts in regard to the results of individual 'exemplary action'. However helpful it may be in some cases, its effects become problematic if the ambient conditions are not suitable. Unco-ordinated individual paradigmatic action can fall flat, or can even, under certain circumstances, aggravate the problem. This may be demonstrated by three by no means unusual examples from the field of transport:

(1) Anyone prompted by the volume of traffic to get rid his or her car involuntarily increases the scope for expansion of those who continue to drive. The parking-space that is vacated in front of that person's house is quickly filled up again. Instead of there being a chain reaction of 'opting out' of the system of personal motorised transport, one has to reckon on a marginal increase in the attraction of the car to others, until the 'gap' is filled again.

(2) Even less successful is the approach of the person who engages in an 'exemplary' renunciation of consumption on competitive markets. If oil prices go down because, for example, energy-conscious drivers have invested in engines that are

economical on petrol, this provides an incentive to drivers with other preferences (e.g. driving at higher speeds) to indulge in increased consumption.

(3) An unco-ordinated individual action can even lead to an increase in the harm caused. A person who decides off his own bat to be 'sensible' in foggy weather on the motorway and adjusts his speed doggedly to visibility whilst hotfoot truckers jet along behind him at 100 miles an hour is setting up a sure catastrophe for everyone involved.

It is clear that the logic of individual example is not a universal answer to the dilemma of rational collective consumer action. It fails where groups with other preferences are involved and the 'suitable' underlying conditions for the realisation of the objective are still absent. In the first two examples cited, the benefit deriving from the individually sensible action should be safeguarded against misappropriation by actors with other preferences (e.g. by cutting back on roads or by introducing an energy tax). In the third example, what is required is the reliable co-ordination of all those involved by means of some common and effective 'rule of play' (monitoring of speed?). Thus a truly rational approach, i.e. one that was both collectively and individually worthwhile, would be to begin by stating one's readiness to engage in conditional co-operation (that is to say, if the others join in), and secondly to do something to ensure the creation of underlying conditions in which co-operation is easier and less risky. Besides this, the examples show why it is not simply a problem of the pursuit of egoistic interests. Problems of this kind, which have to do with the collective good, come about because individual contributions to collective action are examined to see whether they will be effective. They are measured in terms of individual cost, even where an effect is sought on behalf of others (i.e. where altruism is being practised).

A change in values?

Another alternative seems to lie in the hope of a general change in values, as observed in particular in the comparative international investigations conducted by Inglehart.[16] The 'post-materialist' outlooks which are frequently to be found particularly amongst younger age groups do seem, after all, to signal a pronounced environmental awareness and a greater than average readiness to participate in 'grass-roots' politics. Here too, some correcting of misconstrued social facts is required. Follow-up investigations have shown that 'post-materialist' attitudes are indeed now 'measurable' in one-fifth of the population of the Federal Republic of Germany.[17] There is nothing to justify the expectation of a linear trend. Whether younger people will be able (as they were during the 1970s) to gather experiences that support a 'post-materialist' world-view depends on the one hand on the development of their socio-economic environment, an environment which is currently characterised by low rates of growth, a high-base unemployment level, and a technological optimism revived by micro-electronics. On the other hand, the dynamic of cultural and political processes acts as a factor that either stabilises or fragments 'new' values,[18] a fact which explains the very uneven rates of transformation of values in the different countries of the EC.[19] When these external factors in the social 'production' of values and the differences in perception of meaning between various age-groups are taken into consideration, the overall picture is one of the 'pluralisation of values'[20] (i.e. a moderately animated pattern comprising a number of zones of meaning existing alongside each other). There is not the hoped-for unidirectional 'development'.[21] There are now so many different nuances of eco-social thinking that groups which would like to replace 'purposive' discourses about strategy as much as they can with expressive, 'value-oriented' action on the part of their members descend either into self-paralysis or into quasi-theological dispute.[22]

Now that the last niches in which traditional lifestyles, norms, and social milieu have been overrun by industrialisation there is no longer any prospect of an 'organic' alignment of thought and action. The inference from one's own personal development to a parallel development of 'society' is now more inadmissible than ever. The pluralisation of social circumstances, and the individualisation of perceptions of meaning in and between the various social spheres (part-systems), are leading to the creation of a multiplicity of interpretations and attitudes which, though related, have their own separate logics. Radical, strongly normative ecological ways of thinking also have their place within this spectrum. However, even if these ways of thinking could function as a kind of communicative leaven (which, given their tendency to concentrate on self-portrayal, is doubtful), the surrounding circumstances are not suitable as 'dough'. However much they 'knead' different opinions, different ways of being, radical approaches, and expressive approaches with the most varied interpretive content, they will never succeed in making a cake out of them. Most importantly, attempts to make pronounced views even more pronounced (what is seen by those involved as 'radicalisation') themselves fall entirely within the prevailing trend towards differentiation. The result of these attempts is scarcely any different from that produced when one relies on homogeneous, rational, advantage-oriented interests, namely the self-immobilisation of the actors involved.

Interim conclusion

In view of these findings, the answer to the question contained in the title of this paper must be 'yes'. Ecological consumption, as defined in terms of classical consumer-interest and of the political interest-grouping, is indeed a generalised collective interest which is unable to attract sufficient mobilising force. We can go even further and say that ecological consumption has a chance of being organised at best only as a particularised or special interest that is tied to one specific subcultural lifestyle. This outside chance is lost if ecological consumption becomes a generalised interest no longer based purely on philosophical considerations but pursued from rational motives.

A dispassionate appraisal of the situation makes it clear that we must bid farewell to unfounded expectations and inappropriate alternatives for action. In their place, we should give more careful consideration to the remaining opportunities for action, beyond the domain of belief and hope. In other words, is there an alternative way of enforcing ecological consumer-interests? The following section will supply an answer to this question. Are there still, in certain circumstances, possibilities for improving our handling of that instrument of limited appropriateness, the 'interest-group'? Two proposals concerning this will be made in the final section.

Consumer politics in the workplace

The design principle underlying this alternative to ineffective consumer-politics ties in theoretically with the functional differentiation of society into self-referential partial-systems. In concrete terms it relates to what is, as far as our problem is concerned, the decisive separation of the functional roles of production and consumption, of the work-sphere from the other spheres of life. As is well known, this separation stimulates conflicts between individual desires and the rationalising approach of organisations on issues such as job security, working conditions, and working-hours. What is even more serious, it is an effective but, most importantly, a one-sided barrier to the import into the workplace of worker-initiated, 'non-company-related' social appraisals of the production process.

Anyone who has a go at dislodging this barrier has undoubtedly hit one of the main nodal points in the global network of social problems. However, all effort directed at this spot is wasted if one thinks only in terms of opposition, contradiction, and conflict. What one should do instead is admit, without attempting to gloss over the situation, that the subordination of the social interests of workers to the employer's power of disposal is by no means solely a product of the logic of the wage-agreement. It also springs from the need for co-operation which characterises complex business enterprises and which workers are wont actively to tolerate. The latter rightly expect that the self-imposed limitation of their interests will have positive effects on company profitability, and thus also on the remunerations that depend on this. The market, where businesses secure success and continued existence, creates a structural community of interest. Under the banner of the 'good of the company', the 'productivity alliance' which exists in the workplace[23] embraces not only a zone of legal incitements to co-operation, but also in many cases a zone of illegal incitements of this kind, based either on blackmail or on projections of profits.

Although this is, for the best of intentions, readily overlooked, it is a fact that workers co-operate with management in maintaining a narrow company perspective, out of an understandable concern for job and career prospects, even if this runs counter to the good of the rest of society. They may, for example, construct valves for emptying toxic-waste tanks into the Rhine, or fit bypass flues to desulphurisation plants, complete production or shipment procedures for illegal arms-exports, treat data about non-observance of emission limits or other infringements of the law as company secrets, or fail to make public privileged information about dangerous products, production procedures, and product-applications.

'The immense knowledge of waste, fraud, negligence, and other misdeeds which employees of corporations, governmental agencies, and other bureaucracies possess' constitutes, according to Ralph Nader,[24] a largely unexploited and underestimated potential for precluding the effects of the 'institutional irresponsibility' of organisations. Tapping this potential would mean organising 'consumer protection from the production level onwards'[25] and significantly levelling the barriers between the functional role of wage-earning labour on the one hand and that of the consumer, the domestic budget, and the citizen on the other, by 'on-the-job citizenship', as Nader calls it. A number of preconditions would be needed for this which are probably less difficult to set up than is an all-embracing consumer-organisation.

Something that would be useful in this connection would, of course, be 'appropriate countervailing positions of power within companies themselves'.[26] This is, safeguards in industrial law and industrial-relations law for those workers who promote the good of the company. They would do this by considering the longer-term effects of company operations and standing up for general interests inside as well as outside the company. Workers would help the company, if necessary without its bidding, to conform to the requirements of the social and natural environment.

It would be too optimistic simply to append the issue of 'consumer protection in production' to the list of desiderata drawn up by the unions for implementation in the event of a complete, worker-friendly overhaul of industrial law. What is at issue is not so much the introduction of new kinds of rights but the enforcement of perfectly well-founded and, for the most part, long-since legally established norms, particularly in regard to the observance of laws, regulations, and agreements. What must be done above all is to indemnify the personal risk which the situation of blackmail prevailing in the workplace occasions to workers who are looking out for the common good. To do this, a network of legal, material, and moral support (the latter to include professional ethics) is required which will give those who sacrifice their careers with a company for the sake of the common ecological good alternative security, social recognition, and new opportunities. Such a network is one of those things that is not at all easy to initiate but which, once it acquires greater social importance, tends to necessitate the input of less, rather than more effort.[27]

Dynamic forms of organisation

By brushing the 'logic of collective action', that is to say the thesis of the improbability of co-operation for the sake of a generalised interest, somewhat 'against the grain' (though not against its own logic), one discovers two other secondary routes to the representation of the interest in ecological consumption. First of all, associations could be formed to champion other consumer interests besides specifically determined ones. Secondly, the prospects of being able to form a coalition out of a variety of motives for participation are relatively good.

Intentional non-correspondence between the purpose of an organisation and the interests of its members becomes problematic only if the goals that are actually promoted by the organisation lie outside, or run counter to those interests of the members that are relevant to the organisation. This is not necessarily the case in every kind of 'deviation'.

Consumer interests are prone to self-immobilising tendencies only when they are defined in general terms, i.e. when they are not embedded in specific attitudes, lifestyles, and ways of looking at problems. If, on the other hand, they are part of a kind of subculture, they may not be socially representative, but they do have a certain degree of amenability to organisation. Hence the problem of providing the collective good in question is amenable to partial solution. Associations with particularised orientations can more easily mobilise support and thus become 'more powerful' than those which attempt to represent general interests.

If, therefore, the present situation, in which not enough committed people come together who regard themselves primarily as ecological consumers continues, it will none the less be possible to represent interest in improved preconditions for ecological consumption as a variety of the ecological interests that exist have already been organised. It is conceivable that, for example, groups working for nature conservation, the movement for the ecological reform of agriculture, ecological insfrastructures in the fields of transport or finance (e.g. the Verkehrsclub der Bundesrepublik Deutschland, or the Ökobank), and a whole variety of environmental initiatives would come together to form a functionally specialised umbrella-organisation. The authority of such an organisation in matters of ecological consumption would then derive from its being rooted in a plurality of ecological interests, and not in its connection with the far too general consumer role. Naturally, however, the influence of such an organisation would be not so much economic as primarily political, and this would be a result of the force of information and open debate, not of any compulsorily co-ordinated action on the part of its members (e.g. in boycott actions).

Better prospects for collective action may be expected from heterogeneous coalitions. By this is meant the rational co-operation of groups which, though they have differing values and views of the world, do have some things partly in common. This alternative requires that, when organisations are being formed (be they social movements or associations with formal memberships), one should give up the habit of looking for homogeneous motives, that is to say unidirectional motives of a single kind. Instead, there should be a conscious effort to achieve a pattern of 'plural' organisation, and to guard against the traditional ideal of homogeneity. The arguments in favour of this contra-intuitive solution are furnished by rational choice analyses of the emergence of social movements (as repeated co-operative multi-person interactions).[28]

Detailed observations (for example of the anti-nuclear and peace-movements) show that what facilitates the take-off and (partial) stabilisation of the dynamic behind a movement is not a flat uniformity of motives for action and readiness to act but an optimum degree of dissimilarity in these. It is quite usual for the risks and costs of co-operation to decrease as the number of participants increases, once committed activists have functioned as a 'critical mass' and overcome initial difficulties. Their action is guided more by a notion of identity ('Who am I?') than by any notion of advantage ('What do I get out of it?'). In many cases there is something in the nature of an avant-garde consciousness: 'If you don't do it, nobody else will'.[29] Of decisive significance is the fact that thanks to the non-utilitarian activists, an infrastructure is created which makes possible the participation of individuals who are only prepared to co-operate conditionally, in other words, if they know that their contribution is needed and is not in vain. If, thanks to this second group, the goal of the co-operation becomes attainable, the coalition becomes attractive to hangers-on and fellow-travellers, who either wait for the maximum marginal utility to be achieved before climbing aboard, or begin to worry about which side they will end up on if they continue to 'stand on the sidelines and watch whilst a good thing happens'.

In this model, collective action comes about because of the heterogeneity of motives and preferences, and not, as was expected in the tradition of the labour-movement, as a product of similar interpretations of the same social situation. It is also subject to jeopardy by participants who imagine they are on a unifying trip and are occasionally shocked by the pluralism of the objectives. One other notable feature is that suitable motives for 'hetero-strategies' can be found without difficulty, whereas the appearance of unitary motives for comprehensive homogeneous organisations is becoming less likely.

In sum, a strong ecological consumer-movement, if it is at all possible, should be imagined not as a quasi-mechanistic aggregation of similar interests but as a highly differentiated and only 'loosely bound' network of interaction which allows actors with different preferences to become strong together, for example, because the ends of one group function as the means of another. Such a network would have room both for pragmatic 'initiators of movements' and for fundamentalist 'enlighteners'. It would consist of co-operative neighbourhood circles and local consumer co-operatives. It might become a forum for public reflection on consumer needs and on the criteria by which these should be appraised,[30] and it would be kept on a developmental course by means of centralised administrative services and opportunities for the large number of not wholeheartedly committed individuals to participate loosely and at a distance.[31]

In conclusion, I should like to point to the common pattern underlying the various alternatives proposed, namely that they do not attempt to tackle the problem of political mobilisation in highly differentiated industrial society with the social theory of the nineteenth century, which still allowed one to hope that 'structures' would guide disparate motives and false beliefs towards noble historical goals. Instead, they pick up on the idea of a better-developed understanding of the obstacles to, and remaining options for purposive action. Only those who feel content in the no man's land between doom-laden scenarios and self-help slogans will regard this kind of 'elucidation' as grounds for despondency. Others, meanwhile, may find this glimpse at some practicable ways round the problems useful. They do not guarantee properly targeted action within complex systems, but they do increase its likelihood. If there should ever be such a thing as a theory of the post-modern shaping of society, it must, to be 'strong', confine itself to these kinds of details and be adept at managing heterogeneity and differences of opinion.

Notes

1 On the measurement of ecological awareness, cf. Dieter Urban, 'Was ist Umweltbewußtsein?', *Zeitschrift für Soziologie*, 15 (1986), and Alexander Pawelka, 'Ökologie im Alltag' *Zeitschrift für Soziologie*, 16 (1987), pp. 204–22.

2 Operating with the logic of a reversible causal chain allows one to seek 'radical' measures, i.e. measures that go back to the roots of the problem. Although system analyses can also point up measures that are aequate to the problem and effective, they clearly lack an equivalent imagery.

3 Cf. Helmut Wiesenthal, Chapter 6 above. This offers a critique of the referential framework of unrealistic claims regarding direction.

4 A sceptical attitude towards the political potential for direction is quite compatible with a positive assessment of the capacity of the political system to learn and innovate, a standpoint vindicated by the establishment of the Greens as a fourth party and by the success of the social movements in putting certain issues on the agenda.

5 The phenomena of the separation of operational spheres or functional nexuses, as described in the theories of Habermas and Luhmann, are not merely intellectual constructs. Even if one rejects this social scientific terminology, it is none the less true that such factors hinder political action. They may, if one so wishes, be described as 'alienation' and 'self-dependence'. Cf. Jürgen Habermas, *Theorie des kommunikativen Handelns*, 2 vols., (Frankfurt/M.: Suhrkamp, 1981). Also Niklas Luhmann, *Soziale Systeme* (Frankfurt/M.: Suhrkamp, 1981), and Niklas Luhmann, *Ökologische Kommunikation* (Opladen: Westdeutscher Verlag, 1986).

6 This is why presidents of the German employers' federation (BDA) and chairmen of the German association of trade unions (DGB) are also free to have their own ecological conscience, provided they do not forget their responsibility to preserve the decision-making premises that lie within the interests of the organisation (premises relating to wages, and to economic, and socio-political conditions).

7 Gerhard Scherhorn, 'Die Entstehung von Verbraucherproblemen im Spannungsfeld von Konsum und Arbeit', *Zeitschrift für Verbraucherpolitik*, 4 (1980), pp. 102–14.

8 Cf. the paradoxicalness of introducing rationalisation objectives such as factor productivity, increased pace of work, and time-saving into the consumer field.

9 Claus Offe, 'Ausdifferenzierung oder Integration', *Zeitschrift für Verbraucherpolitik*, 5 (1981), pp. 119–33.

10 To the extent that consumer interests are determined 'exogenously', i.e. by action on the supply side, they are proof of a special kind of 'market failure'. A consumer who not only has a preference for a particular brand of cigarettes but also has the meta-preference (completely consistent with his 'first-order preference') for becoming a non-smoker can, in his capacity as a participator in the market, express only the first-named preference but not his meta-preference (to be spared the cigarette industry's offer). Cf. David George, 'Meta-preferences: reconsidering contemporary notions of free

choice', *International Journal of Social Economics*, 11 (1984), pp. 92–107.

11 Wilfried Nelles *et al.*, 'Alternativen der Verbraucherorganisation' in Gerd Fleischmann (ed.), *Der kritische Verbraucher*, (Frankfurt/M. and New York: Campus Verlag, 1981), pp. 241–257.

12 The 'co-representation' of consumer interests by trade unions is considered less effective. Cf. Klaus von Beyme, *Gewerkschaften und Arbeitsbeziehungen in kapitalistischen Ländern*, (Munich: Piper, 1977), pp. 138 ff.

13 In contrast, in a market economy geared to innovation and obsolescence, absence of comment on falls in turnover is the rule. On the logic behind the migration (exit) and protest (voice) options for action, see Albert O. Hirschman, *Exit, Voice and Loyalty* (Cambridge: Cambridge University Press, 1970).

14 Claus Offe, 'Solidaritätsprobleme in der Arbeitsmarkt- und Sozialpolitik', Mimeo, University of Bielefeld, 1985.

15 Mancur Olson, *The Logic of Collective Action* (Cambridge: Harvard University Press, MA, 1965).

16 'The emergence of new political issues can . . . lead to the revival of older value-oriented dividing lines which were established in pre-industrial society. . . .' See Ronald Ingelhart, 'Traditionelle politische Trennungslinien und die Entwicklung der neuen Politik in westlichen Gesellschaften' *Politische Vierteljahresschrift*, 24 (1983), pp. 139–65. (p. 159). Also Ronald Inglehart, *The Silent Revolution* (Princeton: Princeton University Press, 1977).

17 Detlef Jahn and Ferdinand Müller-Rommel, 'Krise der Arbeitsgesellschaft und Politische Kultur', in Dirk Berg-Schlosser and Jakob Schissler (eds.), *Politische Kultur in Deutschland* pp. 344–55 (Opladen: Westdeutscher Verlag, 1977).

18 Helmut Thome, 'Wandel zu postmaterialistischen Werten?', *Soziale Welt*, 36 (1985), pp. 27–59.

19 Jahn and Müller-Rommel, 'Krise der Arbeitsgesellschaft'.

20 Helmut Klages, *Wertorientierungen im Wandel* (Frankfurt/M. and New York: Campus Verlag, 1984).

21 Inglehart, *Silent Revolution*.

22 This can be observed regularly in the green party.

23 This enjoys the support of works committees even where it is a question of redundancy programmes or of avoiding the recruitment of new workers.

24 Ralph Nader, 'Action for Change' in Nader (ed.), *The Consumer and Corporate Accountability* (New York: Harcourt Brace Jovanovich, 1973), pp. 367–75. See also 'A Citizen's Guide to the American Economy', pp. 4–18 of the same volume.

25 Offe, 'Ausdifferenzierung'.

26 Offe, 'Ausdifferenzierung', p. 131.

27 Its impact would depend primarily on the anticipation of developments that were disagreeable for the company (social pressure plus the departure of qualified workers) and not so much on the effects of concrete interventions (and would thus be analogous to the power of influence on the conduct of workers). It is a scheme which, to be realistic, one should envisage more as a mixture of some trade organisation and Greenpeace rather than as a sub-section of the co-determination department of the DGB.

28 See for examples: Jon Elster, *Making Sense of Marx* (Cambridge: Cambridge University Press, 1985) pp. 351, 367, 364 ff.; Pamela Oliver, 'If You Don't Do It, Nobody Else Will: Active and Token Contributors to Local Collective Action', *American Sociological Review,* 49 (1984), pp. 601–10; and James W. White, 'Rational Rioters: Leaders, Followers, and Popular Protest in Early Modern Japan', *Politics and Society,* 16 (1988), pp. 35–69.

29 Pamela Oliver *et al.,* 'A Theory of the Critical Mass: Inter-dependence, Group Heterogeneity, and the Production of Collective Action', *American Journal of Sociology,* 91 (1985), pp.522–56.

30 Scherhorn, 'Die Entstehung'.

31 It is almost superfluous to note that a multi-layered organisational network would provide a suitable framework for the solidary back-up of 'on-the-job citizenship', and could also be appropriate as an individual membership base for an umbrella organisation representing interests relating to ecological consumption.

8

Unheeded problems and enticing utopias

Conditions and opportunities for a green social policy

What's the latest in social policy? Even at first glance the field of social policy does not appear exactly clear-cut, embracing as it does the health service, pensions, benefits in case of sickness, incapacity for work, or unemployment, as well as various other forms of welfare. It is only at second glance that the real picture emerges, that each of the named areas harbours several problems, with two or three different solutions vying to resolve them. There are insignificant solutions, which can be disregarded, and there are more significant ones. The latter marry up with one or two other problems and are thus upgraded to the status of a socio-political issue. Depending on the standpoint of the observer, the emergence of the social policy issue is treated either as a basis for reform or as a social catastrophe.

An interesting special case occurs where more than three problems are grouped around a single solution, as happens in very popular concepts for reform such as the 'restoration of full employment', the 'global shift to self-help', or the 'introduction of a guaranteed basic income'. The multiplicity of beneficial effects claimed for these recipes by their advocates deprives them of much of their political impact. They are then labelled 'utopian' and move out of the public debate and become the personal property of prophet politicians and politically committed feature-writers. Analytical and pragmatic criticism bounce off them without effect. Whilst they gather groups of trusting believers round them, experienced politicians go back to sticking more wieldy spokes in each other's wheels.

This too is part of social politics, being aware that not everything that is important in this area can profitably be made into an issue, although more can be made an issue of than it is possible to deal with in the relevant circumstances. The experts adapt to this situation by specialising only in single areas or in regulatory details. They decline to enter into a dispute about priorities and leave the political parties great scope for genuinely political choices. Just how rich the choice is becomes clear simply from casting an eye on the schemes proposed by the SPD and the Greens.

Subject to the resolutions passed at its party conference in Bremen, the SPD intends (according to its draft programme of 2 March 1989) to effect a radical turn-around to a preventive type of social policy which depends on foresight, a policy in which there is no longer any trace of disadvantage to women or special privilege for particular professional classes (e.g. civil servants). In particular, the SPD is pursuing the idea of a form of basic social security, as a complement to the contributory security that applies in the case of old age, disability, or unemployment. What it has in mind are basic allowances in the form of minimum payments which may be claimed in the absence of any other kind of income. In addition, employers' contributions are to be readjusted in line with a new calculatory basis, that of 'value creation'. One alternative scheme originating in Schleswig-Holstein even recommends, *en passant*, that in addition to the basic social security there should be a guaranteed basic income for all citizens. This will presumably not be achieved during the next parliamentary term.

There are, after all, major tasks calling for attention in other areas. In the health service, there is to be an expansion of out-patient care, accompanied by the abolition of the own-risk arrangement. The newly discovered female electorate is promised drastic reductions in working-hours, in the form of a universal six-hour day (as usual, no mention is made of the indispensable corollary to this, namely increased shift-working), more crèches, and more all-day schools. Both parents can look forward to paid parental leave during the first three years of their children's life, with the time taken to bring up and care for their offspring being included in the calculation of retirement provision.

As usual, the elderly will receive 'secure' pensions – though the level of these is not specified. They are told not to take too much notice of the recent foundation of a party for the elderly (the 'Grey Panthers'). They are also promised cover for the financial risks associated with care, more in-home social services, housing and urban planning that caters for old people's needs, and adequate numbers of places in esablishments providing care for the elderly. In general, there will be much more help and decentralised social services for children, old people, the sick, and the disabled.

The kinds of yardsticks according to which future (social democratic) social policy will be lauded or criticised has been made clear by experts from the Deutsche Gewerkschaftsbund (Alfred Schmidt and Erich Standfest, 'Die Sozialpolitik der Bunderegierung und die gewerkschaftliche Vorstellungen', *Gewerkschaftliche Monatshefte*, 40, 1989 pp. 97–105). For them, the top priority is the project, tried and tested by the vindicatory route, of the generation of full employment through 'an active state employment policy, backed up by reductions in working-hours and a well-targeted job-market policy'. In the health service, more attention must to be paid to prevention, particularly *vis-à-vis* the causes of chronic diseases. Finally, as a sort of rounding-off of a successful overall scheme, 'poverty is to be abolished' by union-based means, namely the extension of the principle of national insurance and the gradual reversal of the dismantling of the social system. The authors also indicate the only areas in which deviations from the guideline of a strictly labour-related social policy seem tolerable, namely the claim of women for independent pensions, and 'certain elements relating to a system of basic social security'. Sceptics may see this as betraying some doubt as to the attainability of the target of full employment.

The Greens, for their part, are far less vague in their pronouncements than is often supposed (1987 federal election manifesto). They too want a system of basic social security (to operate in the case of unemployment and old age, and instead of supplementary benefits), and they set the level of this at DM 1,200 per person. The same figure is proposed as a child-care allowance to cover fifteen months of child care. In the case of the elderly, there are plans for a care allowance, graduated according to the degree of care needed, on which no figure is put, but which would probably be higher per individual than the above sum. Because of the time at which the proposals were made (the programme dates from 1986), the target for reduced working-hours is confined to a thirty-five-hour week. Nowadays this would no doubt be a six-hour day. In addition, the programme states that the general reduction in working-hours is to be accompanied by the creation of opportunities for part-time work that is subject to the safeguards of social and industrial law, and by the institution of employee-oriented 'sovereignty over time'. The topicality of these goals has been confirmed by the SPD, which has included them in its own draft manifesto.

The mixture of traditionalism and enthusiasm for innovation that characterises social policy schemes from the centre to the left indicates that one would, in the classic case, have to reckon on two typical conflicts. First, there would be a public conflict about the quantitative extent of existing and new demands. This would be resolved to the advantage of the potential beneficiaries only if non-beneficiaries could be persuaded to increase their contributions or taxes and to accept doing without any measures to their advantage.

Secondly, and cutting across the last argument, there is the conflict conducted by political professionals about what sort of innovations in social policy make suitable material for electoral campaigns and talk shows, in other words what, in view of the future decisions of voters, should be moved on to the agenda of public debates. Besides other important matters, this conflict determines, *en passant*, the principles according to which social problems are defined and tackled. Are the various systems to continue to follow the paradigm of full-time, life-long, male employment, despite the extensive differentiation of working and living conditions? On the income side, should the principle of contribution based on non-civil-service employment be replaced by compulsory contributions for all citizens? On the expenditure side, should the strictly defined conditions of entitlement be supplemented with a general civil right to minimum social security?

If these questions received the attention they really deserve in party manifestos, they would probably act like a bacterium, revealing as they do a split between interests shaped by the past, and interpretations of problems which look forward to the future. The standpoints based on history do not guarantee either a complete overview of the problems or up-to-date knowledge about how to act. This accounts in part for the ignorance shown by the *Volksparteien* in regard to such questions. The Greens, however great their sympathy for harmony-enhancing measures, should not imitate them. For this reason, I propose at least to list those problems which are readily overlooked in centre-to-left declarations of intent.

(1) First there is the insidious long-term problem of demographic change. By the year 2030 the number of the elderly as a proportion of the total population will increase in such a way that, stated crudely, there will have to be either a doubling of the level of

pension contributions or a reduction by half of present pension-
levels. This will keep doubts about pension security alive and will
perhaps mean that the issue of the lengthening of working time is
raised before the six-hour day has been achieved.

At the same time, if the present structure of social services is
maintained, a considerable 'gap in care' will emerge, because soon
many more people than today will need part-time or full-time care,
whereas the number of individuals of working age will decline, and
there will also be a decline in willingness to undertake voluntary or
poorly-paid caring work. Both the contributory principle and solutions based on insurance miss the mark here. What is needed is
money and concrete forms of help.

(2)   The dependence of the various types of national insurance on
the labour market poses the problem of the poor productivity of the
major source of income here, namely social security contributions
from earnings. With continuing unemployment and the inadequate
cover which the earnings-related social security system provides for
many of those eligible for work, we have ended up with an extremely
asymmetrical distribution of the contributory burdens. They are
concentrated on wage-dependent workers who fall below the upper
limit for national insurance contributions. These individuals pay for
non-payers who are entitled to claim, they relieve civil servants and
the self-employed from the obligation to share liability and, as a
result of increased incidental wage-costs, they involuntarily put out
undesirable signals as regards economic decisions. Reliance on the
principle of contribution shows that the welfare state in fact functions as a 'workfare state' (Guy Standing), and this, via the 'increased
incidental wage-costs/cuts in expensive manpower/higher social
security contributions' chain, contributes to the diminution of
demand for manpower. No social reform of any promise can avoid
establishing a solid 'finance through taxation' income base, protected from the grasp of the exchequer.

(3)   One factor that is ignored politically but will persist in the
medium term is the social effects of long-term or recurring unemployment, which are also appearing in increasing concentrations.
What is meant here is the 30 per cent of workers who have been
without work for more than two years, the 10 per cent or so who
have been repeatedly affected by unemployment, and workers living
on their own, particularly single mothers (about 300,000 of these
receive less than DM 800 monthly; cf. Hans-Ludwig Mayer;

'Erwerbslosigkeit 1987 – auch im internationalen Vergleich', in *Wirtschaft und Statistik*, 12, December 1988, pp. 849–63). Clearly the unnuanced talk of a prosperous 'two-thirds society' on the one hand, and another third, united in collective poverty, on the other, conceals an enormous disparity of impact simply among the victims of modernisation.

(4)   To round off the catalogue of problems, mention should be made of the parlous state of the health service, which even at a cursory glance fragments into a collection of reduced claims, high contributions, and inhumanely formal procedures. A closer look reveals a political abdication ranging from resignation to complete ignorance of the problems. The reaction of the Greens, when they come up with demands drawn from the realms of Third World work, environmental protection, preventive action, democratisation, and respect for human rights, is basically one of helplessness. There is a widespread refusal to tackle the phenomenon of a mixture of social indispensability and ambiguity in many medical services. This lends power to the professionals and which even reform-minded politicians are forced to regard as effectively blocking attempts at reform. This uncertainty, which starts with the patients and presents politicians with the electoral puzzle of calculating what level of dissatisfaction with income makes it difficult for doctors to adhere to their professional ethic, is by far the stoutest bastion against possible projects for reform. Because what is needed here is not further regulation with new monopoly premiums, but competitive structures and differentiated alternatives (e.g. in the public health service). The health system remains a taboo area. Structural improvements would result initially in greater demands for money instead of bringing immediate savings.

The list of problems and solutions relating to social policy, including the unheeded problems and the enticing utopian solutions, must be irritating to any outside observer. It is easy to come to mistaken diagnoses that are more suitable for reinforcing a political circle's image of itself than for providing practical therapies. Either social policy seems like a party game, in which all the different groups can take it in turns to try out their pet ideas, because there seems to be less call here than elsewhere for security and continuity. Or else society appears to be overburdened by a flood of existing problems relating to provision and security, with the result that the only option left is to organise an 'orderly' demise by means of spontaneous and unco-ordinated partial solutions.

The point of taking this fictitious outside perspective is to demonstrate not only the virtue of emotional restraint but also the improbability of reality. In order to interpret the latter correctly, one has to remember two things. First, since at least 1976, the discussion about social policy in the Federal Republic has been constantly circling round the same issues, positions, and demands. Full employment versus self-help, expansion versus cuts, job-related criteria versus the principle of need, etc.

Secondly, since 1957 old age pensions have been index-linked. This area of politics has, for understandable reasons, developed only via gradual reforms. This has a lot to do with what is technically termed the inclusivity of social policy, which has now reached a level of over 90 per cent. Almost everyone is affected by any financially relevant change, whether in entitlements or in liability to contributions.

Thirdly, solutions in social policy are always controversial on several counts. They are expected to be equitable from the point of view not only of distribution but also of cost. Even those who would receive a larger slice of the national-product cake would react with annoyance if, because of this, the overall size of the cake diminished. For this reason, when it comes to social security it is never only a question of effectiveness, but one of efficiency as well. If more efficient solutions emerge, even 'just' remedies can abruptly lose their legitimacy.

Fourthly, although this area is regulated by the State and answered for by the political parties, its amenability to reform is dictated mainly by the degree of tolerance of extra-parliamentary actors. Chief amongst these are the associations representing the parties involved in the job market, followed in second place by professional and business associations, and lastly by the welfare bureaucracy, comprising state-run and associative elements. These bodies can hinder changes by forecasting undesirable effects, some of which they themselves can influence and others of which they can merely spot early on. In order to gain attention, all that is needed is some non-committal forecast, e.g. of plans for investment perhaps having to be modified because of rising labour-costs, or of wage-demands being made to offset increased social contributions, or of capacity in non-state welfare-work being jeopardised. Anyone who ignores this inertial factor will, under certain circumstances, have to take responsibility for consequences which he did not intend, for example, in the form of a loss of votes.

Not all the special features of social policy concern the Greens to the extent that they concern the established mass parties. In favourable circumstances, they may actually be what gives the smaller party in a ruling coalition its strength. Such a party is able to initiate, and accept joint responsibility for reforms which a party of the people would have difficulty in putting through on its own, because of the difference in interests within its own ranks. Whatever the case, one is still left with the problem of selection. It cannot be solved by choosing only those packages of measures which express some noble guiding principle (e.g. equality or compensation, state provision or subsidiarism, market or control) in a way that involves the least compromise. Reality, in its principle-less complexity, would only strike back all the harder.

A further factor commands attention. Interventions by the State do not just express political will, they also tend to alter the will both of those affected by them and of those looking on. For example, in the latest fiasco over taxation of income at source, anyone who, year-in year-out, had done his duty and included the interest on his savings on his tax return because he did not want to be counted amongst the country's cheaters, was inundated with incentives to change this stance. He was shown not only the unusualness of his action, and the personal disadvantages it brings, but also his power as a voter. It was made clear that he would throw away this power if he continued to want that which, in strict legal terms, he ought to want, namely to pay taxes rather than save them.

If it is the case that even those politicians who willingly 'leave well alone' have to reckon on substantial changes in people's wishes, how much more more true will this be of those who are concerned to bring about very specific changes! Only when they include the future wishes of others more or less accurately in their calculations will the truly intended effects move into the realm of the possible.

Even where there is 'less' democracy, there is no better alternative than the sensitive weighing-up of possibilities. The most unlikely developments and the greatest deviations from the prescribed values of state regulation are currently being recorded in, of all places, countries with real socialist regimes, in other words, in places where, by virtue of the nature of the State, people should not have wanted (or should not want) what they do want. Paradoxically, politics in those places has produced many unwanted effects.

In contrast, the atmosphere in a democratic arena, with its uncertainty and its tendency to put any original thought rapidly into perspective, offers at least a slight chance of making the guiding principles of political decision-making comprehensible and attractive. With a bit of luck, one may even see the appearance of a 'self-propelled surge' of desire for reform.

What follows from these reflections, in terms of the choice of emphases in social policy? In all probability, the Greens' influence in shaping society comes not so much through their participation in the quantitative determination of flows of income and expenditure, but rather through the attention and acceptance (achievable by force of argument) which they manage to win for qualitative innovations. It is undoubtedly still right to campaign for high levels of child-allowance, minimum pensions, etc. But in so doing one has to be prepared for two things. First that, simply on arithmetical grounds, sensitivity to the unwanted effects of higher taxes, contributions, and public borrowing will be incomparably greater in our coalition partner than in ourselves. Secondly, that the maximum achievable level of expenditure will never be so high that the underlying social problems can be regarded as 'solved'. It will, however, quickly reach a level too high for enough resources to be left over to stop or slow down the mechanism that generates the problems. This, precisely, is what constitutes the predicament of a bad social democratic concept of the welfare state, namely making the solution of social problems dependent on accurately targeted flows of funds whose course could only be influenced 'with certainty' if one were not reliant on them.

The decline of belief in industrial progress and the successful stabilisation of the Green Party are not totally unrelated events that are only coincidentally happening at the same time. This fact should be reflected in the criteria according to which the main priorities in social policy are chosen:

First criterion: Green social policy must strive to bring about structural innovations that take into account the fact of increasing differentiation in the various spheres of life and in individual biographies. In other words, these innovations must in principle be suitable for a variety of life-styles and problematic situations. Needs and behavioural options must not be made to conform to the irrevocably lost 'standard' of a life long, linear professional or employment career.

As far as tackling social differentiation is concerned, there are two possibilities. One is to bring about improvements specifically for those who have had the misfortune to end up in uncomfortable niches. Another is to provide incentives for individuals to leave the more comfortable niches from time to time and engage in a kind of game of tag. The obstacle to the first of these routes is that resources are never sufficient to bring everything up to one and the same high level. The target-level itself is constantly moving on, and the whole thing is a race without end. The second route is made easier by the fact that, during their lives, people develop different needs and desires: full-time work, desirable for a thirty-year-old, may be too much for a sixty-year-old.

To follow the second route, therefore, would mean increasing the number of bridges between paid employment and non-wage-earning activities, and reinforcing these bridges, instead of regarding them as loci of an abnormal, or even prohibitable, kind of individual behaviour. By doing this, one would be taking account of the fact that there are a whole range of other criteria by which one can sensibly shape one's life besides that of economic rationality, which incidentally is neither trivial nor straightforward, and that social acceptance of these criteria facilitates, at least indirectly, ecological reconstruction.

The first step must be to reduce the isolating and intimidating effects of a system in which sources of income are dependent on the labour market. What is meant here is crude 'either/or' classifications such as that which affects those in receipt of social security benefits. On the one hand, every single Deutschmark of supplementary income that these individuals may have earned off their own bat is taken into account in assessing their claims for assistance, but on the other hand they can be ordered off to do quasi-unpaid compulsory work. A situation that does not reinforce self-help but illustrates how anyone who is dependent on this 'help' is forced into a choice between apathy and illegality.

This blackmail mechanism does not exist only in the form of the 'poverty trap'. Even qualified employees get to feel the steely limits of labour-based society if they try to fit their extra-professional activities in with company timetables, either because of unavoidable family commitments, or because of a desire for creativity, for the freely chosen stress of group activity, or out of a simple lust for life.

Attempts to obtain leave to care for children or others, or in order to fulfil extra-professional commitments, still have to contend with the paradigm of the textbook career, unreal except as a reference point for disappointment and sanction.

Second criterion: Whatever measures we propose, they must not only be technically effective and economically efficient. They must also be capable of being thought 'just'. More than this, the odder they appear against the background of the wage-earning norm, the more stoutly they must stand up to the criteria of social justice and need. However, ideas about what constitutes justice are anything but simple. Any measure of justice that is fit to be put to practical use has at least three sides. It must do justice to the situation of the 'intended' recipients, it must make sense in the eyes of the non-affected, and it should not ignore wholesale all the arguments put forward by the net payers. What has for some time now been known to be the case in our treatment of nature also applies to social policy in a competitive democracy, namely 'there is no such thing as a free lunch'.

This means that our innovations in social policy must be fashioned in such a way that they make sense not just for a narrowly-defined social group, but, where possible, for a great many other people as well. Not for everyone at the same time, but for particular stages of life which everyone goes through at some time. This would mean making politics with options, and these options, instead of establishing a further special status for a few, would generate opportunities for many. Optional politics offers us a way of coping with the extensive individualisation of social problems and organising collective security for various types of personal situation. In contrast to selective prevention, it requires no great knowledge of future needs. This kind of innovation is suited to a society whose dynamic transformation no one can forecast reliably, let alone direct. It offers link-up points, rather than a means of demarcation, for varying interests, motives, and goals.

Two complexes of ideas which satisfy both criteria seem to me to have been sufficiently honed by public discussion to be regarded as realistic goals of an ecologically conscious social policy. Without the intiatory role of the Greens, these ideas have very little chance of being realised, since they do not follow the 'fire-brigade' principles of targeted elimination of symptoms and selective indemnification.

Optional working-time

The first complex involves getting personal rights in regard to individual arrangements and the taking of leave from work on to a firm legal footing. This would take the form of a policy of optional working-time for employees in the emergent information and service-based society. The area of suitable measures ranges from parental leave and a (temporary) changeover for parents and non-parents to protected part-time employment. Extended opportunities for compensatory free time for overtime and periods where workloads are heavy. The enforcement of very specific personal requirements in regard to time (requirements for which, in the case of unpaid leave, no justification need be given).

Clearly, the creation of new legal opportunities does not guarantee that these opportunities will be used. What it can do is acknowledge a social need, one that even business magazines such as *Capital* have begun to register with a certain degree of feeling. Since the point is not least to achieve a moral upgrading of the plural culture of the industrial society, a culture that has long since become a reality, the relevant regulations must not be group-specific. Only when it has become perfectly natural for men to step off the treadmill of full-time employment for a while will women, young people, or old people cease to be given dirty looks for wanting something of which they have long been regarded capable. There are a whole series of ideas on this which go far beyond what was formulated in rather conservative terms in the Green election manifesto of 1987 as a demand for 'individual power of disposal over the time gained through cuts in working-hours'.

Objections raised will generally relate to the cost which such measures will occasion the company, and also to poor uptake by workers, and to the supposed luxury of these kinds of arrangements. The costs are indeed hard to calculate as long as the degree of uptake remains unknown. It would be advisable to seek solutions in the setting-up of funds that would limit the risks to individual companies through horizontal redistribution. At least for small-scale businesses, we should be thinking of something along the lines of the compensatory procedure covering the continued payment of wages in case of sickness. The argument about demand must be countered by market methods, since what is involved are innovations of the same order as the car, the non-stick pan, or the telex machine, the demand for which was supply-induced. The reproach about luxury is a more serious one. It emanates from our own ranks and suggests that more 'social progress' could be achieved by more accurately directed monetary benefits. This, however, is to ignore the above-mentioned, and admittedly less attractive aspects of the idea of justice, namely those relating to the degree of tolerance of third parties and their willingness to pay up. In addition, no account is taken of the fact that there are two sorts of currency involved here. It is envisaged that anyone who wants to and can afford to should be able to secure more time instead of more money. With the result that, given the right circumstances, there will be (more) earned income for those who have too much time but too little money.

Eliminating the poverty trap

The second complex of ideas is rather less clear-cut and more explosive in social terms, but is no less well primed. It relates to the proposed reform of welfare. There are basically two opposing concepts involved here. Those in charge of social policy, their advisers, and the various associations that determine events in this area recommend an increase of about 30 per cent in normal allowances, which would, however, offset only part of past monetary depreciation. A 'dilute' alternative with lesser financial effects envisages changing the basis on which need is calculated from the 'shopping basket' model to the results of consumer spot-tests. However, this variant need not concern us here, a 'full-strength' proposal involving a refashioning of supplementary benefit (in accordance with the Federal Law on Welfare) and unemployment benefit is also being proposed as an alternative to the idea of a gradual improvement in welfare rights, currently based on the notions of disadvantage, family subsidiarity, and the obligation to work.

What is involved here is some kind of non-discriminatory subsistence/allowance for individuals whose income and assets are insufficient to finance basic needs. What is not involved (and this is regrettable) is a lead-in to some kind of guaranteed basic income. Specific aspects of a 'needs-oriented basic social security' may be regarded as also constituting steps towards the establishment of a universal basic income. These aspects have their own justification and do not need such a label in order to make sense in the light of the above-mentioned criteria. Supporters of the idea of a guaranteed basic income, currently classified as belonging to the utopian tendency of social policy, will nevertheless observe that a reform which fosters both the worth of those entitled to welfare and their freedom of decision can also have the desirable side-effect of clarifying the sense of a civil right to income.

Three changes in particular need to be made to current legislation. The financial viability of these is set out in a report prepared for the Greens by Walter Hanesch and Thomas Klein:

(1)   Family subsidiarity should be limited to spouses/partners. That is to say, the income of the parents or children of those entitled to assistance should not be taken into account.

(2)   The so-called 'stepping-stones to work', on the basis of which about one-tenth of all those in receipt of welfare are forced, according to arbitrary local criteria, to engage in non-paid community work, should be abolished.

(3)   The obligation to work and the inclusion of all monies earned in the calculation of benefits should be replaced by a positive incentive to take up paid work, in the form of a tax allowance or a proportional reduction in the amount of income included in benefit assessment.

We are not yet talking about technical details, but about the choice of a basic perspective of reform which aims to guarantee minimum subsistence. If welfare legislation can be made an issue of ecological–social reform, we should, despite all the difficulties in dealing with bureaucratically colonised spheres of interest, avoid the easy route of quantitative perpetuation and venture into the battle for structural enhancement. Even if the initial sally should not bring a decisive victory, the arguments about ecological restructuring must be voiced, and voiced emphatically.

The elimination of the 'poverty trap' would create the scope for individual combinations of (voluntarily or involuntarily) limited wage-earning activity and guaranteed subsistence-allowances, thus taking into account the irreversible differentiation of employment conditions that has occurred below the level of normal working circumstances. If the full inclusion of wages in benefit assessment is abolished, even a modest social income will guarantee its recipients a minimum of freedom of decision. They can use it either as a basic income, or as a wage-subsidy, or as 'a basis for refusing to engage in certain activities', as Georg Vorbruba has pointed out (*Frankfurter Rundschau*, 27 Jan. 1989).

Such a scheme of reform will give rise to various objections, only three of which I propose to mention and respond to here. The first two derive from the discussion about a guaranteed basic income, the third seems to me to be important, even though it is hardly mentioned in public.

(1) As an alternative to guaranteeing minimum subsistence by monetary means, the linking of individual income-needs to society's labour-needs, in particular in the welfare services, is pointed to as a supposedly better option. A moderate obligation to work would, it is supposed, not only counter the loneliness and social isolation of those in receipt of assistance; it would also help tackle other social problems.

I cannot subscribe to this view. It seems to me to set the benefits of work-derived self-affirmation at all too abstract and high a level. These benefits must be offset against the experience of discrimination that results from the obligation to work. The norms of work-based society draw a firm line between those who work for a work-related income, and those who work for the sake of a non-work-related income.

In addition, there is nothing to suggest that those who (without welfare) would be lacking the minimum required for subsistence possess exactly those skills that are required to solve social problems. Welfare income for the income-less requires no other justification but the rejection of a 'lifeboat economy' (Claus Offe) whose watchword is 'It's bad luck on anyone who gets left outside.'

(2) Another objection was set out recently by André Gorz (in *Critique of Economic Reason* (London: Verso, 1989)). According to Gorz, there are two ways of bringing industrial society, currently split into those without work and those overstressed by work, together again. The first is via a universal right to (basic) income, the other is the fair distribution of work amongst all (by means of reductions in working-hours). To Gorz, the social philosopher, it is the second of these alternatives which, perhaps after discussion with West German trade-unionists, seems the better. The congenial appearance of this argument is deceptive, the appropriate institutions and organisations needed for a complete and sufficiently flexible redistribution of work do not exist.

No one in Germany, least of all the unions, is going to devote their energies to a strategy of national wage-cost increases (resulting from compensation and recruitment expenditure). Reductions in working-hours, which convert gains in productivity into free time and act as incentives to further increases in productivity, will not lead us back to classical full employment. Of course the unions deserve sympathy when they find themselves unable to dispense with the redistribution illusion as an aid to pushing through further reductions in working-hours. It remains none the less an illusion. In contrast, the alternative of an income guaranteed, in whatever form, directly by the State has the advantage that the necessary institutions do not have to be dreamt up. State, treasury, and welfare benefits are already a reality.

(3)   The final point concerns the supposedly unavoidable adaptation of legislation on national insurance and taxation. If the claim to non-work-dependent income is guaranteed, then every kind of wage-related income must be treated as liable for social security contributions. This points in the direction both of the elimination of the special provisions for 'minor employment', for which demands are already being made, and of the downward extension of liability to national insurance. Although such a move would mean that many workers in 'precarious' employment would finally obtain their own claim to security, and that the incentive to employers to break up normal jobs into small time packages would diminish. One would have to be prepared for objections from quite a different quarter, namely from those who live or proft from illicit working.

In this connection, there might have to be a decision of principle in favour of a non-discriminatory guaranteed subsistence for those who 'bear the brunt' of the modernisation of industrial society. Such a decision would take the wind out of the sails of those who counter any ecologically dictated limit on production by pointing to the social hardship that will result. In what way do the measures proposed here differ from the normal course of things? At the heart of both complexes lie opportunities for dealing with social differentiation through the establishment of universal civil rights, rather than through the extension of legislation on poverty, of contingency provisions, and of guarantees in regard to standards of living. Both complexes are informed by an insight summarised by Ralph Dahrendorf in a single sentence. 'The methods of work-based society are no longer sufficient to keep that society going' (*Die Zeit*, 17 January 1986).

Both proposals are concerned with creating socially acceptable options. They offer a wider circle of people increased opportunities to shape their individual situations and their situations in society. Of course, they result in costs, to the extent that people avail themselves of them. With the policy of optional working-time the problem of take-up by the wrong parties does not arise. The institution of a social income that includes wage-earning incentives increases individual prospects of one day being able to stop claiming that income. Instead of leading to a hardening of the divisions between social groups, such measures will facilitate movement between them. Besides this, they are strong enough to withstand social debate.

PART III

9

The German Greens: preparing for another new beginning?

I Introduction

The German Greens are an exception. Not because their career as a political party began relatively early and thus secured attention for ecological issues in the political system of their country as early as the first half of the 1980s but because they have become, much more than any other green party in Western Europe, the object, indeed the victim, of a myth. Although the well-intentioned myths about Germany's Greens have fostered a positive view of the chances of Green parties in other countries, they nevertheless hinder understanding of the convoluted and irritating course of development followed by the party 'Die Grünen'. Unless one knows the background to the Greens' emergence, and the problems associated with their organisation, their assimilation of experience, and their elaboration of strategy, one cannot understand why, in the process of German unification, the Greens ended up on the periphery of political events, and even lost their seats in the Bundestag.

One of the chief myths is the notion that the foundation and early electoral successes of the German Greens were due to a particularly strong ecological/pacifist mood in West German society. 'Ecological issues' have indeed become a 'standard topic' in the media and amongst a large number of younger people, but this is not sufficient to account for the existence of the 'Greens'. Unconditional pacifism and the tendency to engage in an ecological critique of civilisation are features confined to a tiny segment of the population, and to only a minority of green voters. Combative commitment to the environment was, in any case, not a German speciality. The anti-nuclear and environmental movement in 1970s France was markedly stronger, but it was only about ten years later that a viable green party came into being there. Again, the West German subcultural milieu never attained the creativity and radiating power of the new age 'consciousness revolution' which began on the west coast of the United States in the 1960s and left its mark all over the world, even in places where green parties have remained unheard of to this day.

Also mythical is the belief that the German Greens are the successful creation of charismatic personalities such as Petra Kelly or Rudolf Bahro. However important the role of such personalities was in bringing together groups and individuals during 1979 and 1980, the fate of the Greens took shape largely uninfluenced by the wishes and actions of their prominent founders.[1] Another myth, finally, is the notion that the activities and conflicts of the Greens were always, and primarily, concerned with the issue of ecology, with ecological values and the critique of industrialism. There is a very important difference here between the picture which the media painted of the Greens (and which for many years determined public perception of them) and the issues on which they actually concentrated as they formulated their objectives and conducted their disputes. Thus, until very recently, the Greens were accused of being a single-issue party, although from the very beginning they had concerned themselves with the full range of global and social themes, as well as pursuing the ambitious programme of a movement of democratic and moral renewal.

The various chapters of this book, most of which were written as contributions to the strategic debate conducted in the circle around the Greens, would have remained unwritten if there were only those kinds of Greens evoked in the myths. The real Greens, both members and party officials, experienced a different reality – a deep gulf between favourable opportunities for effective social action on the one hand, and immense internal party difficulties on the other. Many an internal conflict gave rise to hostilities that were more intense than any dispute with other parties. If, despite this, one can currently observe a positive trend in the development of the Greens, this is due primarily to the commitment and sacrifice of countless local activists, who refused to trust in any favourable-looking trend, and who, despite the factional disputes going on in all the different bodies, sought repeatedly to give public proof of the Greens' political potential.

Whereas the other chapters of this book deal with the rival strategic concepts and material options of green policy, this chapter attempts to plot an interpretive framework within which questions about organisational development and organisational structure may be answered. What were the institutional conditions under which the unique phenomenon of 'greenness' emerged (section II)? What marks have the Greens left on society (section III)? What is the explanation for their dual ideological identity (section IV), and for the ambivalent results of the grass-roots experiment (section V)? And finally, where do the Greens stand today, twelve years or so after their foundation and in an unexpectedly united Germany (section VI)? The chapter closes with an analytical summary of the problems which any party of reform now faces in shaping itself (section VII).

II Attractions and handicaps: the opportunity structure

Comparative political science views the emergence of the new social movements and green parties in Western Europe as part of a profound change in the social structures of industrial society. From this standpoint, the environmental movements and parties appear as new forms of participation by new social categories, in particular the new middle classes.[2] Unfortunately, however, this characterisation can only capture the common aspects of a phenomenon which presents itself in nationally and culturally highly varied permutations. Since the phenomenon does not exist anywhere in a 'generalised' or 'average' form, it becomes interesting, and comprehensible, only through its peculiarities. Thus it should come as no surprise that the emergence, development, and prospects of the German Greens have all been influenced to a great degree by the peculiar historical and cultural features of the Federal Republic.

Naturally, the influence exerted on the Greens by historical/ cultural factors can be seen clearly only when one looks back over a sizeable stretch of development. As far as the shaping of political image is concerned, this influence has manifested itself in a decidedly 'left–green' bias, with strong traits of a 'generation-based party'. For one thing, the party has maintained an outlook on society and political conflict that was prevalent amongst substantial sections of its membership at the time of its foundation. In addition, the generations associated with the party's foundation, these are primarily contingents with birth-years falling between 1945 and 1965, form a disproportionate percentage of the membership in relation to the population as a whole. In somewhat overstated terms, one can say that the Greens still 'think' like their founders, and, since their way of thinking is shared less and less by younger generations, they are also 'ageing' with their founders.

In order to understand the political and cultural image of the Greens, one has to recall some of the peculiar features of German post-war history. West Germany, here for once regarded not as a symbol of the economic miracle, but as a political/cultural syndrome, was obliged to 'reinvent' the Germans' collective view of themselves, their social and political values, following the downfall of the Hitler regime. As is well known, early post-war policy (i.e. the governments of Chancellor Adenauer) discharged this task through unconditional political and economic attachment to the West, and through two equally resolute 'separations'. One was the dissociation from National Socialism, and the other was the strict rejection of all things 'communist' or 'socialist'. These latter were equated with Stalinist domination and repression.[3]

Both the climate of opinion, characterised as it was by repression and taboo, and the political leanings of the Christian Democrat governments prevented the demarcation from National Socialism and from the crimes of the Hitler regime from being carried out as honestly and consistently as was the rejection of everything that could be associated, however remotely, with any manifestation of 'Soviet domination'. Thus it was that until well into the 1960s, official policy displayed an obsessive McCarthy-like anti-communism, whereas the National Socialist past was treated as a taboo subject (i.e. was suppressed from public discussion). It is one of the paradoxes of post-war Germany that in 1956 the Communist Party (KPD) was outlawed, whilst associations of former SS and SA members were tolerated, and met with considerable success in their socio-political demands. Later on, the infamous Berufsverbot or professional ban was introduced for use against any members of the German Communist Party (DKP), labelled 'extremists', who wanted to work as teachers, railway workers, postmen, or civil/public servants. During this same time, former Nazi judges were still at work, and concentration-camp superintendents who were being sought for murder and torture could expect their crimes eventually to come under the statute of limitations (until its application to Nazi murder was abolished in 1979).

Post-war Germany was characterised not so much by social divisions as by moral/cultural and political 'cleavages'. In comparison with the majority, probably 90 per cent − of consumer-minded, security-oriented, and politically abstinent citizens, there was only a small minority of left-wing, left-liberal souls. They had an eye for the past and a critical attitude to cultural developments, though they were no more interested in institutional politics than were the majority. It was only in the years around '1968' (now the symbol of democratic awakening) and as a 'joint product' of internal political democratisation and the external relaxation of relations with the East, and also as a belated effect of the student movement[4] that the present liberal, pluralist society of the Federal Republic, with its capacity for self-critical analysis, emerged. Only a generation after '1945', in the 1970s and 1980s, did knowledge of the National Socialist past combine with moral horror at the fact that this past had been possible and was irreparable.

Only once did that Old German authoritarian state, with its unashamed propensity for stirring nationalist emotion, for snooping into people's political convictions, and for conducting witch-hunts against intellectuals, seem to resurrect itself. This was in 1977, a year of 'extreme events' in politics, the high point of a wave of left-wing terrorist actions[5] and the last surge of the mass movement against the construction of nuclear power stations. A number of large-scale demonstrations were literally fought down by police using quasi-military means. If '1968' had been the symbol of a phase of liberalisation overloaded with utopian revolutionary ideas, '1977' became the negative symbol of a 'German autumn' which not only provoked justified worries in civil society about politically motivated terror, but also served as a reminder of the dangers that emanate from a ruling elite that is unnerved but, equally, has great power of interpretation and repression.

When, after 1977, following the blossoming of the 'citizens' initiative' movement, 'green' electoral associations began to be formed at local and state level, the protagonists of these groups regarded themselves as being motivated not only by ecological considerations of the natural 'limits to growth', by the fear of a 'silent spring' (Rachel Carson), and by the risks of nuclear energy, but also by their desire for a genuinely democratic kind of politics, open to participation and moral scrutiny. However, the greater willingness to take part in collective action which manifested itself in the extensive participation in civil action groups and mass demonstrations was not transmitted to the political parties. Whereas the social democrats had still managed, at the end of the 1960s, to recruit young people as members and supporters with their watchword of 'daring more democracy', the Greens developed, from 1979, from a very small base of members who were ready to undertake organising activities. These were representatives of the first 'green' lists, individual pioneers of the ecological critique of civilisation, disillusioned social democrats, and, last but not least, the remains of the groups and small-scale parties left over from the student movement, some of undogmatic 'socialist' bent, others of decidedly 'Marxist–Leninist' outlook.

With this mixture of policy-related motives for participation and 'anti-capitalist' standpoints (as is well known, the student movement was accompanied not only by the expansion of the education system, but also by the return, with considerable impact, of Marxist and 'critical' theories to the universities), the Greens became the first party to succeed in defining itself discursively and independently[6] in terms of a quest for social reform, of criticism of the repression of National Socialism, and of an anti-institutional understanding of politics and democracy. In so doing, they filled a gap in supply of a kind that was unknown in the political systems of other Western European states, namely the specific German lack of a socialist opposition, resulting from the division of the country, the Cold War, and the semi-official anti-communism. They found themselves pushed into this role, and were simultaneously the subject and object of an unexpected 'push effect': as interlocutors and representatives of social minorities,[7] as systematic advocates of the effective enforcement of equal rights for women, as champions of egalitarian principles and morally sound decisions.[8] It goes without saying that this brought pitfalls as well as opportunities. 'Structural' overstrain of the Greens was to some extent pre-programmed. The more pleasant consequences of the task of multiple representation will be discussed in the next section.

The fact that the Greens did not collapse under this strain but managed rather to establish themselves within the network of political actors in the Federal Republic might be described as an effect of various institutional 'pull-factors'. Thanks to comparative political research, these factors are well known, and mention of four special features of the Federal German political system will therefore suffice to give a rough picture of what, for many sceptical observers, was an unexpected chance of institutionalisation for the Greens.

(1)   The first, and probably most important, condition of success

is satisfied by German electoral law, under which all parties at the various levels of representation obtain parliamentary seats in proportion to the votes cast. Whether a member of parliament has stood for election in a constituency and and won that constituency, or whether she owes her mandate (parliamentary seat) solely to her place on her party's list of candidates (the so-called *Landesliste*) is of no significance once the election is over. This means that even parties with only small reserves of voters have some chance of success, and the securing of absolute majorities by a single party are the exception rather than the rule in the multi-party system that results from these arrangements. Thus the various parliaments are, in principle, open to any interest that shows itself capable of organisation and is able to win at least 5 per cent of the votes (this is the so-called *Sperrklausel* or 'barring clause'). In addition, because in certain circumstances majorities come about only when coalitions are formed between a number of parties, the 'small parties' also come in for consideration as potential participants in government.

(2)   The '5 per cent clause' performs the function of preventing a fragmentation of the party system. It is supposed to ensure continuity and predictability. Not every viewpoint, not every minority interest is to be able to send its own representative (or handful of representatives) to Parliament. As far as the creation of the Greens is concerned (who incidentally support the abolition of the *Sperrklausel*), this rule was a strong incentive, perhaps the decisive incentive, to construct the party as an alliance of at least four variously oriented forces. In addition to green, the 'spectrum of green colour-theory' contains a hefty dash of of 'red' (in the form of Marxist, Leninist, Maoist, Trotskyist, anarchist, and Spontaneist groups), as well as the somewhat weaker streak of 'lilac' of the feminist movement.[9] At any rate, had it not been for the institutional pressure to put aside the many differences that existed, the Greens would not have emerged in 1980, and not in this form. Neither could any single current have asserted itself alone.

(3)   The party system in the Federal Republic owes its stability not only to the 'constitutional patriotism' (Jürgen Habermas) of its citizens, but also to systematic precautions taken by the political parties, who were keen to safeguard themselves against unwelcome competition.[10] The CDU/CSU and SPD, operating as 'catch-all parties', came to an agreement very early on with the much smaller, and therefore organisationally very weak Liberals (FDP) to

'unshackle' themselves from the fluctuating commitment of their members in regard to participation and financial support. They created a legally based system of party finance, the stoutest pillar of which is the so-called *Wahlkampfkostenerstattung*, or refund of electoral campaign costs. According to this, all parties taking part in state or federal parliamentary election campaigns and receiving at least 0.5 per cent of the vote are awarded a certain sum of money for every vote,[11] although on the one hand this arrangement makes the older parties markedly less dependent on voluntary commitment, and thus less dependent on the political will of their members. It also constitutes a kind of spur to innovation, operating to the benefit of small-scale parties which cannot themselves finance repeated candidacies. Because, in accordance with democratic principles, the system of subsidy to parties begins to operate a long way below the 5 per cent hurdle, parties with shares of the vote between 1 and 5 per cent receive a reliable aid to organisation. This explains why twenty to thirty other parties, besides the four parties in the Bundestag, regularly woo the voters. And it also explains how an initially small party like the Greens, despite many handicaps and the absence of any donations by financially strong members (let alone industry), managed to build up a network of party offices and an electoral campaign organisation.

(4) Finally, the federative structure of the German political system provides comparatively favourable opportunities for new parties to develop. It is relatively easy to acquire initial experience and a public profile through participation in local elections (for seats in the city council) or in elections for the State Parliament. The State Parliaments and governments may be subject to federal decisions in many important areas, but because of their responsibility for education, for the promotion of the economy, for developmental and structural planning, and for monitoring local-authority operations, they offer many opportunities for 'new' political approaches to make their mark. Less striking are the effects of the principle of democratic proportional representation which is part of German federalism. According to this, representatives of all the parties present in Parliament are, in time, sent to take part in consultative and supervisory organs of the most varied kinds. In addition, members of parliament receive invitations to discussions and educational events, by no means uninfluential, at academic institutions associated with the Church, the trade unions, or the universities. Thanks to the many

opportunities for participation, even small parties can benefit from the multiplicatory effect of media coverage.

Summarising the combined effect of these four elements of relative openness in the political system, one can say that the 'political opportunity structure' is definitely favourable as far as a green party is concerned. As regards the chances of success for social movements, the responsiveness of established politics may appear slight, as Herbert Kitschelt[12] observes, but for newly arrived political actors the institutional obstacles are perfectly capable of being overcome. Indeed, as long as it is possible to mobilise increased potential support and secure re-election, self-assertion within the political system brings a series of 'feelings of achievement'. The new actor receives incentives to view his survival as an endorsement of his political programme and of his interpretation of reality, even though they contradict those of the other parties. In the case of the Greens, this meant not only that they were subject to the temptation to satisfy society's 'demand' for a resolutely left-wing party, but also that they found themselves being 'rewarded' with institutional recompenses and increasing opportunities for influence, the more they played this role. In addition to the various advantages flowing from a gradual adaptation to the set forms and routines of the political system (on this, see the detailed analysis by Claus Offe,[13] there were also premiums for non-adaptation and for the demonstrative pursuit of 'otherness'.

III   The Greens as a stimulus to social learning processes

Society and politics in the 1980s were characterised not only by the revival of conservative and liberal forces but also by the rise of the Greens. In 1983 they succeeded in getting into the Bundestag and won seats in nine out of eleven regional parliaments.[14] Here and in countless municipal and district councils the agenda and style of political debates was transformed under the influence of the Greens. It sometimes seemed as if the journalists in the press and in broadcasting, and even individual civil servants in the various administrations, had just been waiting for the change initiated by the Greens. They seized on quite a few 'green' themes, provided the Greens with useful background information, and thus secured greater public attention for the Greens. The Greens did not function only as vehicles for environmental interests and the concerns of disadvantaged groups but also as monitors of the conduct of governments, mayors, and administrations. With great persistence they set about uncovering corruption, tacit partnerships between politicians and business, and instances where competencies had been exceeded. The influence of the Greens is thus scarcely measurable in terms of votes. Their very presence, their politics, and even their internal disputes have left unmistakable marks. Four points illustrate this.

(1) The general acceptance and 'normalisation' of the environmental issue, including the related problems of the link between the industrialised and developing countries, of agricultural policy, of energy policy, etc., are not, of course, due solely to the Greens. Nevertheless, their effect as a catalyst and reinforcer of this set of issues was and is enormous. By transporting the doubts, critical viewpoints, and anxieties of the social movements into the political system and securing a hearing for 'counter-experts', they ensured greater variety in the relevant information and arguments. Thus, although the nuclear industry's abandonment of three large-scale projects[15] during the second half of the 1980s is not attributable directly to the activity of the Greens, the fact that politicians regarded the continuation of these projects as too costly is due chiefly to the changes which the Greens brought about in the criteria for determining political legitimacy and economic reasonableness. A similarly unchartable strand of influence reaches into the environmental ministries at state and federal level. Because the SPD was forced, under competitive pressure from the Greens, to develop a comprehensive environmental programme, the ruling CDU/CSU also found itself unable to carry on with its purely symbolic policy. Measured against the situation in the 1970s, or the environmental policies of other countries, the 'material' effects brought about by the Greens appear considerable. Measured against the much more rapid growth in the problems themselves and in the need for action, they continue to be inadequate. Even in Germany, ecological factors are far from being regarded as the self-evident premises for decisions relating to economic innovation and investment. Thus, although German environmental policy has attained a quite high level (as far as the strictness of standards for emission and licensing procedures are concerned), the majority of the population quite rightly considers that environmental problems are the most urgent and least satisfactorily handled political issues.

(2) Somewhat less striking but no less important is the political

'change of style' fostered (again, not caused solely) by the Greens. Initially, the Greens had a tendency to champion their ideas of egalitarian political participation, of openness and transparency in the political debate, and of unmediated self-expression by concerned interests in a way that was not only provocative but also dogmatic and formalistic. Nevertheless, positive effects of this confrontation are visible in many areas of politics, and even within rival parties. Naturally, the established parties at first tried to deflect the barrage of 'radical' arguments against economic growth, against militarily based concepts of security, and against the multiplicity of social inequalities, and to classify green reasoning as naïve, one-sided, and failing to take consequences into account. They did not, however, succeed for very long with this approach. Whether because of the dialectic of communicative understanding or because of the career opportunities which up and coming 'non-green' politicians saw in a 'serious' approach to green issues. The forms as well as the themes of 'green' politics, and indeed something of the radical impetus of the early Greens, became part of political culture. At the same time, toleration of unusual or differing views has also increased in civilian society. A positive view of pluralism established itself, in which even the representatives of the 'fundamentalist' position enjoyed respect and achieved a certain prominence in the media. Mention should also be made of the successes brought about by the green-inspired 'feminisation' of politics, initially confined to the symbolic but now a yardstick for women's demands and women's presence in all political bodies (women are often more strongly represented than men in the official bodies of the Greens). The Greens' intensive experiments with 'grass-roots' forms of operation had a similar effect. It seems as if the predictability of the lower levels has gradually diminished in other parties as well, as if those at the top of the organisation can no longer rely so easily on the 'obedience' of their members, or ensure discipline simply via the allocation of official positions and career opportunities.

(3)   One of the surprising, and perhaps paradoxical, effects brought about by the Greens is the reinforcement of left–right polarisation in inter-party rivalry. This has several causes. One is related to the 'political ecology' developed by the Greens. The ecological approach would be doomed to failure if there were not simultaneous and equally serious attempts to champion the material needs of the poorest members of society. An environmental policy

that relied solely on change in individual behaviour appeared ineffective, whereas comprehensive intervention by the State in the economic process seemed indispensable. Given that environmental interventions are necessarily mainly restrictive in character, it was calculated that there would have to be trade-offs in terms of income and employment. The Greens therefore attached great importance to social guarantees for workers. They pledged to offset the material burdens occasioned by environmental policy.

In order to fulfil this promise, the Greens had to enter into competition with social democracy in the field of social policy, thus contributing further to the new left–right polarisation. Following its fall from government in 1982, the SPD was in the process of trying, by means of comprehensive employment and social programmes, to suppress recollection of the fact that it was not a conservative but a social democratic government – that of Helmut Schmidt – which had initiated the roll-back in social policy. Because the SPD was afraid it would lose voters to the Greens, it declared itself to be the only socially responsible party and castigated its new rival, the Greens, for focusing exclusively on the environment and for not paying any attention to the unemployed or to workers affected by crisis. The unjust accusation of hostility to the workers greatly affected the Greens, who saw themselves as both critical of capitalism and socially oriented. They responded with even more voluminous programmes of social action, which, like those of the Social Democrats, adhered to Keynesian logic. Because both business and a majority of the electorate were against the idea of higher taxes and higher public borrowing, the Greens soon fell into the same attractiveness and credibility trap as the SPD. An intense competition for precedence in determining opinion within the left-wing spectrum of voters widened the gulf with the government and hindered the updating of both the SPD's and the Greens' programmes.[16]

Finally, the internal competition between Green 'pragmatists' and the ethically motivated 'fundamentalists', may be seen as a fourth causative factor in the increased polarisation. The latter group, who lost their dominant position in the formation of the Greens' political goals and objectives only in 1989, did not just reject any form of continuous political co-operation between Greens and Social Democrats but attempted to depict the SPD as a party of 'right-wing' bent, which now differed only in minor traits from the ruling conservatives. Under fundamentalist dominance, the Greens narrowed down the ecological dispute to class conflict and assumed the role of 'linesman' in the party system. They disallowed any other lines of conflict, besides the crude left–right dimension, along which political alliances, particularly with the Social Democrats, might have been concluded.

(4) The most significant success produced by this competition between Greens and Social Democrats is undoubtedly the trans-formation in programme and 'style' undergone by the SPD. The one-time bastion of 'socio-technocratic' state-interventionism, as represented by ex-Chancellor Helmut Schmidt and the former Defence Minister Hans Apel,is scarcely recognisable any longer. As well as 'green' terminology, the SPD adopted various items from the Greens' programme of action in the areas of energy and environ-mental policy, global economic policy and policy on development, and even peace and (military) security policy. This was both the result of an unconscious 'learning response' to changes in the SPD's constituency,[17] and the intentional effect of a competitive strategy initiated by Oskar Lafontaine. Lafontaine, who, with his unorthodox political proposals and enthusiasm for controversy, has contributed greatly to the revival of German politics (yet was defeated in the 1990 federal elections by Kohl, the 'chancellor of unity'), had from the outset regarded the Greens as a force to be reckoned with, and had overstrained them with his strategy of tactical embrace. Those sections of the SPD which drew their inspiration from Lafontaine (notably in the states of Saarland, Berlin, Schleswig-Holstein, Niedersachsen, Hessen, and Rheinland-Pfalz) adapted a part of the green range of ideas and surprised the Greens, whenever the electoral results seemed to permit this, by putting forward proposals for the formation of joint administra-tions. By so doing, they stoked up the internal dispute between the co-operation-minded Realos and the identity-obsessed Fundis, each of whom occupied diametrically opposed positions on the question of a 'red–green' coalition.

Whatever the result of the conflict, it redounded to the advantage of the SPD. If the fundamentalists won the day, this seemed to prove to the voters that the Greens were politically incapable, and the SPD could then regularly reap a substantial percentage of the 'green' vote for itself at the next election. If, on the other hand, the pragmatists amongst the Greens got their way, the SPD gained a coalition partner with which it shared a greater area of agreement than with the Free

Democrats (FDP). It then had a good chance, working on the basis of joint successes, of building up a new, 'ecological' image, which would improve its prospects with younger voters. One problematic consequence of this double game, however, is that the SPD is trans- forming itself rather too quickly into a 'post-modern' party, i.e. the rate at which it is modernising its image is greater than that of the (post-) modernisation of attitudes amongst its constituency. In the working-class milieu, which is traditionally union-oriented and of industrial–conservative bent, 'Auntie SPD's' new style is frowned upon. One section of the constituency is migrating to the con- servatives. The poor figure cut by the SPD in the five 'new' federal states is a sign of this dilemma. The modern SPD, which was sceptical in regard to German unity, which would like to see a change in the Federal Republic's 'tried and tested' constitution, and which for the most part condemned the Gulf War and regards the delegation of German soldiers to take part in UN operations as a prelude to the remilitarisation of German politics. This party is regarded by many classical SPD voters as a populist version of the Greens. The competi- tion from the Greens, the 'Lafontaine' strategy of adopting green issues, and a number of very successful red–green coalitions in various states have helped the SPD achieve a new and, in the long term, promising image.[18] That what is involved here is not mere superficial retouching of the party image but irreversible changes is demonstrated by the fate of the right-wing Social Democrats. They have lost some of the key positions of influence in the parliamentary party, the national executive, and the cabinets of the state govern- ments.

IV The Greens' dual identity

A brief glance has already been cast, in the second point of the last section, at the history of the Greens' internal conflict. Because the background to this conflict, and the forms it has taken, are one of the most misunderstood aspects of the Greens, it deserves somewhat closer inspection. For this, we may turn to social-scientific analyses which deal with the Greens' fundamental conflict not (or not only) from the point of view of committed green activists,[19] but (also) from that of a critical observer concerned to understand the pheno- menon. This is the approach that characterises the empirical studies conducted by Herbert Kitschelt[20] and Joachim Raschke[21] from which at least the first two of the following three points derive.

In contrast to what uncritical admirers of the Greens (e.g. Fritjof Capra and Charlene Spretnak)[22] suggest, there is almost no proof of the development of a common basic stance or central idea amongst the German Greens. This thesis naturally does not dispute the existence of diverse proposals for a unified green philosophy; it simply records the differences, indeed the rivalry, between these. The great susceptibility of the Greens to ideological conflict is to be explained by the peculiar nature of issues in the 'new politics'.[23] There is no central 'cleavage' along the lines of the 'labour versus capital' split. Instead there is a multiplicity of conflictual aspects touching on almost all social spheres, from production, through upbringing and education, state and law, science and technology, to patterns of consumption and individual lifestyles. Dichotomies between 'true and false', 'good and evil', 'us and them', are of little use. What is required is well-considered decisions that take account of reciprocal relations and learning-processes.[24] The unclear and fluctuating conflictual structure manifests itself in problems of orientation; after all, a party can secure its existence only if it can rely on the stable involvement of its members, and those members, in their turn, are most easily recruited where there are a number of fundamental shared convictions. Given that the Greens' orientation problem springs from a 'simultaneous radicalisation of problems and deradicalisation of the means available for solving these',[25] radicalisation of thought and desire is one way of still being able to stabilise group-identity and involvement.

This is one reason, probably the main reason, why catastrophic scenarios, apocalyptic forecasts, and an impassioned critique of civilisation and capitalism were such marked features of the 'philosophy' of the early Greens. Radicalness in diagnoses and therapies promised to offset the lack of a fully-developed theory, a lack of which those concerned had been painfully aware of since the crisis of Marxism. Also, reference to a radicalised concept of politics provided a means of containing the difficulties occasioned by the model of identity prevalent in the new social movements. That model is subjective, particularist, and marked by a strong preference for autonomy which runs counter to the requirements of any kind of formal organisation. There was another reason why ecological fundamentalism became the most influential current of opinion during the Greens' initial phase. The income from official party funding did not suffice to establish local party-offices with paid officials in every locality. Quite apart from the fact that paying party workers an appropriate wage would have violated grass-roots principles, it was vital to recruit committed members for voluntary, unpaid work. As Herbert Kitschelt[26] shows, only those members who derived some 'private benefit', the corroboration of their own philosophical standpoint by others, or involvement in important organisational decisions, would undertake poorly paid, or even unpaid, work for the party.[27]

Of course, the fundamentalists did not have a monopoly on the organisation. They had to share power with adherents of a basically moderate view of politics, who, because they had participated in the foundation of the party and because conditions of entry to the party were 'lax', could not be refused membership. However, because the fundamentalists were the ones who continually devoted themselves to the development of the organisation and, until very recently, held the majority in party congresses, they had a monopoly on the intellectual interpretation of the party's image. It was thanks to this monopoly that there occurred what for outsiders was an astonishing reversion to the traditions of the early workers' movement, to its rhetoric and its schemes of institutional reform (expropriation and socialisation of the means of production, establishment of a system of councils in addition to Parliament, integration and equalisation of systems of social security). At the same time, issues concerning the organisational 'form' of politics were declared to be key political issues, on the one hand via the establishment and impassioned defence of grass-roots principles (the problems associated with this will be discussed in the next section), and on the other hand by a fetishisation of the role of the parliamentary opposition. True to the principle that political practice consists primarily in the manifestation of identities and intentions, Parliament was to be used only as a 'stage', not as a means of participating in the elaboration of political decisions, let alone the formation of governmental coalitions.

Strictly speaking, the ideological predominance of fundamentalism was broken not so much by 'better' arguments from the pragmatists, but by side-effects of the growth in the green constituency. Lobbyism and parliamentarism contributed greatly to the change in image and in the processes whereby demands and objectives were formulated. I shall deal first with the function of green 'lobbyists', who come in two versions. The first are advocates of the kinds of specific collective interests which figure in the list of issues of 'new politics', for example, representatives of citizens' initiatives, of environmental or conservation groups, of women's refuges. The second group consists of lobbyists who represent not only collective interests but also legitimate individual interests, namely those involved in self-managed businesses or projects (production companies, bookshops, alternative newspapers, cultural centres, music and theatre groups). The 'lobby faction' regularly succeeded in persuading the fundamentalists to support particularised, more realistic and more short-term political objectives. In return, they gave their backing to the fundamentalists when it was a question of occupying positions of influence or of defending 'radical' formulas of identity against the pragmatists' practical view of politics.

However, because the 'lobbyists' now and again, e.g. before important election dates, allied themselves with the 'pragmatists', they were able to hold fundamentalism in check and to stop the pragmatists leaving the Greens. Although the champions of ecological and social special interests began by being scarcely less radical than the convinced fundamentalists, as they experienced the (individual and collective) benefits of parliamentarism, their view of politics came closer to that of the pragmatists. As experts or 'specialist politicians', they enjoyed a certain amount of attention in the media and were respected even by officials of other parties. A fact which had a beneficial effect on the interests which they represented. It gradually became obvious how much social influence the Greens were throwing away when they did not, like the other parties, steer their followers towards vacant posts in civil and public service (e.g. as mayors, public administrators, judges, or school heads). As the political weight of the 'lobby politicians' in the Greens increased, so too did their dissatisfaction with the fundamentalists' anachronistic approach to conflict, which threatened to squander the hard-won influence that had been gained within the political system. It was only in 1988 that they determined to organise a third green current, under the name 'Aufbruch' or 'New Beginning'.[28]

Given the triply fragmented way in which the Greens' experience was shaped, it is no surprise that their image continues to be a disunited one. The tendency to identify adversaries solely as a means of reinforcing the party's own identity, and to evoke an inexorable apocalypse has, it is true, been curbed. Nevertheless the makeshift solution of borrowing various elements from the labour movement (expropriation, council systems) is still current practice. The 'anti-capitalist' impetus is also kept alive through ideological 'rivalry' with certain sections of the unions and of social democracy which see themselves as (eco)socialist. For a long time, this meant that radical but politically ineffective criticism was regarded as an alternative to practicable environmental intervention (e.g. in the spheres of energy, waste, and transport policy). The internal party scepticism in regard to a policy of reform that is necessarily incrementalist but is rejected by the other parties as 'going too far' has now given way to a positive attitude. The Greens too have learned to appreciate the 'effects' of their parliamentarians and ministers. However, the competition to appear as 'left wing' as possible, from which even the pragmatists could not escape, has prevented the elaboration of all those proposals which aim at a loosening of society's dependence on economic development and thus damage the vested interests of workers as well.[29] Again, the idea that at the end of the twentieth century capitalism should more appositely be thought of as a kind of drug-dependency of the whole of society, and no longer as a kind of fist-fight involving only capital and labour, was one that did not occur to the majority of Green politicians.

V Organisational democracy as a test of self

As is well known, the Greens' approach to politics has a formal as well as a material (or policy-oriented) side. There has been an attempt, through the choice of organisational structures and procedural rules, to take account of the fact that attitudes and preferences do not simply flow into the party from outside but are also shaped by the party itself, indeed are in some cases self-generated. What the party wants and how it acts is dependent to an important degree on how it is organised. In order to guarantee the effective operation of members' interests, which in bureaucratic organisations and hierarchical decision-making structures are often at a disadvantage, the Greens expressly pledged themselves to the principles of 'grass-roots democracy'. These principles are familiar from the anarchist and syndicalist traditions of the labour movement. The Greens established the principle of the rotation of official posts, which allows for short periods of office (from one to two years)[30] and excludes re-election of office-holders. They prohibited the simultaneous holding of a number of offices, particularly the combination of a party office and a parliamentary mandate (the 'incompatibility rule'). They experimented with the imperative mandate, which binds delegates to the resolutions of the body that has delegated them. And they tried (prompted also by a lack of money) to fulfil most organisational tasks using voluntary, honorary, and unpaid workers rather than a paid staff.[31] Not much importance was attached to the decisions of executive committees and elected functionaries. What was expected of the latter was not so much political initiative and organisational capacity but a readiness to ensure that the resolutions taken by members' and delegates' conferences were put into practice.

The effects of green grass-roots democracy were, to put it cautiously, highly ambivalent. Above all, one has to distinguish between the effects which it had outside the Greens and those which it had inside, for the Greens themselves. The 'external' effects of the green experiment in democracy can be adjudged to have been unreservedly positive, and may be said to continue to be felt to this day. The fact that organisations could not only function but also be politically effective without permanent functionaries, provided members occupied a 'strong' position and there was a high degree of transparency in all (formal) procedures, came as a positive surprise. There was a 'radiating power', which affected many other organisations (e.g. tenants' and consumers' associations), setting them under pressure to democratise. One has to bear this in mind when one assesses the internal effects, which appear much less favourable.

Grass-roots principles are typically justified with arguments such as those developed by the party sociologist Robert Michels[32] in explaining the emergence of an 'iron law of oligarchy'. Division of labour, power hierarchies, and expert knowledge alienate elected leaders from their constituency, so that the latter's will is either ignored or, indeed, changed into its opposite. It was principally the fundamentalists amongst the Greens who wished to preclude this kind of scenario of detachment, in which those who represent members' interests are wont to change into charismatic leaders who end up managing to impose their own personal will on the membership. In fact, however, the situation of the Greens, as Herbert Kitschelt's precise analysis shows,[33] cannot be likened to the relationship between members and leaders in the Social Democratic Party of the Kaiserreich. Members of the green Party have access to sufficient information and resources to be able to ensure that their interests are enforced. The party does not have an organisational monopoly, with no alternative available. Its members are not prevented by any subjective or institutional factors from themselves seeking higher-ranking offices within it. Quite the contrary, provided they act jointly and not purely individually, members who are at all informed or articulate have a relatively good chance of helping to determine the course of the party by means of 'voice' and (the threat of) 'exit'.

The problems posed by the relationship between members and party are quite different ones in the case of the Greens. Because the overwhelming majority of the members come from the new middle classes, the Greens are presented with some very varied subjective motives for participation. The members do have some normative attitudes in common, but their commitment is based not on any binding ethic but on a desire for self-fulfilment and on high expectations as to the direct benefit of political action. The preconditions for stable group-solidarity are thus scarcely satisfied. If party life makes great demands on members (e.g. by having meetings dominated by ideological controversies and an excess of formal issues), the commitment of the 'average' member quickly dissipates. This discontinuous pattern of participation, punctuated by 'shifting involvements,'[34] became a typical feature of the Greens. Problems developed which were not healed but aggravated by grass-roots principles.

The formal application of the principle of rotation, of the incompatibility rule, and of various other forms of 'grass-roots monitoring' of elected party representatives produced the same sort of tendencies to alienation and detachment as are claimed for a rigid ruling hierarchy. Instead of a lively organisational democracy, what often developed was a 'culture of distrust'.[35] The most serious effects were those brought about by rotation and the incompatibility rule. They prevented the accumulation of experience and the building-up of stable informational and communication links with other actors inside and outside the party. The tight chronological and functional restriction on the mandates ran counter to the interdependent nature of the problems with which green politics is concerned. Because party functionaries and members of parliament were not allowed to stand for office again, they lost an important incentive to communicate with the grass roots, they 'became detached' and concerned themselves only with that which they personally considered to be important. Accountability and willingness to assume responsibility dwindled. Because there was a strict ban on plurality even of party offices (e.g. a member of the regional executive committee could not also be treasurer of the local party organisation), an important channel of communication between the different levels of the organisation was lost.

Two fatal consequences in particular are to be regretted. In the first place, a disproportion developed between the large number of posts that had to be filled and the meagre stock of members that were sufficiently qualified and motivated to fill them. As a result, individuals had to be called on who appeared unsuitable. The only rudiments of competition to be observed, if there was any competition at all, emerged when candidates had to be selected for parliamentary seats. In the second place, the party soon became fragmented into a multiplicity of different spheres of action, in which actors operated in parallel or against each other, instead of co-operating. At local, state, and federal levels the bodies in which posts had to be filled included not only executive committees and delegates' conferences, but also supervisory forums (finance and steering committees) and twenty to thirty specialist working-parties. Because delegates and grass-roots representatives are only willing to commit themselves on a discontinuous basis, the various conferences have a greatly fluctuating make-up, with a high proportion of first-timers and last-timers. In 1990, the executive committee chairperson Ruth Hammerbacher complained in her farewell speech that the basic principle which the Greens had established, namely the 'principle of division' rather than that of meaningful connection, was a false one, indeed that they had made the 'lopping-off of connections into a systematic practice'.[36] She identified a structure of 'fragmented, compartmentalised "stratarchies" '.

Grass-roots democracy became an arena chiefly for two groups of actors. On the one hand, there were those who regarded the formal principles of grass-roots democracy as having great value in themselves, these were the (mainly younger) fundamentalists. Their concern to pledge the party to strict definitions of identity coincided with the opportunities made available to them for gaining self-knowledge and self-fulfilment in public roles and in exciting party conferences. On the other hand, informal networks began to form within the different wings, the members of which prepared the formal decisions through covert arrangements and took it in turns to occupy the most influential posts. The latter happened in full accord with the rotation principle, since this only prohibited standing again for the last-held post, but not for a different one. These two groups determined the shape of the party's work in many areas, and they furnish most of the delegates who are present on a continuous basis. A certain mismatch already exists between the motives for participation in a strongly reform minded party and the complexity of the problems and tasks which are to be considered. Also the difficulties associated with the design of the organisation are multiplied if the party is seen as a means of attaining direct satisfaction of 'aesthetic organisational' interests, in addition to comprehensive social reforms. The directness and ease of evaluation of organisation-related objectives gives such objectives almost automatic precedence over the complex, long-term social goals. Bureaucratic rule is not the only regime able to pervert the claim to a viable and worthwhile society. Grass-roots democracy can also do this.

If the well-considered balancing of different democratic principles (such as representation, participation, pluralism, and accountability) is abandoned in favour of one single principle, this may satisfy participatory desires but it also frustrates participatory motives. The motives of those who wish to participate not so much for reasons of self-fulfilment but more in the interests of long-term collective goals remain unrealised. The predominance of the one democratic principle destroys the others' chances of being realised. When one looks at the situation from this point of view, the fundamental problem of the Greens become clear. 'They are unable to combine legitimacy and efficiency.'[37] What they regard as legitimate, namely laxer rules of membership and a high degree of fluctuation, institutionalised distrust and intense self-reflection is inefficient as far as intervention in society is concerned. The things that would be efficient, the fostering of creativity, the ability to communicate and co-operate, the delegation of responsibility for a fixed term, the acknowledgement and corroboration of successful work, are considered illegitimate. When the Greens failed to secure entry into the first all-German Parliament in December 1990, they were not just paying the penalty with the voters for having shown themselves indecisive and petty-minded *vis-à-vis* the historic opportunity offered by unification. Their predicament was also a consequence of their irritating 'performance', a result of the distrust fomented by Greens against other Greens.

212   *The German Greens*

VI Where do the Greens stand today?

The failure in the federal elections of 1990 profoundly shocked the Greens. All wings of the party, apart from the fundamentalist 'radical ecologists' around Jutta Ditfurth, reacted with impassioned self-criticism. In spring 1991 the organisation's constitution was reformed by a national delegates' conference. Compulsory rotation was abolished, the incompatibility rule was toned down,[38] conditions of pay for executive committee members were changed, a procedure for postal ballots was introduced, and the filling of posts on the national steering committee was assigned to the regional executives. These organisational modifications are being applied to a party which, under the pressure of considerable changes in its milieu, is beginning to project a different ideological image.[39] These changes are: (1) The erosion of green fundamentalism; (2) The consequences of the break-up of the GDR.

The erosion of green fundamentalism
Fundamentalism started to lose support when the option of red–green coalitions began to appear a viable one in more and more states. This in its turn was due more to the growing dissatisfaction of the voters with conservative–liberal coalitions than to any attractive proposals of reform put forward by the SPD and Greens. A certain weariness with the same old fundamentalist plea for a critical attitude to the system and for abstinence from politics, a fall in the number of votes won in the fundamentalist strongholds, and the seemingly attractive opportunitites offered by participation in government meant that even in erstwhile 'radical' regional executive committees majorities emerged in favour of political co-operation and policies of reform.

The readiness of the West Berlin Greens (AL) to form a municipal administration with the SPD in 1989 gave the impression of a real breakthrough to a productive conception of politics.[40] It was the second instance of a red–green administration, the first being the red–green coalition in Hessen, renewed in 1990. The pattern was followed shortly afterwards by the Greens in Niedersachsen. The traditional alliance between fundamentalists and 'left-wingers' in the regional executives of Nordrhein-Westfalen, Schleswig-Holstein and Hamburg began to collapse. As late as 1990, the 'eco-socialists' around Rainer Trampert and Thomas Ebermann left the Greens; in spring 1991 the 'radical ecologists' around Jutta Ditfurth announced their departure.[41] The rump consisted of moderate 'left-wingers', now transformed into critics of the fundamentalism which they had previously supported. There is now a ubiquitous willingness amongst them to team up with the pragmatists, their erstwhile pet enemies, a factor which strengthens the party's capacity for integration and action in most states. Since spring 1991, the national executive committee itself has been made up of a majority of pragmatic 'left-wingers', and these are striving to establish a relationship of co-operation with prominent pragmatists of ministerial status (in particular Joschka Fischer, the Green Environment Minister in Hessen).

Any appraisal of this change of image will necessarily register a 'narrowing-down' of the spectrum of green positions. On the one hand, the Greens have seen the departure not only of the spokespersons of fundamentalism but also of prominent pragmatists (such as Thea Bock and Otto Schily, who are now SPD MPs in the Bundestag). On the other hand, the internal conclusion of peace between pragmatists and left-wingers has meant that the middle-of-the-road current operating under the label 'New Beginning' now feels itself pushed to the periphery. Since it began in 1988, the 'New Beginning' itself has changed character. Originally intended as a melting-pot for specialised (lobby) interests and as a mediator between the mutually hostile Realo and Fundi camps, it is now the sole group in which any reflection occurs about the central ideas and fundamental issues relating to the green concept of politics, an activity that occurs in opposition both to the simplistic left–right thinking of the 'left-wingers' and to the pragmatism of the Real-politiker.

The collapse of the GDR
The collapse of the socialist states of Eastern Europe, the flow of refugees from the GDR, the end of the SED regime, and, finally, the unification of the two German states constituted another shock for which the Greens were unprepared. Their political activity was geared to overcoming confrontation between the blocs and achieving equality of rights and understanding between them. It did not aim for the 'triumph of the West'. They had always advocated acceptance of the dual statehood of Germany and the extension of co-operative relations between the GDR and FRG. The Greens were

far from being supporters of state socialism, and, through their long years of support for civil rights activists in the USSR, Czechoslovakia, Poland, and the GDR, they had helped reinforce the movement for democracy. At the same time, however, they appreciated real socialism as a counterweight to the power pretensions of the Western alliance and also as a symbol of the 'counter-system'. There was always the idea that at least the experiences that had been gathered under socialism could be used as material for a fundamental restructuring of capitalism. Even Gorbachev's 'Perestroika' evoked ambivalent feelings, because it was unclear whether its aim was to improve or to abolish Soviet communism. The actual end of the socialist system initially left the Greens utterly speechless.[42]

Understandably, the West German Greens felt affinities primarily with the left-wing and ecological sections of the civil rights movements in the GDR. They supported both their attempts to organise themselves as well as the goal of converting the GDR into what would be a second democratic but the first 'social-ecological' (because non-capitalist) German state. The explosive growth in the East German population's desire for arrangements to be made as quickly as possible for them to live in the same state and enjoy the same living-conditions as the West Germans astonished the whole left-wing movement in West Germany, including the Social Democrats. East German civil rights movements, East and West German Greens, and the majority of Social Democrats opposed the course to unification which the government and Chancellor Helmut Kohl succeeded in pushing through in the face of the erstwhile allies and, in particular, the USSR. However, the standpoint of the German left, which was somewhat romantic and sidestepped the real needs, was not well received by the voters in West or East Germany. Because the East German Greens and social movements also gave in to the temptation to indulge in profuse self-reflection, they have as yet been unable to solve the problem of their fragmentation into a handful of parallel, small-scale organisations. They managed to overthrow a state, but their influence on the subsequent process of unification and on current developments in the new Germany has been minimal. There is, quite rightly, talk of the decline of the West German left.[43] Even if one adds the votes of the post-communist PDS to the votes of the SPD, Greens, and citizens' movements, the 'strength' of the left at the national level now amounts to only 41 per cent of total votes. The German parties of the left are currently stuck in the minority ghetto.

This means that there is for the present no prospect of the Greens and Social Democrats ousting the Kohl government and bringing a 'social and ecological turnaround' to the Federal Republic. The 'narrowing' of the Green spectrum, the loss of seats in the Bundestag[44] and a jading of the willingness to enter into grand debates about future schemes make the Greens currently appear weaker than they really are. All observers do believe, however, that the Greens will 'survive', even if they do not reappear that quickly in the seat of government. The voters have long since come to regard them as an indispensable part of local and regional politics. At the level of the national party, where the great issues of world-view and strategy were debated, the Greens have caused as much disappointment as they have attracted attention. All in all, therefore, their absence from national politics need not be adjudged negative. One feature that is problematic, however, is the lack of incentives in the present situation for overcoming weakness of ideas and for developing an autonomous left–ecological strategy of reform, independent of the distributive interests of the Social Democrats and trade unions. Confining oneself to ecological reforms which at best impinge only on the purses of big earners no longer seems appropriate, given the state of the problem and the wealth of Western industrial societies. However, any other, more thoroughgoing reforms presuppose a transformation of priorities and institutions, and these, in their turn, can be brought about only by well-founded arguments, attractive partial goals, and judicious strategies based on a well-developed awareness of one's opponents. Only in the wake of institutional change can desires for more thoroughgoing changes develop. The first phase of this endogenous moulding of political preferences was inaugurated by the Greens during the 1980s. Will they also be able to give the signal for a second new beginning?

VII Two analytical conclusions

The green experiment contains a wealth of valuable experience. This seems as yet scarcely to have been tapped, let alone put to use by the green party in shaping itself. Instead of providing a summary, I should like to close this chapter by outlining two perspectives on key problems of the Greens. These relate to the particular problems associated with rational operation in ambient conditions which, from the one perspective may be viewed as systemic links, i.e. a web of non-linear causalities, and from the other as an interdependence between strategic actors.

(1)   The prolific attempts of the social movements (and the early Greens) to awaken a sense of 'involvement' amongst people and to move them to take part in collective protest actions or to become members of the party through exaggerated diagnoses of problems, catastrophic scenarios, and a radicalised conception of the enemy, were by no means unsuccessful. Fundamentalist arguments appear neither illogical nor ineffective. Yet they have no effect on the causal structure of the problems which are the object of their disapproval. There is no channel of influence leading from intensely felt involvement and moral rigorism to causal therapies in the form of institutional changes aimed at bringing about certain effects. Every material or institutional change (of laws, of the premisses on which legal decisions are based, or of collective interpretations of how things hang together) seems to be indebted to at least one additional factor, namely knowledge of the existence of alternatives that can be implemented with a reasonable amount of effort. Moral reasoning may strive to raise the threshold of reasonableness, but success is dependent on realisable alternatives. Alternatives that are inadequate or lacking in credibility do not appear to be increased in value by being linked to an appeal for greater individual sacrifice. The fact that the moral fundamentalism of radical ecology, or of 'deep ecology', is geared to the generation only of the need for action but not of alternatives for action, is what makes it politically weak. Viewed thus, fundamentalism is parasitic, because it remains dependent on the readiness of those with 'other' motives to engage in pragmatic action.

What we have here is probably a problem located in the overlap between individual psychology and cognitive science, one that we regularly observe when emotional affectedness *vis-à-vis* 'global' problems is accompanied by a resolute rejection of the decision-making calculus relating to 'local' political alternatives. Even where this state of affairs is occasionally acknowledged by the relevant actors to be a problem, the latter see this not as a compelling reason to analyse their situation as regards social (or political) action but rather as an invitation to expound their emotions. One explanation for this is that the emotional actor has an intense need to indulge in cognitive simplification and therefore comes to the conclusion that problems regarded as 'big' can only be tackled with 'big' solutions.

However, since 'big' solutions themselves again present one with 'big' problems, the emotional actor becomes the victim of circular thinking. Matching up 'big' problems with what are the only available solutions, namely 'little' ones, is, in contrast, a task that requires not emotionality, but a readiness to tolerate ambiguity. Given the inherent uncertainty, the notion of a chain of 'small' steps precludes any allusion to success. Only such a notion can open one's eyes to the conditions that permit a type of action that is geared to effect and is, to this extent, causally adequate.

The inability to tolerate ambiguities that are real and rooted in the operational context has considerably hindered the Greens in their attempt to develop their potential for influencing society. This was demonstrated in the quasi-confessional formulas used to comment on peace policy (e.g. 'Out of NATO!'), on women's policy (which was always modelled on the lifestyle of the 'most radical' feminists of the day), on German unity (which was declared to be the resurrection of the German Reich), or on the Gulf War (which was regarded as an example of the material colonialism of the West, not as a response to the Iraqi occupation and not as having anything to do with Israel's interest in survival). Abstracting equally well-founded interests, which clearly appear to bear some relation to the one interest that is championed, may relieve one of the effort of having to weigh up all the factors and to present a discriminating case, but it leads to an arbitrary simplification of the true complexity of the world. This in its turn brings about a reduction in potential support, because it expressly excludes – or indeed declares as enemies – those who hold a more differentiated view of the world yet agree on many concrete proposals for action.[45] It is a well-attested sociological finding that voluntary organisations are wont to ensure their cohesiveness by means of emotionally satisfying collective interpretations which regularly prove to be insufficiently complex and of little instructive value when it comes to selecting strategies of action. Sociologists can be content with the elucidatory value of this finding, but actors who wish to influence society in a purposeful and responsible manner face a hard task. They must be constantly guarding against the temptations and consequences of simplification.

(2)   A look back at the 'fundamentalist' phase of green politics seems to prove the case for developing an awareness of ambiguity, for a 'culture of the scale-pan', and for tolerance of multiple rationalities. Indeed, for some time now a number of greens of

academic bent, most of whom consider themselves as belonging to the 'New Beginning' group or to the smaller, pragmatist section, have been expressing great disquiet at the Greens' crudely simplified perspective on problems, and at their rigid 'zero-sum game' understanding of political conflicts. These critics of ecological and political fundamentalism (with whom the author sympathises) cannot acquiesce in a situation where political strategy, whose targets are complex systemic reciprocal relations (e.g. between science, the economy, and culture), is still based on patterns of thought deriving from Newtonian mechanics (i.e. notions of linear causality) on a mechanistic model of social interaction, and an antagonistic conception of conflict. They point to findings in system-theory and evolutionary theory[46] and draw attention to the 'social construction of reality' through interpretive action that has no firm anchor in absolute truths or exogenous preferences.

Resisting the temptation of biologistic 'naturalism', which seeks to explain politics and society on the pattern of non-cognitive organic processes,[47] these critics, aware of the complexity of reality, tend to call for attention to be focused on the procedures and rules of 'sensible' politics. This deferment of issues follows on from a fruitful renaissance of 'institutional' approaches in political theory,[48] and shifts attention towards issues raised in present-day theory of democracy and towards the debate about the preconditions for the development of 'civil society'. Its significance for political actors lies in the way in which procedural norms influence the quality of the outcomes of political decision-making. It is obvious that a more complex knowledge of context and a higher level of reflection within politics would also make possible 'more' consideration of consequences, as well as more accurate strategies. The only 'residual' problem would appear to be the emotional and expressive needs of the members of the organisation, which up to now have been satisfied by crudely simplified world-views and 'gratificatory' organisational routines (e.g. party conferences). These, it is suggested, would have to be 'diverted' into a new democratic organisational culture, such as would appear to be achievable by replacing 'in person' democracy with plebiscitary procedures for participation (e.g. postal ballots).

However attractive such ideas may appear at first glance, they do not offer a way out of the dilemma faced by a party of reform in resolving the issues of participation and the determination of objectives. It only seems as if the substantial fundamentalism that is based on the need to express identity could profitably be exchanged for a procedural fundamentalism which attempts to follow the ethics of communicative understanding as formulated by Jürgen Habermas.[49] A party of reform that wishes to act as the agent of new issues and as the promoter of comprehensive democratisation cannot confine itself to reflexive decision-making and ethical deliberations. Even to win support for such an approach it would need to take strategic decisions in which the strategic options and probable moves of other actors were taken into account.

On the realistic assumption that actors have non-identical preferences and do not share the same world-view (this is not to say which of them must be regarded as 'right' and which 'wrong'), politics will always be a game of strategy, in which 'true' intentions should not be laid bare without consideration of the consequences. In other words, duplicating social complexity in the discourses of the collective actor threatens to make that actor incapable of joining in the strategic game with other actors. The successes, and they are urgently needed, of ecological and social politics will be successes brought about by judicious politics, or they will not be brought about at all. Green politics cannot afford to confine itself to the joys of communicative aesthetics. When some part of the basis of life disappears every day, when lives begin and end without hope, before a single trace of happiness has been experienced, ecological politics cannot display the kind of patience suited to a philosophy seminar. Equally, it must not become addicted to the pleasures of emotion.

The correct response to emotional reductionism is therefore not to be found solely in an increased awareness of complexity and in ethical reflection. It can only come as a result of weighing up defensible against indefensible simplifications, co-operative against antagonistic urges, mobilising against paralysing 'truths', in other words, weighing up 'good' against 'bad' politics. Because the name of that response is 'politics', it has no transcendental premises. It need wait on nothing and no one.

Notes

1   Although Petra Kelly was one of the three chairpersons of the Greens from 1980 to 1982, and was a member of the Bundestag from 1983 to 1990, she took no part in the impassioned factional disputes and debates about strategy which took place in this period. The few (oral) comments which she

220

The German Greens

did make on the development of the organisation had little influence. The same is true of her suggestion – which aroused a lot of interest outside the Greens – that the Greens should be thought of as an 'anti-party party', the object of which was by no means simply to 'freshen up' the other parties by introducing Green ideas to them (Kelly, *Um Hoffnung Kämpfen*, p. 21).

In contrast, Rudolf Bahro, who was a member of the national executive committee from 1982 to 1984, strove to give the Greens the image of a radical force that was critical of civilisation and which, although it determined the topics of public debate, resisted the temptation to participate in political decision-making and the exercise of power. Bahro left the party in 1985, following the party conference's rejection of his proposal of an unconditional ban on animal experiments. In his most recent published work, where he advocates a spiritualistic avant-garde concept of the radical reform of civilisation, the Greens figure merely as 'factotums' of the industrial system (cf. Bahro, *Logik*).

2   On this, see Müller-Rommel and Pridham, *Small Parties*; Dalton and Kuechler, *Challenging the Political Order*, and Kitschelt, *The Logics of Party Formation*.

3   This was comprehensible both to the extent that the assessments of the situation which prevailed at the time – and which were reinforced by the Cold War – saw grave threats emanating from the Soviet sphere of power (one should not forget the Korean War and the blockade of Berlin), and to the extent that the Iron Curtain put up by the hostile power-blocs ran right through the middle of Germany until autumn 1989. Both post-war German states – the FRG and GDR – regarded themselves (though not always explicitly) as 'front-line' states, in the strict sense of the term.

4   The first two factors cited are directly attributable to the participation of the Social Democrats in government, whereas the third factor, namely the student movement, was expressly targeted against the limits to development and notions of order implied in the social democratic model of society.

5   The president of the German employers' federation, Hans-Martin Schleyer, was kidnapped and murdered by terrorist commandos of the Red Army Faction (RAF). The passengers travelling in an aircraft hijacked by RAF supporters and made to fly to Mogadishu were freed by force. Immediately after this, three prominent members of the RAF (Baader, Ensslin, and Raspe) died in mysterious circumstances in prison in Stuttgart-Stammheim. These events, and the circumstances surrounding the death of the prisoners, came to be regarded by a small circle of young militant *Autonomer* (nonconformists) as mystical high-points in the struggle against 'the State'. The German Left, on the other hand, saw them as marking the end of the romantic notion of revolution.

6   I.e. not like the still-marginal DKP, which was duty-bound to criticise German capitalism and the national–socialist past on account of its 'unswerving loyalty' to the USSR.

7   In line with their inclusive concept of representation, the Greens give particular support to the rights of children, young people, and the elderly. Their commitment, as expressed in parliamentary initiatives (parliamentary questions, draft legislation), has been concerned with the social situation of

the jobless, of recipients of welfare, of migrant workers, of asylum-seekers, of refugees, and of ethnic and sexual minorities. For example, the green parliamentary group in the Bundestag took up the case of the Roma and Sinti peoples, who are still being refused compensation for the injustice perpetrated against them by the Nazis in the concentration camps.

8 One of the earliest appraisals of their work in the Bundestag bears the title *Ankläger im Hohen Haus* ('pointing the finger in the house') (Cornelsen).

9 Raschke, *Krise der Grünen*.

10 And were successful in doing this until the appearance of the Greens. Hence the various extreme right-wing and crypto-fascist parties have not yet succeeded in getting elected to the Bundestag. All they have managed to do is get elected – temporarily – to one or two regional parliaments. The pro-Soviet left (DKP) has also until recently been present in only a very small number of local councils (and will have to quit these positions, now that its followers have been surprised by the collapse of real socialism).

11 Parties currently pay themselves DM3.50 per vote. This so-called 'refund of electoral costs' makes up more than half of the total income of all parties.

12 Kitschelt, *The Logics of Party Formation*.

13 Offe, 'Reflections on the Institutional Self-transformation of Movement Politics'.

14 The Greens are not represented in the parliaments of either Saarland or Schleswig-Holstein. These two cases display interesting parallels. Before the election, the fundamentalist-dominated regional executives rejected the offer of co-operation put to them (for thoroughly tactical reasons) by the SPD. The regional SPD groups, led by younger 'carriers of hope' (as Oskar Lafontaine called Björn Engholm), won absolute majorities. As far as the state parliaments elected in October 1990 in what was formerly the GDR are concerned, the Greens are represented by their own members of parliament in Sachsen, Sachsen-Anhalt, and Thüringen. In the state of Brandenburg, where no alliance was formed between the Greens and the democratic citizens' movements, only the latter are represented in the parliament. In Mecklenburg-Vorpommern both the Greens and the citizens' movements, having fought the election separately, failed to clear the 5 per cent hurdle.

15 These were the fast-breeder reactor in Kalkar, the high-temperature reactor in Hamm, and the reprocessing plant in Wackersdorff.

16 Cf. the excellent account of the decline of the party-political left in Germany recently produced by Stephen Padgett and William Paterson 'The Rise and Fall'.

17 On this, see Section 2 of Chapter 2.

18 This development has also been reflected in political science, where the concept of 'catch-all' parties that has prevailed up to now has been revised: *Volksparteien* now no longer appear as slothful and hostile to innovation but as compelled, at the risk of going under, to show sensitivity to changes in society (cf. Czada and Lehmbruch, 'Parteienwettbewerb'; Wolinetz, 'Party System Change'). They only survive if they react flexibly to social change and ensure that new social interests are carried over into the

political system.

19   The reader will have noted that the author is inclined to see himself as belonging to the group of the committed activists, although he likes to adopt the position of a neutral and detached observer – ultimately returning to the battlefield with the insights and arguments he has gained. The observations that follow do not claim anything more than this kind of 'tactical' objectivity.

20   Kitschelt, *The Logics of Party Formation*.

21   Raschke, *Krise der Grünen*.

22   Spretnak and Capra, *Green Politics*.

23   Hildebrandt and Dalton, 'The New Politics: Political Change or Sunshine Politics?'

24   It is no coincidence that normative theories of ecological politics readily borrow from concepts relating to biological systems, and argue the case for 'interwoven thinking'. Cf. Hinchman and Hinchman, ' "Deep ecology" '.

25   Raschke, *Krise der Grünen*.

26   Kitschelt, *The Logics of Party Formation*.

27   'For ideologues, party organization is a laboratory to explore new forms of social solidarity and decision-making. Because the gratifications derived from organizational experiments are immediate and the collective benefits or comprehensive social change are more likely to be realized only in the distant future, ideologues may be more concerned with the party's appropriate organization than with its long-term program' (Kitschelt, *The Logics of Party Formation*, p. 50).

28   The most prominent politician associated with the 'New Beginning' is the former member of the Bundestag and chairperson of the parliamentary party Antje Vollmer.

29   Thus almost all attempts to develop an independent green labour and social policy – e.g. the elaboration of a scheme of guaranteed basic income – have failed. The adoption of current union demands in relation to wages and working-time, on the other hand, have met with approval.

30   The members of the first federal parliamentary party had to give up their seats after two years and were replaced by the so-called 'follow-on brigade'.

31   It is sometimes said that the Greens were to have reached their decisions according to the consensus principle, i.e. they would seek to secure the agreement of all those involved. But this is not the case. Even in the highest bodies such as the national executive committee, majority decision-making was the rule from the outset.

32   Michels, *Political Parties*.

33   Kitschelt, *The Logics of Party Formation*, p. 72.

34   Hirschman, *Shifting Involvements*.

35   Kitschelt, *The Logics of Party Formation*. p. 72.

36   *Ibid.*, p. 72.

37   Raschke, *Krise der Grünen*, p. 10.

38   However, members of the Bundestag may still not stand for a seat on the national executive committee, and vice versa.

39   However, developments have given the lie to those optimistic observers who, like Elim Papadakis ('Social Movements', pp. 433–454), believed that the Greens had managed to develop 'a reflexive and analytical approach both to issues of organization and political ideology', and thus to spare themselves the choice between radicalism and reformism. In contradiction to what Papadakis thought, what one observes instead is that green radicalism did allow itself to be tamed by means of various self-restricting arrangements that were capable of commanding consensus, but only after it had caused considerable losses in terms of power of attraction and effectiveness.

40   The alliance was badly prepared in terms of its political programme, and it lasted only a short time. It was terminated by the SPD on tactical grounds, a few weeks before new elections were held in autumn 1990.

41   A number of prominent adherents of 'eco-socialism' (like Jürgen Reents and Michael Stamm) acted as electoral advisers or press spokespersons for the PDS, the party which succeeded the official East German SED and currently has seventeen members in the Bundestag. The radical ecologists, for their part, are seeking to establish an organisation engaged chiefly in extra-parliamentary work.

42   Speechlessness seems to have become the hallmark of green politics in relation to the fundamental upheavals in Europe. Neither the complex processes of transformation in the new Eastern European democracies, nor the nationality disputes that are erupting at every turn, nor even the bloody civil war between Serbs and Croats had elicited a single clear comment from the diligent Euro-Greens in Brussels and Strasburg before summer 1992.

43   Padgett and Patterson, 'The Rise and Fall of the West German Left'.

44   There are nine individuals from the East German Greens and citizens' movements sitting as MPs in the Bundestag, but because of their origins, the emphases of their individual interests, and the looseness of their links with the Green Party, they are not perceived as representing the West German Greens.

45   In the examples cited above, a number of people felt offended: (a) those who thought Germany had a useful role to play in the transformation of NATO; (b) those who thought women's choice of lifestyle should be left to women themselves to decide; (c) those who recognised in the desire for a united Germany the needs of people who felt frustrated and had suffered years of disadvantage; and (d) those who realised that Iraqi-cum-German poison-gas represented a real threat to the Israeli population.

46   E.g. on multiple causality, autopoietic self-referential processes, paradoxal emergence phenomena, perverse effects of purposive action, and evolutionary selection mechanisms.

47   Hinchman and Hinchman, ' "Deep Ecology" '.

48   March and Olsen, *Rediscovering Institutions*.

49   Drysek, 'Green Reason', pp. 195–210.

Bibliographical references

Bahro, Rudolf, 1987, *Logik der Rettung* (Stuttgart: Thienemanns Verlag, 1987).

Capra, Fritjof, and Spretnak, Charlene, 1984, *Green Politics: The Global Promise* (London: Hutchinson, 1984).

Cornelsen, Dirk, *Ankläger im Hohen Haus: Die Grünen im Bundestag* (Essen: Klartext Verlag, 1986).

Czada, Roland, and Lehmbruch, Gerhard, 'Parteienwettbewerb, Sozialstaatspostulat und gesellschaftlicher Wertewandel', in Bermbach, Udo *et al.* (eds.), *Spaltungen der Gesellschaft und die Zukunft des Sozialstaats* (Opladen: Leske & Budrich, 1990), pp. 55–84.

Dalton, Russell J., and Kuechler, Manfred (eds.), *Challenging the Political Order: New Social and Political Movements in Western Democracies* (Cambridge: Polity Press, 1990).

Drysek, John S., 'Green Reason: Communicative Ethics for the Biosphere', *Environmental Ethics*, 12 1990, pp. 195–210.

Hildebrandt, Kai and Dalton, Russell, 'The New Politics: Political Change or Sunshine Politics?', in Kaase, Max (ed.), *Election and Parties* (London and Beverly Hills: Sage, 1978).

Hinchman, Lewis P. and Hinchman, Sandra K., 1989, ' "Deep Ecology" and the Revival of Natural Right', *Western Political Quarterly*, 42 (1989), pp. 201–28.

Hirschman, Albert O., *Shifting Involvements: Private Interest and Public Action* (Princeton: Princeton University Press, 1982).

Kelly, Petra K., *Um Hoffnung kämpfen* (Bornheim-Merten: Lamuv Verlag, 1983).

Kirchheimer, Otto, 'The Transformation of West European Party Systems', in LaPalombara, Joseph and Weiner, Myron (eds.), *Political Parties and Political Development* (Princeton: Princeton University Press 1966), pp. 177–200.

Kitschelt, Herbert P., 'Political Opportunity Structures and Political Protest: Anti-Nuclear Movements in Four Democracies', *British Journal of Political Science*, 16 (1986), pp. 57–85.

Kitschelt, Herbert P., *The Logics of Party Formation: Ecological Politics in Belgium and West Germany* (Ithaca and London: Cornell University Press, 1989).

March, James G. and Olsen, Johan P., *Rediscovering Institutions: The Organizational Basis of Politics* (New York: Free Press, 1989).

Michels, Robert, *Political Parties: A Sociological Study of the Oligarchical Tendencies of Modern Democracy* (1911) (London: Collier-Macmillan, 1962).

Müller-Rommel, Ferdinand and Pridham, Geoffrey (eds.), *Small Parties in Western Europe: Comparative and National Perspectives* (London and Beverly Hills: Sage, 1989).

Offe, Claus, 'Reflections on the Institutional Self-transformation of Movement Politics: A Tentative Stage Model', in Dalton, Russell J. and Kuechler, Manfred (eds.), *Challenging the Political Order: New Social and Political Movements in Western Democracies* (Cambridge: Polity Press, 1990), pp. 233–50.

Padgett, Stephen and Patterson, William, 'The Rise and Fall of the West German Left', *New Left Review*, 186 (Mar./Apr. 1991), pp. 46–77.

Papadakis, Elim, 'Social Movements, Self-Limiting Radicalism and the Green Party in West Germany', *Sociology*, 22 (1988), pp. 433–54.

Raschke, Joachim, *Krise der Grünen: Bilanz und Neubeginn*, (Marburg: Schüren, 1991).

Wolinetz, Steven B., 'Party system change: the catch-all thesis revisited', *West European Politics*, 14 (1991), pp. 113–28.

Index

eco-libertarianism, in Green Party 11, 36,
 58
eco-socialism, in Green Party 11–12, 15, 88,
 207, 214, 223 n.41
ecocentrism 1, 4–7, 17–18, 88, 212
ecology
 in competing parties 105–6
 'deep' 4, 6–7, 17, 19, 23–4, 216
 human welfare 6, 17–18, 22
 support for reforms 91
ecology, political, normative debates 4–7,
 200–1
economy
 alternative 12, 19, 86, 110, 153, 154–5
 capitalist 136–41, 147–50
 control 145–7, 148, 154
 left-wing policy 134–6, 139–41, 142–5
education, in mobilising support 33, 35, 82
elderly, in social policies 172–3, 174–5
élite, green 85, 86
Elster, Jon 8, 97
emancipation, in green politics 6, 104
emancipation principle 18, 19–20, 24, 53,
 57–9, 61, 65
employment, full 171, 173, 177, 186
energy policies 16, 98, 149
Engholm, Björn 221 n.14
environmentalism *see* ecology, political
equality, sexual 98, 101, 109
ethics, of green politics 17–18
evolutionary theory 6, 218

failure, radicalism through 34–6
family, subsidiarity 183–4
FDP
 in coalitions 112
 and party system 103, 196–7, 203
 and working hours 119
feminism
 and Green Party 196, 200
 radical ecological 11
Fischer, Joschka 88, 213
framework party, post-industrial 92, 104–5
France, environment movement 190
functionalism, structural 9–10
fundamentalism, radical
 erosion 212–13
 and grassroots democracy 210
 in Green Party 92–6, 102–3, 200, 201–6,
 208, 219
 realist critique 2, 7–24, 91–100, 217–18
 and social movements 90, 216
future, orientation to 95

Gehlen, Arnold 125
Germany
 ecological concerns 190–1, 192, 194

 and emergence of Green Party 192–4
 political system 3, 195–8
 reunification 23–4, 211, 213–15
Gorz, André 185
governability 58, 60, 80
green alternative list theory 13, 34, 112, 195
Green Party
 as 'anti-party' party 76, 104
 constituency 78–80, 102–3, 195
 current position 91–100, 190, 212–15
 divisions 11, 66–7, 92–6, 191, 203–7
 and floating voters 75–6
 funding 197, 204–5, 208
 and German reunification 23–4, 213–15,
 217
 identity 203–7
 influence 101, 195, 199–201, 208
 intended/unintended effects 101–3
 on left-right scale 14, 38–9, 112, 192,
 198, 200–1
 and multiple representation 195
 myths concerning 190–2
 'New Beginning' ('Aufbruch') 206, 213,
 218
 opportunity structure 192–8
 organisational democracy 207–11, 212
 in parliaments 2, 9, 10, 28, 62–5, 76,
 77–8, 87, 92, 102–3, 198, 205–6,
 215, 221 n.8
 and party system 102–3, 104
 political power 28
 as post-industrial framework party 92,
 105–6
 programmes 96–8, 104, 106
 and radicalism 2
 Reconstruction Programme 135
 role in social change 1, 10–11, 55–67, 77
 social policies 173–4, 178–84
 strategy debate 1, 10–12, 191
 support for 111–12
 see also politics, green
Greens, the *see* Green Party
growth, economic
 consequences 146
 limits 21–3, 51, 125, 134, 153, 194, 200
Grünen, die *see* Green Party

Habermas, Jürgen 9, 14, 42, 167 n.5, 196,
 219
Hallerbach, J. 128
Hammerbacher, Ruth 210
Hanesch, Walter 184
health service, policies 172–3, 176
Hirsch, Fred 99
Hirsch, Joachim 44
Horkheimer, Max 125